75 CLASSIC RIDES
OREGON

Jim Moore

75 CLASSIC RIDES
OREGON
THE BEST ROAD BIKING ROUTES

DEDICATION

To my wife Pam, who understands why I need to ride and fits it into our life.
To my son Dylan, who thinks riding with Dad is a treat; I hope you always will.
You two are my world, and it's a world of adventure. Let's go find some more.

THE MOUNTAINEERS BOOKS
*is the nonprofit publishing arm of The Mountaineers, an organization founded in 1906 and
dedicated to the exploration, preservation, and enjoyment of outdoor and wilderness areas.*

1001 SW Klickitat Way, Suite 201, Seattle, WA 98134

First edition, 2012

Manufactured in China

Copy Editor: Kris Fulsaas
Cover and Book Design: Heidi Smets, heidismets.com
Layout: Jennifer Shontz, redshoedesign.com
Cartographer: Pease Press Cartography
All photographs by the author unless otherwise noted.
Author photo by Mark Riskedahl.

Cover photograph: *The Oregon Coast offers some of the most spectacular riding opportunities in America, including this access road along rugged headlands to the Cape Blanco Lighthouse between Bandon and Port Orford.* Phil Bard/Cycle Oregon
Frontispiece: *On the Ride Across Oregon, you'll pass through varying climate zones and terrain, from the golden wheat fields here to rugged Cascade passes and on to the Pacific Ocean.* Greg Lee/Cycle Oregon

Library of Congress Cataloging-in-Publication Data
Moore, Jim.
    75 classic rides, Oregon : the best road-biking routes / Jim Moore.—1st ed.
        p. cm.
    Includes index.
    ISBN 978-1-59485-650-1 (ppb)
1. Cycling—Oregon—Guidebooks. 2. Oregon—Guidebooks. I. Title. II. Title: Seventy-five classic rides, Oregon.
    GV1045.5.O7M66 2012
    796.6—dc23
                                                                                    2012002267

Printed on recycled paper
ISBN (paperback): 978-1-59485-650-1
ISBN (e-book): 978-1-59485-651-8

CONTENTS

Overview Map   8
Rides-at-a-Glance   11
Acknowledgments   15
Introduction   17

THE COAST

1. Vernonia to Astoria   37
2. Youngs Bay   40
3. Three Capes Scenic Loop   43
4. Newport–Siletz Loop   47
5. Sweet Creek Falls   50
6. Siuslaw and Smith Rivers   53

PORTLAND METRO

7. Banks–Vernonia Trail   57
8. Hagg Lake   61
9. Bald Peak Two Ways   64
10. Wine Country Tour   68
11. Sauvie Island   71
12. Skyline Boulevard Traverse   75
13. Marine Drive Path   79
14. Eastside Neighborhoods   82
15. Double Volcano   86
16. West Hills Highlights   90
17. Eastbank Esplanade   94
18. Springwater Trail   98
19. Lake Oswego Lollipop   101

WILLAMETTE VALLEY

20. Salem Family Fun Ride   106
21. Silver Falls   109
22. Covered Bridges Ride   113
23. Corvallis–Philomath Trails   116
24. Kings Valley   120
25. Alsea Falls   124

26. Quartzville Creek   128

27. Eugene Bike Paths   131

28. McKenzie View   134

29. Wolf Creek Loop   137

30. Row River Trail   140

SOUTHERN OREGON

31. Tour de Fronds   144

32. Rogue River Ramble   147

33. Cedar Flat Loop   150

34. Applegate Lake   153

35. Bear Creek Greenway   157

36. Old Siskiyou Highway   160

37. The Lakes Loop   163

38. Prospect to Ashland   166

MOUNT HOOD AND THE COLUMBIA GORGE

39. Sandy River Roller Coaster   170

40. Larch Mountain   174

41. Multnomah Falls Out-and-Back   176

42. The Waterfall Ride   179

43. Historic Columbia River Highway (Part 2)   182

44. Twin Tunnels   185

45. Hood River to The Dalles   187

46. Cherry Heights   190

47. Summit to Surf   193

48. Lolo Pass   197

49. Timothy Lake the Back Way   200

THE CASCADES

50. Camp Sherman   204

51. McKenzie Pass   208

52. Aufderheide Memorial Drive   211

53. Cottage Grove to Oakridge   214

54. Diamond Lake to Cottage Grove   217

55. Crater Lake Rim Road   221

56. Crater Lake Up-and-Over   224

CENTRAL OREGON

57. Bakeoven Road   228
58. Lower Bridge Road   231
59. Twin Bridges Loop   234
60. Prineville Reservoir   238

EASTERN OREGON

61. The Windmill Ride   242
62. Fossil Lollipop   246
63. Heppner to Ukiah   249
64. Old Oregon Trail   253
65. Tollgate Pass   256
66. Joseph–Enterprise Loop   259
67. Union Loop   263
68. Baker City to Sumpter and Back   266
69. Summit Prairie   269
70. Burns to Frenchglen via the Narrows   273
71. Frenchglen to Burns via Diamond Valley   277

MULTIDAY ROUTES

72. The Oregon Coast Route   281
73. Willamette Valley Scenic Bikeway   291
74. Ride Across Oregon   297
75. Wallowa Mountains and Hells Canyon Loop   305

Resources   310
Index   313

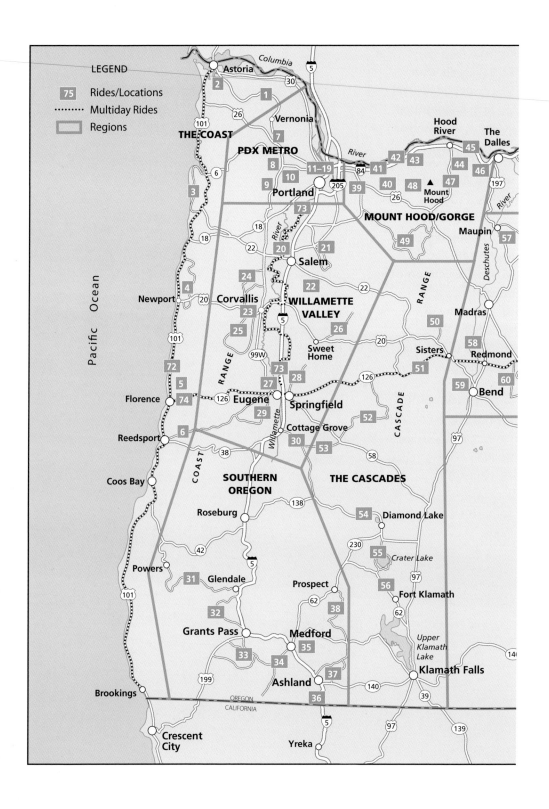

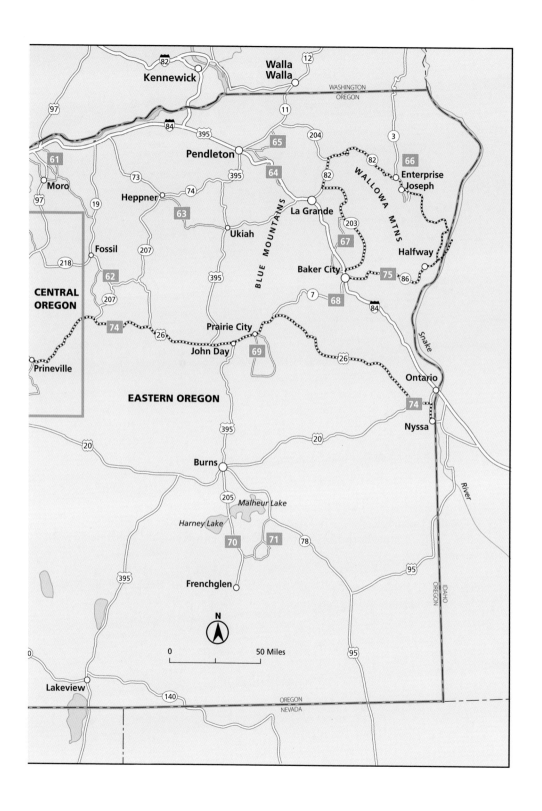

MAP LEGEND

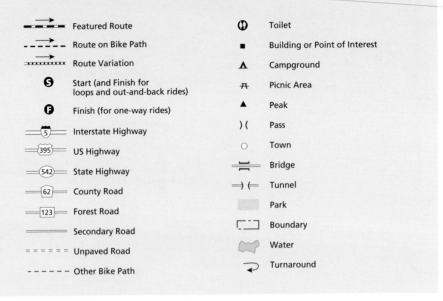

Featured Route		Toilet	
Route on Bike Path		Building or Point of Interest	
Route Variation		Campground	
Start (and Finish for loops and out-and-back rides)		Picnic Area	
Finish (for one-way rides)		Peak	
Interstate Highway		Pass	
US Highway		Town	
State Highway		Bridge	
County Road		Tunnel	
Forest Road		Park	
Secondary Road		Boundary	
Unpaved Road		Water	
Other Bike Path		Turnaround	

With your purchase of this book, you also get access to our easy-to-use, downloadable cue sheets:

» Go to our website: www.mountaineersbooks.org/75ClassicOregon.
» Download a complete set of mileage cue sheets for all 75 rides in this book.
» When you open the document on your computer, enter the code "ORRideQ" when prompted.

It's our way of thanking you for supporting The Mountaineers Books and our mission of outdoor recreation and conservation.

RIDES AT-A-GLANCE

NO.	RIDE	DIFFICULTY RATING	DISTANCE (IN MILES)	ELEVATION GAIN (IN FEET)	TIME (IN HOURS)	POINTS OF INTEREST
1	Vernonia to Astoria	Challenging	66.7	2110	4–6	Coastal forest, rivers, and bays, ending at the Astoria Column
2	Youngs Bay	Moderate	22.3	466	1.5–2	Tranquil coastal bay with extensive wildlife views
3	Three Capes Scenic Loop	Challenging	61.75	2247	4–6	Coastal side road with bays, beaches, and wild headlands
4	Newport–Siletz Loop	Challenging	67.35	1798	4–6	Yaquina Bay, Siletz River, and coastal shoreline
5	Sweet Creek Falls	Moderate	50.3	1050	3.5–5	Series of waterfalls in coastal forest
6	Siuslaw and Smith Rivers	Challenging	76.35	2408	5–7	Up the Siuslaw, down the Smith, to the coast
7	Banks–Vernonia Trail	Easy to Moderate	20.65	938	1.5–2.5	Rails-to-trails path through fields and forests
8	Hagg Lake	Moderate	26.2	719	2–2.5	Rolling hills and lake views from multiple angles
9	Bald Peak Two Ways	Epic	45.1	2589	3–5	Panoramic views of wine country, mountains, valleys
10	Wine Country Tour	Moderate	50.05	1122	3–5	Multiple vineyards and wineries to visit
11	Sauvie Island	Moderate	31.9	581	2–3	Abundant wildlife and quiet roads on the island
12	Skyline Boulevard Traverse	Challenging	20.3	1283	1.5–2	Ridgeline views to north and south, above the city
13	Marine Drive Path	Easy	8.3	79	0.5–.75	Off-road trail with up-close river views
14	Eastside Neighborhoods	Moderate	27.3	554	2–3	Series of revitalized historic neighborhoods
15	Double Volcano	Moderate	18.1	778	1–2	Two extinct volcanoes and great city views
16	West Hills Highlights	Challenging	15.9	1115	1–1.5	Stately homes, leafy boulevards, lofty views
17	Eastbank Esplanade	Easy	3.0	108	0.25–0.5	River-level views of the city, plus floating bridge
18	Springwater Trail	Easy	18.9	476	1.5–2	Urban bike path through variety of settings
19	Lake Oswego Lollipop	Challenging	27.6	1430	2–3	Twisty Terwilliger Blvd., Lake Oswego views, Mountain Park climb
20	Salem Family Fun Ride	Easy	2.05	79	0.25	Cool bridge, indoor carousel, kids' museum, paddlewheel steamboat

NO.	RIDE	DIFFICULTY RATING	DISTANCE (IN MILES)	ELEVATION GAIN (IN FEET)	TIME (IN HOURS)	POINTS OF INTEREST
21	Silver Falls	Challenging	34.05	2133	2–3.5	Quaint Silverton, picturesque Silver Falls State Park
22	Covered Bridges Ride	Moderate	49.1	1112	3.5–5	Five historic covered bridges
23	Corvallis–Philomath Trails	Moderate	12.75	190	1–2	Series of city parks on trails or quiet back roads
24	Kings Valley	Challenging	65.9	1998	4–6	Series of scenic valleys in the Coast Range
25	Alsea Falls	Challenging	58.9	2474	4–6	Coast Range forest, secluded falls
26	Quartzville Creek	Challenging	61.0	2740	4–6	Deep green reservoirs, rushing rivers
27	Eugene Bike Paths	Easy	11.9	92	0.5–1.5	Parks, bridges, wildlife, and riverside riding
28	McKenzie View	Moderate	38.4	525	2–3	Rolling country roads, McKenzie River views
29	Wolf Creek Loop	Epic	65.0	2293	5–7	Cathedral of forest, lofty vistas, stringent climb
30	Row River Trail	Moderate	33.25	755	2–4	Rails-to-trails with covered bridges, lakeside riding
31	Tour de Fronds	Epic	69.7	5466	5–7	Deep-forest isolation, extended climbing, riverside cruising
32	Rogue River Ramble	Challenging	61.3	3127	4–6	Wild and Scenic Rogue, Wolf Creek Inn, Golden ghost town
33	Cedar Flat Loop	Epic	72.6	4334	4.5–7.5	Epic climb, dizzying drop, riding along the rivers
34	Applegate Lake	Challenging	58.4	3212	4–6	Old-West Jacksonville, Buncom ghost town, sparkling reservoir
35	Bear Creek Greenway	Easy	17.7	20	1.5–2.5	Bike path through five towns; parks along the way
36	Old Siskiyou Highway	Challenging	29.45	2146	2–3.5	Ashland, Emigrant Lake, quiet, shady climb
37	The Lakes Loop	Epic	51.35	4229	4–5.5	Green Springs Highway climb, Hyatt and Howard Prairie lakes, thrilling descent
38	Prospect to Ashland	Epic	76.0	4436	5–7.5	Secluded roads, wildflower meadows, alpine lakes
39	Sandy River Roller Coaster	Challenging	32.8	2011	2.5–3.5	Three river crossings, parks along the way
40	Larch Mountain	Epic	46.2	3921	3–5	Sandy River, Columbia Gorge views, long steady climb

NO.	RIDE	DIFFICULTY RATING	DISTANCE (IN MILES)	ELEVATION GAIN (IN FEET)	TIME (IN HOURS)	POINTS OF INTEREST
41	Multnomah Falls Out-and-Back	Challenging	36.6	2339	2.5–4	Women's Forum viewpoint, Crown Point, Multnomah and other falls
42	The Waterfall Ride	Moderate	9.75	545	1.5–2	Seven waterfalls in less than 10 miles
43	Historic Columbia River Highway (Part 2)	Moderate	11.2	724	0.75–1.5	Eagle Creek fish hatchery, Bridge of the Gods, mossy forest trail
44	Twin Tunnels	Moderate	9.0	1115	1–1.5	Stunning Gorge views, twin tunnels, no vehicle traffic
45	Hood River to The Dalles	Moderate	20.2	1407	1.5–2	Gorge views, twin tunnels, orchards, Rowena Crest viewpoint
46	Cherry Heights	Challenging	15.65	1050	1–1.5	Cherry orchards, Gorge views, wildlife
47	Summit to Surf	Epic	64.9	5676	4.5–7	Mt. Hood views, Timberline Lodge, Hood River valley
48	Lolo Pass	Challenging	32.05	2779	2–3.5	Secluded forest climb, Mt. Hood views, extended descent
49	Timothy Lake the Back Way	Epic	68.0	4964	4.5–7	High Rocks view, quiet forest roads, primo descent, Clackamas River
50	Camp Sherman	Moderate	21.4	479	1.5–3	Metolius River views and crossings
51	McKenzie Pass	Challenging	37.0	2152	2.5–3.5	Lava-rock vistas, Dee Wright Observatory, mountain views
52	Aufderheide Memorial Drive	Epic	63.6	4308	4–6	Covered bridge, streamside riding, Cougar Reservoir
53	Cottage Grove to Oakridge	Epic	59.6	5003	4–6	Extreme seclusion, steep climb, and sheer descent
54	Diamond Lake to Cottage Grove	Epic	89.4	3563	6–8	Diamond Lake, N. Umpqua River, Toketee Falls
55	Crater Lake Rim Road	Epic	32.6	3107	2.5–4.5	Crater Lake Lodge, Pumice Desert, jaw-dropping views
56	Crater Lake Up-and-Over	Challenging	58.65	3100	4–6	Annie Creek Canyon, Crater Lake and lodge, long forest descent
57	Bakeoven Road	Challenging	52.0	2845	3.5–5	Deschutes River, high-desert isolation, broad vistas
58	Lower Bridge Road	Moderate	38.0	925	2.5–3.5	High-desert valleys, rimrock canyons, Deschutes River
59	Twin Bridges Loop	Moderate	32.9	850	2.5–3.5	Five crossings of the Deschutes River
60	Prineville Reservoir	Moderate	49.9	1362	3.5–5	Reservoir views, Crooked River canyon riding

NO.	RIDE	DIFFICULTY RATING	DISTANCE (IN MILES)	ELEVATION GAIN (IN FEET)	TIME (IN HOURS)	POINTS OF INTEREST
61	The Windmill Ride	Challenging	49.7	2762	4–5	Hundreds of windmills, rolling wheat fields
62	Fossil Lollipop	Challenging	66.35	5748	4–6	Donnelly Grade, Girds Creek rimrock canyon
63	Heppner to Ukiah	Challenging	46.9	3675	3.5–5.5	Rolling crop fields, climb through pine forest, descent to Ukiah
64	Old Oregon Trail	Moderate	42.0	1266	2.5–4	Emigrant Springs State Park, canyon viewpoint, deliciously twisty descent
65	Tollgate Pass	Epic	73.9	5299	5–7.5	Thorn Hollow canyon, alpine summits, long gliding descent
66	Joseph–Enterprise Loop	Moderate	20.05	577	1–2.5	Wallowa Lake, Joseph, mountain views
67	Union Loop	Challenging	75.9	2710	5–7.5	Catherine Creek, rolling terrain, Pyles Canyon
68	Baker City to Sumpter and Back	Challenging	59.2	1345	4–6	Powder River, Phillips Lake, historic Sumpter
69	Summit Prairie	Epic	65.2	3816	4.5–6.5	Prairie City, Crane Prairie, Strawberry Mountains views
70	Burns to Frenchglen via the Narrows	Moderate	60.1	961	4–6	Wide-open landscape, Steens Mountain views, Frenchglen Hotel
71	Frenchglen to Burns via Diamond Valley	Challenging	96.7	991	6–10	Hotel Diamond, Diamond Craters, Crystal Crane Hot Springs
72	The Oregon Coast Route	Epic	359.8	12,809	4–8 days	Rugged capes, sandy beaches, coastal forest
73	Willamette Valley Scenic Bikeway	Moderate	132.9	1758	2–4 days	Agricultural bounty, Champoeg Park, river views
74	Ride Across Oregon	Epic	452.0	16,440	5–8 days	Incredible variety of terrain, McKenzie Pass, coastal finish
75	Wallowa Mountains and Hells Canyon Loop	Epic	313.6	19,218	4–6 days	Wallowa Lake, Hells Canyon, Halfway

ACKNOWLEDGMENTS

No author yet has been able to say, "It was all me; I did this on my own." This book is the product of a broad group of wonderful people with a collective love of cycling, nature, Oregon, and the best things in life.

I am so thankful to be able to regularly combine my cycling and writing worlds; that's largely due to Cycle Oregon, Travel Oregon, and *The Oregonian,* which all let me write about and stay involved in what I love—and help me make a living in the process. Jerry Norquist, Tara Corbin, Ingrid Nylen, Steve Schulz, and Ken Chichester with Cycle Oregon have been wonderful to work with and have provided many resources and much support. Kristin Dahl of Travel Oregon and David Lowe-Rogstad and his crew at Substance have made the Ride Oregon website a rich resource and fun joint effort. Alex Pulaski and Laurie Robinson of *The Oregonian* buy my stories and let me claim to be a travel writer, which is a really sweet gig.

Thanks to my parents, Jerry Moore and Dee and Marty Rotto, for instilling a sense of adventure and wonder; to Jeff Welsch for talking me into my first real taste of riding in Oregon; and to a group of friends I've shared two-wheeled adventures with: Steve and Diane Zipper, Mike and Erica Lurie, Mark Riskedahl and Melissa Powers, Mike Ruff, and Pat Lynch; they've dragged me up many hills and made me a better rider. And a nod to my riding buds in the Portland Wheelmen.

Thanks to the folks at The Mountaineers Books for handing me this project on a platter, and to Phil Bard, who volunteered his time and expertise to try to make me an adequate photographer.

Forest Road 1828 plunges deep into the forest on the flanks of Mount Hood, rising steeply but serenely up to Lolo Pass. My friend Erica remains undaunted by the grade.

INTRODUCTION

As I was reriding the very last route for this book—Lolo Pass—my friends and I stopped for a photo break. We were on a one-lane Forest Service road, surrounded by vast swathes of evergreen forest, and through a gap in the trees straight ahead, Mount Hood towered above the landscape.

It was a perfect summer day and a fantastic ride. I took in the scene and couldn't help myself: I yelled out, "*I love living in Oregon!*"

While I do love living here, what I really meant at that moment was that I love *riding* in Oregon. I'd just finished crisscrossing the state over many months, revisiting dozens of routes and checking out a few new ones. And my culminating thought at that moment was simple: This is a stupendously good place to ride.

Call it a local's pride, but I just don't know of anywhere that offers a better variety and atmosphere for road riding. Within a few hours' drive you can choose from a menu of cycling pleasures: Ride above crashing ocean breakers, high on a coastal cape; pedal smoothly through a silent old-growth forest; roll past fields of bountiful crops and majestic century-old barns; complete a scenic loop around a river in the middle of a bustling city; swoop down through a red-rock canyon in the high desert; spin on sagebrush-lined roads so wide open that you can see 10 miles down them; or climb a mountain pass next to the music of a rushing stream.

I want to share all these experiences with you—so you can hit the road and experience them yourself. Whether you're a visitor trying to pick out the places you want to ride on a vacation, a resident looking to expand your in-state adventures, or even someone who's just decided to start riding, you're going to find rides in this book that will deliver the essence of Oregon road cycling.

PREPARING FOR A RIDE

Like a whole lot of things in life, the 10 minutes you spend making sure you're actually prepared will make your 30 minutes or two hours or eight hours of bike riding a much more successful endeavor. You're about to get on a fairly complex moving vehicle and take a trip, likely miles from home, in the outdoors, for an extended period of time. Don't minimize the need for some basic planning. You know those stories you read about some hiker in shorts, a T-shirt, and flip-flops who gets caught out overnight in the woods and later says, "I was just going for a little walk"? Do not be that person on a bike.

I find it's much easier to prepare in a certain order; a little systemization is a good thing. Here's a suggested order and some critical considerations.

FIT THE BIKE AND GEARS

The baseline for staying a bike rider is that your bike has to be comfortable to ride. This is a matter of finding the right bike for your purposes and then—and I can't stress this enough—making sure it fits you. Sitting on a bike seat, leaning over handlebars, and pedaling for extended periods are not natural situations for our bodies. Some professional help can make a huge difference. Whether you're considering buying a first bike, buying a new bike, or continuing to ride your current bike, it should be fitted for you and only you.

There are two critical elements here. The first is to get a seat you're compatible with. Big advances in seat design over the last two decades have produced a wide variety of choices, including female- and male-specific models that combat common pain points. If you have discomfort from your seat, talk to a knowledgeable retailer about exactly

At an overlook point just south of Bandon on the Oregon Coast Bike Route, a group of friends soak up the scenery. Phil Bard/Cycle Oregon

what hurts (don't blush; they've heard this all before), and the salesperson should be able to narrow it down to the best options for you.

The second element is the geometry of your ride. If you want to spend significant time on your bike, the best money you can spend might be to have a professional bike fitting. A good fitter will interview you, measure numerous body parts, closely examine you on the bike, and then make adjustments as needed, whether it's adjusting seat or handlebar height or position, realigning your pedals or shoes, or something more esoteric. It can make an amazing difference.

Another critical component to your bike is its gearing. Mechanical engineers will tell you that the bicycle is one of the most efficient machines ever invented, and gearing is a principal reason for that. There are a lot of different configurations on the market—ask any gearhead and see if your brain doesn't start reeling at the string of numbers that come spewing out—so again, seek the advice of a plain-talking expert. Basically, there are three setups to choose from: triple, double, and compact. A triple ring has three chain rings in the front, giving you the widest range of gearing (for example, three in front and nine in back equals 27 gear combinations).

A triple is particularly good for climbing if you're not a pure-power rider; the wider range allows more low-end gears for spinning a higher cadence on steep uphills. A double is two chain rings in the front—the standard for a long time for all "serious" riders. However, all but the strongest riders will run out of low gears on big climbs. Hence the compact was invented: a two-ring configuration that uses a wider range of gearing (basically, size as measured in the number of teeth on the ring) between the front and rear rings.

CHOOSE THE ROUTE

When you've decided when you want to ride, start by choosing wisely *where* to ride. The joke with my friends is that when we meet and someone says, "Where should we go today?" the answer always starts with, "Let's go up (fill in the name of a climb) and then …" But a climb is always what we're looking for. It may sound simplistic, but when you're picking your route, ask yourself what your goal for the ride is: An easy spin? A high-intensity flat ride? A hill-climb training session? Take into consideration your training level, the weather, how much time you really have, and who you're riding with (and what *their* goals might be).

Print out or copy a map of the route, as well as turn-by-turn directions (mileage log). Put them in a waterproof, sealable bag, especially if they're going in a jersey pocket, where they could get sweaty. Some people like to use a clip on their handlebars that's designed to hold a map; the waterproof bag is still a good idea.

If your route includes any kind of seasonal road, check if the road is open; you might be surprised what's not open in the middle of summer. This is also the time to jump on the computer and look up a current weather forecast and radar map; these tools are so sophisticated now that you can almost pin down to the half-hour how long you have before the rain hits. (Note that I said "almost.")

PICK YOUR OUTFIT

Besides a reliable, comfortable bike (and a certain level of fitness), there's nothing more important than having the right gear for your ride. Because you're exposed to the elements, you have to carefully consider every single piece of your clothing. It's always wonderful that first time each summer when you realize all you need is a jersey, shorts, socks, and gloves—but this is Oregon, and that's just not going to cut it most of the year.

The Banks–Vernonia Trail is a perfect place to ride with the whole family—in any configuration that works. That's my son, Dylan, riding second-seat.

Again, I like the systematic approach; I go top-down. This may be elementary for experienced riders, but I'll aim for those who may be just learning.

Do you need something on your head? While the conventional wisdom that you lose half your body heat out the top of your head is not true, frosty ears are no fun. Next to fingers and toes, I think ears are the most vexing thing to have too cold; even on a brisk morning, you might want something light up top. Skullcaps, headband-style ear warmers, or even wraparound ear muffs that go around behind your neck below your helmet are options.

What about eyewear? Most riders prefer glasses to keep wind, glare, and bugs out of their eyes. Wraparound styles are good for deflecting all these things. Some models have interchangeable lenses with different tints, which is a good idea. In the winter, in the rain, or on evening rides, a pair of clear or yellow-tinted lenses is best; in the summer, darker shades are better. But don't fall for the marketing that you need a $130 pair of name-brand cycling sunglasses—plenty of modestly priced shades work fine and won't get you laughed at.

Perhaps the single most critical question is about a base layer. If it's not sweaty-hot out, you may want something between you and your jersey. A lightweight base layer is a great way to keep your torso warm, and, to paraphrase: If the torso ain't warm, ain't nothin' warm. You can choose from synthetic fibers or wool, or blends of these; just try to find a material that breathes. You don't want a base layer that's going to make you sweat and then trap that moisture. I'm a big fan of modern wool blends—they breathe really well, provide impressive warmth even in thin layers, don't start to stink after one wearing, can actually be washed in a machine (although I still recommend hanging them to dry), and feel very nice next to the skin—no itching anymore.

Note that I referred to a jersey in the above paragraph. That's not to say you have to rush out and spend a wad of money on the latest Tour de France team kit, but the key here is, don't wear a cotton shirt to ride a bike if you're going to sweat. There's a reason jerseys are not cotton: You want something suited to riding, sweating, and moving through air. Plus, jerseys usually have very handy pockets in the back. As with sunglasses, you don't necessarily need an expensive jersey unless its advantages are truly important to you. A couple hints: If you're going to be riding a while in hot weather, a jersey that zips down quite a ways in front can be nice for ventilation (even with a sports bra), and long-sleeve jerseys are a good idea for when you're certain you'll want to cover your arms for the whole ride; otherwise, think about arm warmers, which are more versatile.

What about outerwear? You have a lot of choices here. My recommendation is that if you plan to ride in Oregon, you should have two jackets: a lightweight rain jacket and a heavier rain jacket. Unless, of course, you're going to ride only between July and September—then you'll maybe need only the light jacket. The light jacket should be breathable and water-resistant, because you should wear it when you might get rained on just a bit. (By the way, I don't believe any manufacturer that says a jacket is both breathable and water*proof*; maybe I'm wrong, but I haven't worn one yet that is.) The heavier rain jacket doesn't need to be highly breathable; you want something that will truly keep you dry. The better ones have zippered underarms and other venting mechanisms to keep you somewhat cool. In addition, some riders like to have a vest, which provides a good windbreak and helps keep the torso warm without enveloping your upper body.

Arm warmers are one of the best things about cycling. For some reason, just having them on can keep your whole body warmer when you're starting out on a cool morning that will warm up later, or in other conditions where it's just a tad chillier than you'd like. And they're versatile; you can pull them down around your wrists if you heat up on a climb, then pull them back up for a descent, or you can wear them in the morning and then roll them up and stow them in a jersey pocket for the rest of the ride.

Some new riders I've met have asked me why a cyclist needs gloves. Here are a few reasons. When it's cold, well, that's obvious. Options range from lightweight running gloves under (or even over, for easy removal) regular fingerless riding gloves, to medium-weight water-resistant gloves for warmer rainy days, to substantially insulated and waterproof gloves (and even mittenish "lobster-claw" styles) for true foul-weather riding. But when it's hot, gloves still serve some purposes. One is padding on the palms, which helps a lot of riders avoid hand cramping or numbness. Another is grip; when your hands get sweaty, gloves help you keep a firm hold on your handlebars. And most good biking gloves have terry or other soft material positioned to help you wipe sweat away from your eyes (or, OK, snot from your nose), which comes in quite handy.

Ah, cycling shorts ... the tired old jokes about "spandex pants" still persist even though the correct pejorative these days would actually be Lycra. But any semi- or more serious cyclist will tell you that a good pair of cycling shorts is an absolute necessity. Our butts (and other nearby parts) aren't really meant to sit on a seat like that and get pumped back and forth thousands of times in a row; that's why cycling shorts have chamois in them. The number-one deterrent for new cyclists (especially females) is what would be euphemistically referred to as "seat discomfort." Your saddle (seat) choice is the biggest factor here, but even the best seat still needs a little help. Pick shorts that provide a comfortable amount of padding for you and don't chafe. This is one article for which I counsel spending a little

Oregon's small towns, like Joseph (shown here), are a blast to ride through, and they tend to be very welcoming. Cycle Oregon

but over the shoulder, your basic bathroom functions become a lot more complicated. But bibs also never ride down your waist or roll or pinch there, they provide nice support through the stomach and lower back, and somehow they're just actually more comfortable for most people. A friend who's a former pro racer told me, "Bibs will change your life." I wouldn't say that's entirely true, but I do like them.

Once you've got a base layer or jacket for your upper half if it's cold or rains, what about down below? Starting from the lightest option, knee warmers are a good choice when the temperature is borderline. They function just like arm warmers, except they cover only the joint (you don't want to roll them down to your ankles; that would be dangerous and just wrong). A basic guideline I've read is that you should cover your knees if the temperature is below 60 degrees F. You can also get leg warmers, which extend from midthigh to midcalf. The next step is to get tights, which vary a lot. You can find pairs that don't have a chamois and go over your normal shorts; there are also tights that have their own chamois. Tights can be primarily for warmth or offer various degrees of rain (and wind) protection. You can also get rain pants, which don't fit as tightly but just go over your legs.

Socks are pretty straightforward. Yes, you can wear regular footie-socks or even ankle socks, but cycling-specific socks do offer specific advantages, such as ventilation, support, and some really fun designs. If you'll be riding in winter, invest in some heavier wool pairs; for summer, lightweight models let your feet breathe better.

Biking shoes are inextricably linked to pedals. For some riders, old-school flat pedals and a pair of tennis shoes work just fine. If you're interested in getting more efficiency from each turn of the pedals, the next step up is toe clips, or toe cages, which provide a little structure for your feet to slip into, allowing you to pull up on the pedal, not just push

money—the difference between cheap and good is pronounced. Talk to a bike shop you trust about this; don't just pick up a pair at some large retailer or online.

What if you just don't want to wear something that tight or of questionable fashion value? There are good options available—casual-style shorts with padded linings, women's "cycling skirts" (or is that "skorts"?) that go over the Lycra layer—again, talk to a reliable cycling retailer.

Last consideration here: bibs versus shorts. The large majority of riders wear bike shorts, but if you pay attention to pro riders or even amateur racers, you see that they pretty much all wear bibs (essentially, bike shorts with shoulder straps). There are pros and cons: Bibs tend to cost a little more (but not much, really), and because they go under the jersey

down—a real boost. Again, almost any pair of shoes will work here, although bulky boots don't tend to fit in the cages very well. The ultimate level is what are called clipless pedals (although they actually do clip in—who named that?): A cleat on the bottom of a cycling shoe is paired with a corresponding pedal style so that, essentially, the bottoms of your feet are attached to the pedals. This is the standard for serious riders, because it makes a serious difference in transferring power from the legs to the pedals. It takes some getting used to, remembering to "clip out" when you come to a stop (and 99 percent of clipless riders have fallen over at some point), but the advantage is worth forming the habit.

There are several major styles of clipless systems; turn to your local bike shop to learn more and make a good choice. Another fork in the road is whether you want bike shoes you can walk around in—many high-end road shoes are not at all made to walk in. But you can also get what are called "mountain-bike-style" shoes that have a recessed cleat and allow you to walk like a normal human being. It may cost you racer cred, but you don't have to waddle when you walk in them.

There are also multiple rain-protection options for your feet. Soggy feet can make you miserable pretty fast, so make a good investment here. The challenge of cycling booties is that because your shoes typically attach to your pedals, there has to be an opening on the bottom of the bootie, and an opening means . . . an opening for water. So get some good advice on booties; some lightweight models, just like rain jackets, are designed for slowing down water, while some

A smooth single-lane road, slicing through a pristine forest, and friends ahead to catch—this is the good life. Greg Lee/Cycle Oregon

increasingly substantial models are more serious about keeping it out.

ADD FUEL

Cycling is one of the most efficient ways to burn calories, which is one reason it's a great way to lose weight (another being that it's not load-bearing on your joints, reducing strain on them). But most of those calories need to be replaced. If you're not interested in losing weight, *all* those calories need to be replaced. So fuel is absolutely critical. If you've never experienced "bonking"—when your body basically shuts down from lack of fuel during exertion—trust me, you don't want to.

Liquids are just as important as solid food (remember, you'd die from lack of water way before you'd starve to death). Most research shows that you should ingest liquids in small, regular doses during a ride. But it's a good idea to "load up" before you set out. My experience is that on a hard ride, it makes a difference whether I'm well hydrated not just the morning of the ride, but the day before. So think about drinking good fluids—we're not talking alcohol or other diuretics here—the night before and again the morning of your ride. If you're riding later in the day, it's good to have a healthy amount of water or sports drink before you set out.

You should take, at a minimum, one full water bottle of liquid on any ride, two for any ride where you can't easily refill for more than an hour or two. Using a bottle in a cage attached to your bike frame is the best way to go, because you're more likely to remember to drink if you can see it there. You should drink a long sip or two at least two or three times an hour.

And don't forget to continue hydrating after your ride. That celebratory beer is fine, but have a good chaser, too. Not to be too graphic about it, but the color of your urine is a pretty reliable indicator of your level of hydration; the lighter the better. (Notice that after a hard ride it tends to be darker yellow.) If your urine is more toward clear, that's a very good sign.

And what to drink? Other than some basic advice, that's absolutely a matter of preference and trial and error. A broad rule is this: If you're riding hard or for more than an hour, water alone isn't sufficient; bring along some kind of sports-specific concoction. It can be a mass-market sports drink, a cycling-specific one you buy at a bike shop, or a special home-made formula—whatever works for you.

Food is even more a matter of personal preference; what works for one person is never guaranteed to work for another. I know riders who can eat fast food in the middle of an ultra-endurance race, and I know people who can barely tolerate solid food in their stomach on a ride. The key comes down to calories—you have to replenish what you're burning, with a combination of drinks and food. This is a common approach: Before a strenuous ride, make sure to have a meal that includes both carbohydrates and protein—you'll need both. Here's something I learned by trial and error on morning rides: When you've fasted during your overnight sleep, your normal breakfast might go mostly to making up for lost time, so to speak. I've become a fan of Second Breakfast—if I don't eat again right before the ride starts, I bonk.

During the ride, focus more on carbs. Popular choices include energy bars, gels and gelatin-based energy products, bananas, even small sandwiches like the pro racers in Europe have traditionally eaten. Once again, there are so many choices that you just have to find what works for you. I know an endurance racer who says Pop-Tarts are perfect ride food; he's also tried drinking a can of Ensure every hour. And don't forget to eat recovery food—your body keeps burning calories after a hard ride, and the first hour after you get off the bike is crucial for recovery. Try for something healthy, again with a mix of carbs, some protein, and a little fat.

CHECK YOUR BIKE

It sounds like something your mother would tell you: Don't leave without checking your bike! Well, Mom's right. You're trusting your steed to take you where you want to go, safely, so take a couple minutes to do at least a basic check before you set out.

Over the long haul, you should build a relationship with a local bike-shop mechanic—this is the person who will look for problems you might not be able to find yourself and who will remind you about regular maintenance. (This is a good reason not to buy all your gear online to save a few bucks. Buying regularly at a local bike shop is how you build that relationship. And under no circumstances may you use your local bike shop to figure out what you want and then go order it online; you will be so overdrawn at the karma bank that they might close your account.)

But in the short term, this is what you should check regularly, especially before each ride:

Look at your tires—examine them for nicks, embedded items, and unusual or excessive wear. Check the tire pressure before you ride. (Your tire is designed for a particular range of pressure; it should be printed on the sidewall. If you ride typical skinny road tires, 80–90 pounds per square inch (PSI) will give you a smoother ride; many riders like 100–120 PSI because it *feels* faster.)

Then go over the brakes and wheel rims: How is the brake-pad thickness? Is there grit or grime on them and the rim? Are the pads properly aligned with the rim for effective braking? Is there an unusual wear pattern on the rim? Is the brake-handle play or pressure right for you? And a reminder: If you have to flip up the brake-release lever to take a wheel off for any reason—such as putting it on a rack or changing a tube—be sure to check that the lever is back down before you ride.

Check the rest of your wheels, too—finger the spokes to make sure none are loose, make sure your quick-release lever (the way most

The beauty of this shot is that you can't even tell where it is; it's one more remote climb that mixes pain and scenery—just ask Ken here.
Phil Bard/Cycle Oregon

bike wheels are clamped on) is tight, and lift each wheel and spin it to make sure it's not lopsided (out of true) and rubbing the frame or brake pads.

Next, look at your drive train—the chain, derailleurs, and gears. While they will pick up dirt and grime over time as you ride, there shouldn't be excessive amounts on any of these parts. You can buy basic chain-cleaning systems and use a brush on the chain rings and rear cogs; lube your chain regularly (although doing it immediately before you ride is not the best; if your lube hasn't dried, your chain will pick up everything that touches it).

Finally, make sure you have your equipment necessities, whether they're in a saddle-bag, a jersey pocket, or wherever else you figure out. Always take a spare tube, a patch kit, a tire lever, and some way to pump up a tire. Carbon dioxide cartridges are becoming more popular—they're basically one-tire, one-shot inflation devices (carry at least two; occasionally you'll get a dud), but many riders don't trust them enough to not also bring a portable tire pump. Smaller pumps can fit in a pocket, or you can get a frame-mounted model that's easier to operate. Oh, and here are two other considerations: Do you need to lock up your bike at any point during the ride? If so, bring what you need for that. And don't forget sunscreen—there's really no difference between lying on a beach for three hours and sitting on a bike for three hours (well, you can't turn over on the bike for an even tan). Hit all the exposed spots, but pay particular attention to your nose, the back of your neck, your forearms, and the top of your thighs. And remember: A biker's tan is something to be proud of—no matter how freaky you look in the shower.

DO A SAFETY CHECK

Before any ride, several basic safety elements should be covered. First is that most important piece of equipment: your helmet. (How important? If I hadn't been wearing a helmet on a simple ride home from kindergarten with my son in 2010, I might not be here to write this book; a truck knocked us over and my helmeted head bounced off the street like a basketball. I had just bought a new helmet; I was able to ride three days later.) Make sure it fits right: snugly enough that you can shake your head and it doesn't slide in either direction, but not so tight as to give you a headache. It should be worn down on the forehead close to your eyebrows, not pushed back. And if you've dropped your helmet hard or ever fallen and hit it on the ground, get a new one. Helmets should be replaced every few years in general because their components gradually break down in sunlight and heat.

Next thing to think about is information.

Here's more basic advice you should follow: Always tell someone where you're going and when you think you'll be back. It may sound lame, especially if you live alone, but just drop a friend a text or something—if you're out on a back road and anything happens, someone needs to know where to look. And always carry identification—even if you're riding to the store. You can order a customized ID wristband, or figure out a system to carry some essentials. I always carry a waterproof packet with my driver's license, a card with emergency contact phone numbers, a business card or two (hey, cycling is great for networking), a credit card, and my cell phone (which I've heard referred to as a "cellular repair kit"—call for a ride and fix whatever broke when you get home).

THE TEN ESSENTIALS

Yes, even cyclists can benefit from putting together a Ten Essentials checklist for each ride:

1. Navigation: map and mileage log in a waterproof, sealable bag
2. Sun protection: sunglasses and sunscreen
3. Insulation: extra clothing such as arm and leg warmers
4. Illumination: bright white headlight and red rear light or reflector
5. First-aid supplies
6. Fire: hand-warmer gel packs for winter rides
7. Repair kit and tools
8. Nutrition: extra food
9. Hydration: extra water
10. Emergency protection: wind- and raingear

SAFETY ON THE ROAD

It goes without saying that you need to ride safely on the road—but it's not just to save your own hide. An unsafe rider imperils everyone around, and that includes other riders. Cyclists do not appreciate riding with bozos who flout laws or are a danger to others; they give us all a bad name, escalating tension with drivers, and if they crash, they can take us down with them. But let's assume you're one of the "good" riders and want to ride as safely as you can. Here are some thoughts.

First of all, ride in a stable position. The strongest position is with your hands in the "drops" (the section of a curved handlebar closest to the ground); next strongest is "on the hoods" (hands over the brake-lever covers); coming in third is "on the top" (between the hoods and the stem). Of course, if you have straight handlebars, your choices are pretty limited: Keep your hands wide for stability. The most common position for most riders is on the hoods (easy to drop down to the brake lever and to shift), but if you're in a crowd or in a strong wind, the drops are a better choice (keep your hands forward enough to quickly grab a brake or shifter). Really, on the top is OK only if you're not in close proximity to others or you have the kind of bike-handling skills that allow you to sit up and eat a plate of spaghetti while going 25 miles per hour.

More basics: Ride as far to the right as possible in almost all situations. Riding in the middle of a lane or a one-lane road is tempting, but you'd better be pretty sure there's nothing coming up behind you. And riding two or three wide is OK only on lonely roads, on exceptionally wide bike lanes or shoulders, or on a closed course. If you're chatting side by side and a car comes up from behind, quickly communicate who's going in front and who behind, and get into single file right away.

On a related matter, a beginning rider should invest in a mirror. It can be mounted on your helmet, on your left handlebar drop-end, or on the top of your left handlebar (you can even mount one to your glasses). Getting used to it can take a while, but a lot of riders swear by it. However, a different lot of riders would never use one. If you're not going to use one, learn to listen really well and how to turn around to look over your shoulder: Put your right hand on the top bar, right near the stem; put your left hand on your left thigh or your left butt-cheek, then twist around and look over your left shoulder. Do this correctly and you won't swerve to the left like an amateur; practice it when no one's around first.

If you're riding in groups much and trying to go as fast as you can, you'll eventually run into pace-lining, which in basic terms is an entire group riding in a single-file line, taking turns riding at the front and rotating from there to the back. This is also known as drafting, and it can be more than 40 percent more energy-efficient to ride in, say, the third position than in front. It's also fun if done right. The intricacies and "rules" are too complex to delve into here, but here are a few basic ideas: Don't ever make a sudden move or brake when you're in front of anyone; don't overlap wheels with the rider in front of you (if he or she goes right or left suddenly, you're probably both going down); don't trust riders you don't know (how close you ride to the person in front of you is a matter of your trust in them and yourself).

Riding in traffic can be scary, but it's also an inevitability if you do much road riding. Here's a set of basic principles to keep in mind. First, remember that in Oregon bicycles are bound by the same set of rules and traffic laws as cars—the motor vehicle code applies to bikes, so think as much like a really good driver as possible. Second (something I learned from a veteran when I first got a motorcycle), the safest way to ride is to assume everyone behind the wheel of a motor vehicle is dumb as a post. This isn't a commentary on them personally; just expect the worst as you ride your best, and you'll do better. And finally, think of yourself as an official ambassador of bicycling every time you hit the road. There's an undeniable amount of tension between drivers and riders, anywhere—even in the bike nirvana of Portland, many drivers hate us. So try to be the rider

Oregon's Willamette Valley is one of the most fertile places on Earth—and a great place to ride through wide-open spaces. Greg Lee/Cycle Oregon

who makes a driver say, "Wow, those bike riders can really be polite." If a driver does something nice, such as wait for oncoming traffic to clear before passing you from behind, give a thank-you wave. If one waits for you to pass on the right in a bike lane before making a right turn at a corner, try turning and actually mouthing the words "thank you." It goes a long way.

SIGNALING

When riding in a group, learn to call out "Car back" when a car approaches from behind, especially if you're at the rear of the group—that's kind of your job back there. But anyone can make the call, especially if someone has better ears than the others. And "Car up" is good to call out when an oncoming car approaches if you're on any kind of narrow road or if people are riding abreast. The same calls can apply to riders, walkers, wildlife, etc.

Here are some other signals you should know: Turns should be signaled with a straight arm, out to the left or out to the right. The old crooked-left-arm signal for a right turn is a vestige from days when cars didn't have turn signals and drivers' arms couldn't reach out the right window; do it on a bike and it looks as though you're waving at someone from a parade float.

If you're riding in a group, especially in the front spot, and you see anything in the riders' path—glass, garbage, rock, dead animal—it's often easiest to just strongly point down at it rather than try to articulate what it is. You can call out "hole" (concave) or "bump" (convex), preferably before you hit it or the next rider is right on top of it. If you need to stop or slow down, put your hand out and down, palm facing backward, and call "Slowing" or "Stopping." There are other, more specialized signals ("Railroad tracks" is an up-and-down with one arm, behind your back), but generally just pointing or calling will alert people to look ahead for trouble.

OREGON LIGHTING LAWS

Bob Mionske, a Portland attorney, *Bicycling* magazine columnist, and nationally recognized expert in legal issues related to bicycling, provides the following information:

In Oregon, a cyclist *or* a bicycle being operated on "any highway" must be equipped with a light and reflectors under "limited visibility conditions." Let's take a look at what those terms mean and then what equipment is required.

First, in Oregon, a highway is defined as "every public way, road, street, thoroughfare, and place, including bridges, viaducts, and other structures within the boundaries of this state, open, used, or intended for use of the general public for vehicles or vehicular traffic as a matter of right." In other words, just about everywhere but your garage.

Oregon law defines "limited visibility conditions" to be "any time from sunset to sunrise." But in addition to nighttime, "limited visibility conditions" is also defined as "any other time when, due to insufficient light or unfavorable atmospheric conditions, persons and vehicles are not clearly discernible on a straight, level, unlighted highway at a distance of 1000 feet ahead." This means, for example, that a rainstorm or snowstorm that limits visibility is also a "limited visibility condition."

So in Oregon, when a bike is being operated on a "highway" at night or under other conditions of limited visibility, the bicycle *or its rider* **must be** equipped with lighting equipment that meets the following specifications:

» The lighting equipment must show a white light visible from a distance of at least 500 feet to the front of the bicycle.
» The lighting equipment must have a red reflector or lighting device or material of such size or characteristic and so mounted as to be visible from all distances up to 600 feet to the rear when directly in front of lawful lower beams of headlights on a motor vehicle. **Note:** This means that the bicycle or its rider must be equipped with either a red reflector or a red light or other material that meets the same requirement for visibility to the rear.

The bicycle or its rider *may be* (but is not required to be) equipped with additional lights and reflectors.

Keeping Bob's information in mind, my bottom-line recommendation is this: If you're riding in any kind of conditions where visibility could be an issue, have a bright white light pointing forward and at least one bright red one pointing to the rear.

RIDING TIPS AND TECHNIQUES

While a guidebook is principally a listing of routes, it doesn't hurt to offer a few tips for new riders, novices, or maybe those just looking to pick up a few pointers. Here are some basic riding techniques.

PEDALING

Because your pedal stroke is your sole means of propulsion, its efficiency is of paramount importance. Most people learn to ride a bike by pushing down on one pedal and then pushing down on the other; however, that's neglecting half the cycle of each pedal circuit. This is where cleats and clipless pedals make the big difference: You learn to "pedal circles," both pushing down *and* pulling up on each revolution. (Of course you're already pedaling in circles, because your chain rings are round, but if you're only pushing down, that's referred to as "pedaling squares." Don't ponder the geometry; just go with the larger concept.) First of all, pedaling circles increases your power, because you're using both legs at any given time instead of just the one pushing down. Second, pedaling circles uses different muscles, spreading the work out so it's not just your thighs carrying the load.

It's not natural for most riders to pedal circles, and it takes considerable concentration and practice to train yourself to simultaneously push and pull. A common mental image trainers invoke here is to scrape the mud off the bottom of each shoe when it reaches the bottom of the pedal cycle. Mimicking the motion you would make to wipe your feet on a doormat will help you pull through the bottom of each stroke. Work on this when you're riding by yourself so you can concentrate on it. And understand that even the best racers don't really get 50 percent of their power from the upstroke; just try to help out the downstroke a bit.

Other pedaling thoughts include these: Try not to point your toes down at any point during the pedal stroke—keep your feet as parallel to the ground as possible; this is more efficient and will reduce leg fatigue. And your ideal pedal stroke would be a smooth circular action with no hitches, no knees thrown out to the side . . . think of your leg action like two engine pistons—smoothly up, smoothly down, in line.

GEARING

What gear to ride in? Most training experts recommend maintaining a steady 80–90 revolutions per minute for normal riding. Riding in a bigger gear than necessary is hard on the legs—joints and muscles both—and can lead to pain and injuries. A smooth, fairly rapid cadence is ideal for most riders. But not all—anyone who ever watched Lance Armstrong and Jan Ullrich riding up a hill side by side (Lance spinning, Jan mashing) knows this is something you'll have to figure out for yourself. This is especially true for climbing. A simple test is to ride a short but significant hill in a low gear, timing your climb or assessing your perceived exertion. Then the next day or next time you ride (so you've recovered

fully), try it again in a higher gear. Compare times, perceived exertion, and recovery.

Same thing for climbing seated or standing; conventional wisdom is that sitting while climbing takes less overall energy, but some riders (I'm one) are more effective or comfortable standing, even for long stretches. Even if you sit most of the time, standing for a burst of power through a hairpin or steep stretch or just to stretch out your back and move the effort around in your leg muscles is a good idea. When you're standing, try to be as still as possible, and don't wrench your upper body around or pull up on the handlebars; it's still your legs doing the work.

CORNERING AND DESCENDING

This book isn't a training manual, but here are a couple basics that I found extremely helpful as I was working on my bike skills as a new rider. Cornering and descending skills can make a major difference in not only your safety but also your speed and enjoyment. These surface-level concepts might get you started on improving your own skills.

When you're approaching a corner, the most important thing is to have a plan. Look through the corner, down the road a bit, to assess the situation: How sharp is it? Can you see through the entire corner? Can you see oncoming traffic? Assess and make a plan based on your comfort and safety levels.

Let's say it's a smooth 45-degree curve, and you can see all the way through it; your most efficient line is outside-inside-outside. That is, pick as straight a line through the curve as possible, starting wide, cutting across to the inside of the arc, and exiting out to a wide line. This is more efficient and safer than hugging the inside of the curve all the way around. Be aware of riders around you—don't cut anyone off—and only cut to the inside as far as it's safe given the road and your ability to see what's coming the other way.

One of the attractions of riding in Oregon is the sheer variety of terrain. Here, east of Baker City, time and distance stretch out like the horizon. Greg Lee/Cycle Oregon

The second thing when approaching a corner is this: Just as in a car, if you need to brake for a corner, do it before you enter it. Scrubbing your speed entering the curve will allow you to power through it, giving you momentum coming out of it instead of losing momentum by braking in the middle of the curve. And know that your front brake has far more slowing power than your back one—but it's also connected to the wheel that's doing the steering, so blend your braking to your comfort and skill levels; never jam on the front brake in a cornering situation.

Here's a third consideration: If you want to get faster through long corners—twisting descents, in particular—ride with the pedal on the inside of the curve up and the one on the outside down, and press hard on the outside (down) pedal as you lean into the curve. It's the opposite of how you'd make a hard turn on a ski, but on a bike it has the same effect: You carve through the corner. Be cautious trying it for the first few times, but it's a blast when you get the hang of it.

HOW TO USE THIS BOOK

I've divided Oregon into eight geographic regions, from the Pacific coast inland and from Portland south. Routes might be a one-way out-and-back, loop, or "lollipop" configuration: an out-and-back with a loop at the far end. The structure in each route description is pretty straightforward. The first thing you'll find is an information summary that gives you a feel for the route. It includes a pithy description ("If you were going to describe this ride in seven words or less"), followed by the following data.

DIFFICULTY RATINGS

The difficulty of each ride is a combination of three main factors: length (distance), elevation gain, and riding environment. If a route is long, hilly, or has high traffic levels, one of those factors by itself is going to bump it up a level of difficulty. If it has more than one of these factors, it's going to be rated even more difficult. Here's my rating system:

» **Easy**—A ride anyone who is fit enough to ride a bike should be able to handle. There are no significant climbs (or very few, or very short ones), and the distance is something a beginning rider or a child riding on his or her own can likely handle. Easy rides are also typically not on public roads—they're either on rails-to-trails conversions or dedicated bike-pedestrian paths.
» **Moderate**—These rides head out onto the open road but are still doable for the majority of adult riders of all ages and speeds (as with anything rated above Easy, you'll have to be the judge of your kid's ability to take these on). While there's not a strict mileage range for Moderate rides, they typically can be completed in an hour or two and don't have extended or steep climbs.
» **Challenging**—A ride that has some combination of length and climbing that means it's suitable only for those who ride often, have regularly done rides of several hours or more, and have a positive working relationship with climbing. Again, it's more about terrain than length.
» **Epic**—A signature ride for the hard-core cyclist who rarely if ever meets a hill too high or a ride too long. I'm talking thousands of feet of climbing and hours of work. Of course, the rewards are usually commensurate with the effort.

A quick note on the difficulty ratings: This book does lean toward more difficult rides. In fact, it's been suggested that it could have been called *75 Places to Suffer on Your Bike in Oregon*. Of course, that's not true . . . it just has the element of truth to it. When I hear "classic ride in Oregon," I immediately think

of mountain passes and memorable challenges. But I've tried to include a reasonable number of rides to suit anyone's tastes. Tried.

TIME

It's difficult to estimate times, of course, given the wide range of speeds possible on a bike. My approach is to consider an average of 15 miles per hour as the upper end (I know, I know: Some of you are faster than that, but not many, and not that much, over a long route), and that results in the shorter time estimate. For the other end of the time range, I used about 10 miles per hour, which is a nice leisurely pace. The time estimate comes into play only on longer rides, really, and my reasoning is that if you're taking on a Moderate or Challenging ride, you can average 10 miles per hour.

DISTANCE

In the interest of consistency, I mapped all these routes on a computer using the same mapping program. As I've ridden and driven on my research, inevitably small inconsistencies have shown up. My bike's computer and the mapping program tend to line up quite well; my car's odometer, not so much. So I've gone with the mapping program. Just realize that you may have to give a little leeway here and there; in the mileage logs (turn-by-turn directions), 13.95 miles might turn out to be 14.05 miles on your cyclometer. Hey, maybe you turned around and went back to look at that waterfall again or swerved over to the espresso shack across the road. It's more about the directions than the exact mileage.

ELEVATION GAIN

The total amount of climbing over the entire route, in feet, is a good indicator of the overall difficulty of the ride in terms of climbing: It might be long and steady, it might be shorter and steeper, but 3000 feet is still 3000 feet.

Note that I wasn't able to clock elevation gain on my bike computer for all routes, so again, in the interest of consistency, I went with the mapping program's total. But I often found significant inconsistencies between my bike computer's reading and the mapping program—I'm talking 1000 feet different on Epic rides—so I'll just say that the Elevation Gain listing is an indicator of overall difficulty; as they say in the fine print, your results may vary.

BEST SEASONS

The listing of best seasons is based on a typical year, which is difficult, given the vagaries of winter weather; 2010–11, for example, was a drastically bad winter and spring for rides in higher elevations (the Rim Road at Crater Lake didn't open until July 28, for instance). If there's any question of a road's being open, check with a local government agency. For a lot of the mountain passes, that is the US Forest Service, and they're generally easy to contact and quite helpful.

ROAD CONDITIONS

I've included this listing when there are notable circumstances of the road surface, traffic levels, or shoulder existence, width, or condition. The default on most back roads, forest roads, and small highways is little or no shoulder; that by itself doesn't merit a mention in this book. If there are particularly serious concerns, look for this heading.

GETTING THERE

I've tried to start directions to each ride with a general location such as Portland or one of the main freeways, guiding you to the ride's start from that point, with increasing specificity as you get closer. The majority of rides begin at public parks, for two reasons: free parking, plus restrooms and water. In some cases that's not possible or advantageous; occasionally I

recommend you ask a store owner in a small town for permission, where I've had luck doing the same.

ROUTE VARIATIONS

I include this listing when there are options for a longer or shorter ride, a connection to another route in the book, or any other variation from the route as mapped and described.

OTHER INFORMATION SOURCES

Oregon has a bounty of bicycling organizations that provide information you can use to augment what's in this book. Check out the Resources at the back of this book for some good choices. In addition, here are three particularly noteworthy Oregon-specific resources.

OREGON'S SCENIC BIKEWAYS PROGRAM

Oregon has initiated a unique (so far) program for cycling, creating a "Scenic Bikeway" designation to parallel the Scenic Byways highway programs in place across the country. The idea is to create a network of mapped, signed, and promoted cycling routes that represent the best cycling Oregon has to offer. Of course, that's the same basic goal of this book, so I'm a big proponent of the Scenic Bikeways program. Oregon is the first state with such a program; it's managed primarily by the Oregon Parks and Recreation Department, but it has the fingerprints of many groups and people on it. Routes are nominated by local residents who feel their area has something great to offer, and a committee reviews the routes, rides them, assesses their potential, and then approves or denies the application. The Willamette Valley Scenic Bikeway (Ride 73) was the pilot project, and it's been well received and heavily traveled. As of 2011, a new group of Scenic Bikeways has been approved, and individual routes have been publicly announced. The state prepares highly detailed maps that include camping possibilities and other amenities; I encourage you to check out what's available at www.oregon.gov/OPRD/PARKS/BIKE/.

CYCLE OREGON

No discussion of road cycling in Oregon is complete without a nod to Cycle Oregon, an annual event that has had an immense impact on bicycling in Oregon in its 25 years of existence. What started out as a bit of a lark—get a few people together and do a weeklong ride to see some of the cool parts of Oregon—has turned into a powerful force in tourism, economic development, and bicycle advocacy. One of the original goals of the event was to provide economic benefits to Oregon's rural communities—many hit hard by changes in industries such as timber— by taking people through these towns and pumping some money into them. Besides

paying a fee to communities that provide volunteers for the event and serve as host sites for the 2000-plus riders each year, the Cycle Oregon Fund provides grants for specific projects, some related to cycling, some just to help communities with needed projects. Cycle Oregon has provided literally millions of dollars to Oregon communities across the state—more than 100 different towns have hosted the event. In addition, Cycle Oregon has worked tirelessly on the local, state, and national levels to advocate for bicycle-related causes—most notably to get more bike funding, infrastructure, and awareness, so more people can and will ride bikes.

One of the results of Cycle Oregon's longevity and popularity is that the event has covered seemingly every road in the state that's navigable by a large group of riders. And that means there's a good bit of overlap between past and present Cycle Oregon routes and what you'll find in this book. Neither I nor Cycle Oregon sees that as a problem—a great route is a great route, and we want you to ride

The unique floating-bridge design of Portland's Eastbank Esplanade means the ramp's angles change by the season, based on Willamette River water levels.

here—and Cycle Oregon exposed me to a significant number of these routes.

RIDEOREGONRIDE.COM

Travel Oregon, the state's central tourism agency, has created a bicycling-tourism website called Ride Oregon (www.rideoregonride.com) that contains a wealth of information on cycling in Oregon, including hundreds of road routes as well as a plethora of related resources. It's a one-stop information clearinghouse for planning cycling trips in the state—and another source for some of the routes in this book. The site is set up for users to generate content, add comments, and connect with each other; go there and add to the storehouse of Oregon cycling knowledge.

BEST OF THE BEST

Everyone loves lists, it seems—so here are a few for you to ponder. I thought about trying to rank them, or make them all the same length, but that proved nearly impossible, so I wimped out and just included all the best rides for each category and ordered them alphabetically.

BEST FAMILY RIDES

Banks–Vernonia Trail (Ride 7): Train trestles, deep forest, smooth pavement

Bear Creek Greenway (Ride 35): Pick your segment; lots of restrooms and even play areas

Eastbank Esplanade (Ride 17): The best view of downtown Portland on a bike, and it's like a human parade

Eugene Bike Paths (Ride 27): Shady and interesting, with a ton of places to stop and hang out

Marine Drive Path (Ride 13): Sailboats on one side, airport on the other; kids will be fascinated

Salem Family Fun Ride (Ride 20): A bridge, a museum, a carousel, a paddlewheel boat; it's a playground

Twin Tunnels (Ride 44): The best views anywhere, on a broad and smooth path; plus, tunnels!

PRETTIEST ROUTES (WATER DIVISION)

Applegate Lake (Ride 34): Riding the edge of a picture postcard when you reach the lake

Aufderheide Memorial Drive (Ride 52): Follow one river up, follow another down, and then a sparkling reservoir

Crater Lake Rim Road (Ride 55): Crater Lake . . . from every angle

Newport–Siletz Loop (Ride 4): First half, a deep-forest stream; second half, riding along the ocean

The Oregon Coast Route (Ride 72): 360 miles of bays, capes, beaches, and headlands

Quartzville Creek (Ride 26): Reservoirs and river; the water views never end

Rogue River Ramble (Ride 32): One Wild & Scenic River, plus two tumbling creeks

Three Capes Scenic Route (Ride 3): A full taste of the Oregon Coast in one compact route

The Waterfall Ride (Ride 42): Seven waterfalls in 10 miles; enough said

PRETTIEST ROUTES (LAND DIVISION)

Crater Lake Up-and-Over (Ride 56): Meadows, canyons, one big volcano, old-growth forest

This view out to a prime piece of coastal real estate comes on the Otter Crest Loop, a serene road with a stellar bike lane.

Fossil Lollipop (Ride 62): A variety of stunning geology on display

Lolo Pass (Ride 48): Deep green forest and sudden views of Mount Hood

McKenzie Pass (Ride 51): A unique lunar landscape of lava

Siuslaw and Smith Rivers (Ride 6): Maybe the coolest forest road of all

Summit to Surf (Ride 47): Alpine canyons and forest, a climb to Timberline Lodge, and a glide to the Columbia Gorge

SMALL-TOWN HIGHLIGHTS

Applegate Lake (Ride 34): Yes, it's touristy, but Jacksonville is Old West cool

Joseph–Enterprise Loop (Ride 66): Joseph may enjoy the prettiest setting in Oregon

Silver Falls (Ride 21): Silverton is a quiet, pretty burg with a great downtown

Three Capes Scenic Loop (Ride 3): Get away from coastal kitsch and explore some real beach towns

Vernonia to Astoria (Ride 1): Two towns working hard at renaissances; Astoria is in the lead

TOP CLIMBING CHALLENGES

Bald Peak Two Ways (Ride 9): You climb it twice, and the second time part of it is 18 percent

Cedar Flat Loop (Ride 33): The steepest sustained climb in the book

Cottage Grove to Oakridge (Ride 53): Relentless and steep, deep in the woods

Larch Mountain (Ride 40): It's pretty much uphill all the way, for 20-plus miles

Timothy Lake the Back Way (Ride 49): Half-mile warm-up; 13-mile climb that gets steeper at the top

Tour de Fronds (Ride 31): This one just seems to hurt the most, for some reason

Wallowa Mountains and Hells Canyon Loop (Ride 75): From Halfway to Joseph, three tough climbs in a row (plus another one to an overlook)

BEST DESCENTS

Applegate Lake (Ride 34): Long, swoopy, and satisfying; it just keeps going and going....

Aufderheide Memorial Drive (Ride 52): A magic-carpet ride along the river and through the woods

Bald Peak Two Ways (Ride 9): Probably the fastest descent you're going to find

Cedar Flat Loop (Ride 33): The most exacting technical descent; don't look down

Cottage Grove to Oakridge (Ride 53): A giant slalom course on a bike

Old Oregon Trail (Ride 64): Switchback heaven, with a long runout

Timothy Lake the Back Way (Ride 49): Miles of smooth one-lane bliss

ROUTES YOU CAN CONNECT TO MAKE A TOUR

The Coast Route from Portland: Connect Banks–Vernonia Trail (Ride 7), Vernonia to Astoria (Ride 1), and Oregon Coast Route (Ride 72)

Mount Hood to The Gorge: Connect Lolo Pass (Ride 48), Summit to Surf (Ride 47), and Hood River to The Dalles (Ride 45)

Northeast Oregon Explorer: Connect Union Loop (Ride 67) and Baker City to Sumpter and Back (Ride 68)

Southeast Oregon Explorer: Connect Burns to Frenchglen via the Narrows (Ride 70) and Frenchglen to Burns via Diamond Valley (Ride 71)

Willamette Valley to the Coast: Connect Willamette Valley Scenic Bikeway (Ride 73) and Siuslaw and Smith Rivers (Ride 6)

Crater Lake to Ashland: Connect Crater Lake Up-and-Over (Ride 56), Crater Lake Rim Road (Ride 55), and Prospect to Ashland (Ride 38)

Cascade Passes Tour: Connect Crater Lake Up-and-Over (Ride 56), Crater Lake Rim Road (Ride 55), Diamond Lake to Cottage Grove (Ride 54), Cottage Grove to Oakridge (Ride 53), Aufderheide Memorial Drive (Ride 52), and McKenzie Pass (Ride 51)

A NOTE ABOUT SAFETY

Safety is an important concern in all outdoor activities. No guidebook can alert you to every hazard or anticipate the limitations of every reader. Therefore, the descriptions of roads, bike paths, routes, and natural features in this book are not representations that a particular place or excursion will be safe for your party. When you follow any of the routes described in this book, you assume responsibility for your own safety. Under normal conditions, such excursions require the usual attention to traffic, road and path conditions, weather, terrain, the capabilities of your party, and other factors. Keeping informed on current conditions and exercising common sense are the keys to a safe, enjoyable outing.

—*The Mountaineers Books*

THE COAST

Here's the best thing to know about the Oregon Coast: No one can own the beach—anywhere. State law. That spirit of unfettered public access, along with it being an awesome natural playground, makes the Oregon Coast a pleasure to ride. There aren't many inland roads that aren't passes, but I've included some good ones—or you can just pedal the whole beautiful coast.

1 VERNONIA TO ASTORIA

FROM COASTAL FOREST TO COASTAL BAY

Difficulty: Challenging
Time: 4 to 6 hours
Distance: 66.7 miles one way
Elevation Gain: 2110 feet
Best Seasons: Year-round

ROAD CONDITIONS: Road to Astoria Column narrow and windy, with no shoulder—but traffic is pretty much at sightseeing-tourist speed.

GETTING THERE: From Portland, take US 26 west past where SR 6 splits off; turn off onto SR 47 toward Vernonia and follow it into town. When you come into town, main road turns 90 degrees to right and becomes Bridge St. in downtown Vernonia. Go four blocks and turn right on Adams Ave., following it roughly three blocks south to entrance to Anderson Park. Free parking available if you swing around the park past camping spots and almost back out of the park; restrooms are right next to this parking area.

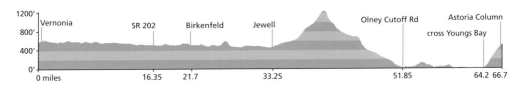

When people ask me how to ride from Portland to the coast, first I ask them how many miles or days they have in mind. If they want to make it two days, I'll tell them to head west into Washington County, connect with the Banks–Vernonia Trail (Ride 7), and

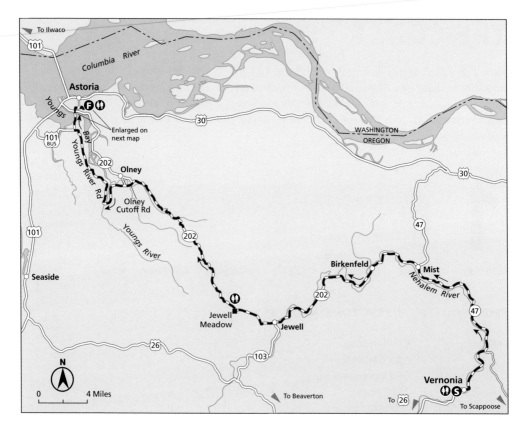

then go from Vernonia to Astoria. If they have only one day, I tell them to start in Vernonia, as this route does.

This idyllic ride along placid rivers and through coastal forest ends up at Astoria, the oldest city in the Northwest, positioned right next to where the Columbia River enters the Pacific Ocean. But one of my favorite ways to describe this route is to simply explain that it goes through a town called Mist. That tells you this route is lush and green.

Start in Vernonia, a town bouncing back from devastating flooding in 2009—when it was already bouncing back from decades of decline due to the timber industry's waning fortunes. It's not a bad little town, and it's fighting back hard. From rustic Anderson Park, get back to the main drag, State Route 47, and follow it up and over a small rise, using a separated bike lane. Follow the bike

lane to the bridge over the Nehalem River— the first of several crossings of this mostly tranquil stream. Take a left just after the bridge to remain on SR 47.

The shoulder eventually gets smaller and then disappears. On this stretch you're dancing with the river, following it, then crossing it twice more. After passing the junction for Scappoose at 5.35 miles, you're riding literally on the bank of the river at times. Traffic drops off here, and you see pockets of pastureland in the foreground and a patchwork of logged and replanted forest parcels behind.

Look for a piece of roadside bike art on the left at 10.7 miles, and at 12.6 the Natal Grange Hall and a one-room schoolhouse built in 1908 are worth a quick stop. At around 16 miles you come into the aforementioned Mist, staying to the left at 16.35 miles to turn onto SR 202. The road is generally gentle rollers. At Birkenfeld (21.7 miles) there's a nice little store. The road surface is a little uneven here—patchy in some spots and superb in others. After an intervening half-mile climb and corresponding descent, at around 35.5 miles the Jewell Meadow elk viewing area extends along the road for a mile.

At 37.8 miles there's a small county park, after which the climbing begins. It's narrow and curvy, but you'll be distracted by deep forest and a mossy creek, summiting at 40.6 miles. From there the elevation chart plunges like a bad electrocardiogram; it's a fun plummet, but be careful with the road surface.

At this point the proximity to the coast brings an elevated level of mossiness to the forest, as you first break out briefly to broad, panoramic views and then drop down to a deep-green creek bed. As you creep up on 50 miles, you'll start to see signs of civilization; at 51.85 miles turn left onto Olney Cutoff Road (although there's a cool little store-saloon just ahead on SR 202 if you need it).

From here the route follows the latter part of Ride 2, Youngs Bay, coming into Astoria on the US 101 business route.

Route Variation: Just for fun, I've ended the ride at the Astoria Column; if you don't want a stiff bit of climbing at the end, you can just roll into town somewhere. But if you want to end the route with a panoramic view, follow the mileage log directions carefully.

The ride up to the Astoria Column scales 600-foot Coxcomb Hill, with views back toward Youngs Bay to the south. Greg Lee/Cycle Oregon

0.0   From Anderson Park in Vernonia, head north on Adams St.
0.15   Right onto SR 47 (Bridge St.).
1.2   Bear left to stay on SR 47 after bridge.
5.35   Bear left to stay on SR 47 at junction to Scappoose.
16.35   Left onto SR 202 at Mist.
21.7   Enter Birkenfeld.
33.25   Enter Jewell.
37.8   Pass entrance to county park (restrooms) on right.
40.6   Reach summit.
51.85   Left onto Olney Cutoff Rd.
52.2   Bear right to stay on Olney Cutoff Rd.
52.65   Left onto Youngs River Rd.
62.85   Bear left onto Warrenton–Astoria Hwy.
63.2   Right onto US 101 business route.
64.2   Cross Youngs Bay.
64.6   Bear right onto Fifth St.
64.7   Cross SR 202.
64.8   Right onto Nehalem Ave.
64.9   Left onto Seventh St.
65.35   Right onto Niagara Ave.
65.8   Left onto 15th St.
65.9   Right onto Coxcomb Dr.
66.7   Finish at Astoria Column.

2 YOUNGS BAY

A COASTAL RIDE WITH AN INLAND FEEL

Difficulty: Moderate
Time: 1½ to 2 hours
Distance: 22.3-mile loop
Elevation Gain: 466 feet
Best Seasons: Year-round

ROAD CONDITIONS: Tricky little transition at 0.7 mile where you have to get in left-turn lane to stay on SR 202, but that's about the worst bit, and it's out of the way early. At 3.8 miles a bridge has a section of metal grate in the middle—be very careful if it's at all wet. At about

13 miles, road surface goes pretty bad for 0.5 mile; evidence of road-slide damage, then pavement is on-and-off for a while. At 21.4 miles choose roadway or sidewalk when crossing the bridge; sidewalk is safer, but it's blocked at midpoint.

GETTING THERE: Head to Astoria on US 101 from the south or US 30 from the east; at traffic circle at east end of Youngs Bay Bridge, head southeast onto W. Marine Dr. (SR 202). Turn left off SR 202 to enter Tapiola Park, and drive up a slight hill to parking area (free).

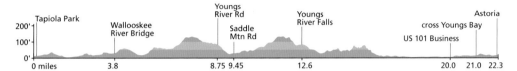

Sometimes you want to ride right on the ocean . . . and then again, sometimes you don't. Here's a pleasant, scenic, and moderate ride that serves as a counterpoint to the levels of weather and traffic you may encounter near the beach.

Starting at Tapiola Park—only because it's conveniently located—head out of town on State Route 202. The early section affords a shoulder that ranges from adequate to broad; Youngs Bay laps at the shore just feet away, and gulls hover above while seabirds float on the water.

The shoulder eventually peters out, and you transition to riding along the banks of the Youngs River. Around 6.5 miles, enter a straight woodsy stretch broken up by pockets of pasture. A barely perceptible climb takes you to 7.8 miles, where you drop down into a lazy serpentine.

At 8.7 miles is the Olney general store–café–saloon; just past it, take the turnoff to the right for Youngs River Loop. A quick drop down and then it flattens out; at 9.45 miles, at the intersection with Saddle Mountain Road (feel like a big climb . . . ?), bear right. At 12.6 miles you can take the turnoff for Youngs River Falls; it's a short climb up for a nice view. Then it's the horseshoe section of the loop and the beginning of a short, steady rise.

The next stretch is positively pastoral: small, tidy cottages to the right, dairy barns below,

fishermen in rowboats out on the water. The road skirts the base of hills bordering the river valley, taking you on small rises and drops as you follow the contours. At 17.9 miles, don't miss the fence on the right made up of old bicycles used as flower planters.

At 18.9 miles, start a series of sharp corners,

The pleasant ride around Youngs Bay makes for a nice meander. And apparently it induces friendly feelings in riders. Cycle Oregon

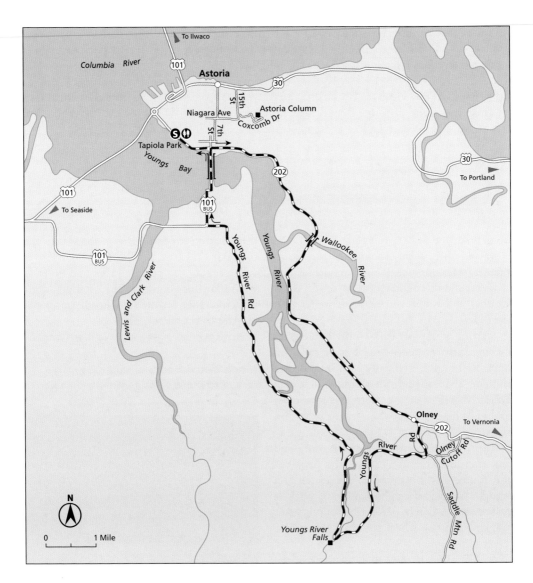

culminating in a 90-degree left at 19.6 miles. Soon after, reach a triangle intersection and veer right, through two stop signs. Once across the bay bridge, you'll bear left to con- nect to SR 202; beware of cars merging in from the right. Then pedal past the school on the right and back to the park.

MILEAGE LOG

0.0	From Tapiola Park, head southwest on Tapiola Park Rd.
0.05	Left onto SR 202 (W. Marine Dr.).
3.8	Cross Wallooskee River.
8.7	Pass Olney store on left.

8.75	Right onto Youngs River Rd.
9.45	Bear right to stay on Youngs River Rd.
12.6	Pass turnoff for Youngs River Falls.
19.6	Bear left to stay on Youngs River Rd.
20.0	Right onto US 101 business route.
21.0	Cross Youngs Bay.
21.5	Left onto SR 202 (W. Marine Dr.).
22.25	Right on Tapiola Park Rd.
22.3	Finish at Tapiola Park in Astoria.

3 THREE CAPES SCENIC LOOP

OFF THE BEATEN (COASTAL) PATH

Difficulty:	Challenging
Time:	4 to 6 hours
Distance:	61.75-mile loop
Elevation Gain:	2247 feet
Best Seasons:	Year-round

ROAD CONDITIONS: Unfortunately, some of the worst pavement in the state; coastal roads are tough to maintain, so this route is for confident bike-handlers only.

GETTING THERE: From US 101 in Tillamook, turn west on Eighth St. and go three blocks to Stillwell Park. Free parking; go through YMCA lot.

Oregon's North Coast is a beautiful place, with accessible beaches, rocky headlands, and towering capes. It's also the part of the coast closest to the majority of the state's population (meaning Portland). The result is that US 101 can resemble a rush-hour freeway on nice weekends. And, personally, I'm not that big on T-shirts-and-trinkets shops. So when I go to the coast, I like to stay in Oceanside, on the Three Capes Scenic Loop. Same thing goes for riding: It's off US 101, it's gorgeous, and it's quiet.

The route starts in Tillamook; pedal right out of town on the Netarts Highway, cross the Tillamook River, turn onto the Three Capes Loop at Bayocean Road at 1.95 miles, and you're in blissful quietude. A glassy, calm section of Tillamook Bay is on your right for miles.

At 6.8 miles, stop to read the information sign about Bayshore, a really-old-school planned community with a sad (or ironic) ending. Just after, turn left onto Cape Meares Loop Road. A hint: When the word "cape" is involved, gear down. About 1.5 miles of pretty bad pavement later, you're at the top, for now. A half-mile later is the entrance for Cape Meares State Park—a good side trip (with restrooms) if you're inclined.

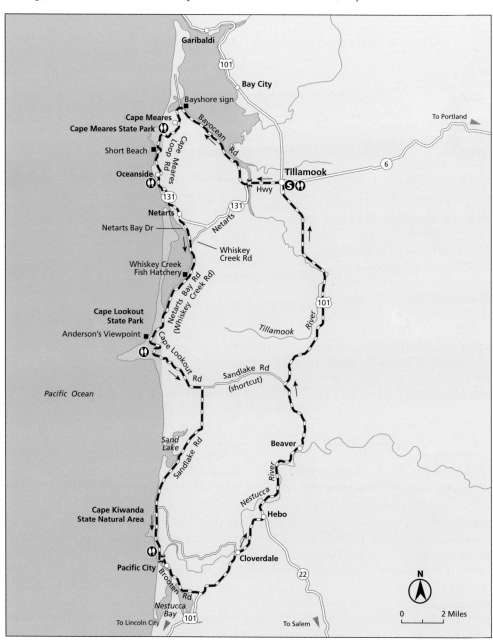

It's hard to resist the simple beauty of a lighthouse—in this case, the one at Cape Meares. Stop in for a great view and a rest from the road. Oregon State Parks

From here the road goes downhill fast—in both senses. Dance carefully around the potholes; when you bottom out at 10.4 miles, consider a stop at Short Beach. Find the tree-tunnel of a trail down to a cool, secluded beach with its own "waterfall."

Climb more, then drop down into the funky little town of Oceanside at around 11.5 miles. Again, this is a good beach stop—head north on the main beach and go through a dark rock tunnel to another beach. Back on the road, turn left, skirt a broad beach, and then climb steeply to 12.4 miles, followed by sharp rollers. At 14 miles hit Netarts, cool town number two; there's a store about a block to the right.

Here the road drops down alongside Netarts Bay—the first flat stretch in a long while. You may see clammers in the tidal flats. At the stop sign at 15.4 miles, bear right; at 16.8 the Whiskey Creek Fish Hatchery has a visitor center.

When you start climbing Cape Lookout—a formidable climb—you get an actual bike lane, which is downright heavenly at this point in the ride, even if it gets a little mossy in places near the top. Stop at Anderson's Viewpoint at 20.3 miles—just look back, and you'll understand—and then finish the ascent at 21.8 miles, just before the entrance to Cape Lookout State Park (restrooms). Enjoy a sharp, twisty descent, and then when it flattens out you'll end up beside a big area of dunes—heaven for all-terrain vehicles.

At 25.5 miles, turn right on Sandlake Road, which starts out mostly flat, through pastures and tidal flats, before rising up at 30.9 miles. Go straight through the stop sign, finish one more small climb, and then drop down in Pacific City, below Cape Kiwanda and its state natural area (restrooms).

Pacific City is the "big city" of Three Capes. When you first hit town, the area on the right is a surfing hot spot with a good beach for exploring and a giant dune to climb and then slide or tumble down. There's a popular brewpub here, too, and a store on the left. Cross the Nestucca River and end up on Brooten Road, following the estuary of the Nestucca all the way to US 101.

The benefit of being on US 101 is good pavement; the drawback is more traffic and intermittent shoulder. There are stores at Cloverdale, Hebo, and Beaver ("groceries and firearms" in one stop!). You're going through dairyland here; after Beaver you get a great bike lane all the way to Tillamook. South of town on the right is the Tillamook Air Museum, with its massive blimp hangar; return to Stillwell Park.

Route Variation: At 25.5 miles you can stay straight on Sandlake Road, following the Coast Bike Route signs back to US 101, then left to head back to Tillamook for a shortcut option.

MILEAGE LOG

0.0	From Stillwell Park, head north on Stillwell Ave.
0.25	Left onto Third St. (Netarts Hwy., SR 131).
1.75	Cross Tillamook River.
1.95	Right on Bayocean Rd.
6.95	Bear left as it becomes Bayshore Dr. (Cape Meares Loop Rd.).
9.25	Entrance to Cape Meares State Park (restrooms).
10.4	Pass Short Beach.
11.6	Enter Oceanside.
11.75	Bear left as it becomes Netarts–Oceanside Hwy. (SR 131).
14.0	Enter Netarts.
14.2	Right onto Netarts Bay Rd. (Whiskey Creek Rd).
15.4	Bear right at a stop sign to stay on Netarts Bay Rd.
16.8	Pass Whiskey Creek Fish Hatchery visitor center.
20.3	Pass Anderson's Viewpoint.
22.0	Entrance to Cape Lookout State Park (restrooms).
25.5	Right onto Sandlake Rd.
33.2	Entrance to Cape Kiwanda State Natural Area (restrooms).
34.35	Right onto Pacific Ave. in Pacific City.
34.55	Left onto Brooten Rd.
37.3	Left onto US 101.
42.7	Bear left to stay on US 101 at SR 22 in Hebo.
47.2	Enter Beaver.
47.35	Bear left to stay on US 101.
61.3	Bear right as US 101 splits entering Tillamook.
61.6	Left onto Eighth St.
61.75	Finish at Stillwell Park.

Variation—Sandlake Shortcut:

25.5   Go straight as Netarts Bay Rd. becomes Sandlake Rd.
29.8   Left on US 101.
40.3   Bear right as US 101 splits entering Tillamook.
40.6   Left onto Eighth St.
40.75   Finish at Stillwell Park.

NEWPORT–SILETZ LOOP

A TRIPLE SCOOP OF COASTAL FLAVOR

Difficulty:	Challenging
Time:	4 to 6 hours
Distance:	67.35-mile loop
Elevation Gain:	1798 feet
Best Seasons:	Year-round

ROAD CONDITIONS: Short stretch of narrow, rough road just before Toledo; no shoulder on SR 229, but pavement is good and traffic is light.

GETTING THERE: From US 101 in Newport, just north of Yaquina Bay Bridge turn west on SW Minnie St., go three blocks, turn left on SW Mark St., and go one block to entrance to Yaquina Bay State Recreation Site, at SW Government St. Parking available at several points within the site, as well as restrooms—but to match mileage log, start at north entrance.

This ride is like a triple-scoop ice cream cone, at the beach—you get three distinctly different flavors in one wonderful treat of a ride: back-bay tranquility, wild coastal river-forest, and drop-dead-gorgeous coastline views.

Start at the Yaquina Bay State Recreation Site, with its lighthouse as well as great views of the twin jetties in Yaquina Bay. Take a right to go under the huge US 101 bridge (don't

follow the Oregon Coast Bike Route signs; that comes later). Once under the bridge, take the first right onto SW Naterlin Drive, hook a right at the stop sign, and turn left onto Bay Boulevard—the main drag of Yaquina Bay. Weave among the tourists and fisheries workers, or grab a meal or some saltwater taffy before you get to the serious riding.

Once you escape the hubbub, enjoy a

smooth road with ample shoulder as you meander peacefully for a dozen miles of bayside biking, past oyster farms and fishing docks. Just before you reach Toledo, the road pitches up sharply and gets narrow and rough—but it's a short stretch of this before dropping down into town. Go left at the stop sign and wind your way up to the US 20 crossing; stay right at the Dairy Queen and cross US 20 straight onto State Route 229.

On SR 229, ride north through farmland at a steady ascent—at first barely noticeable

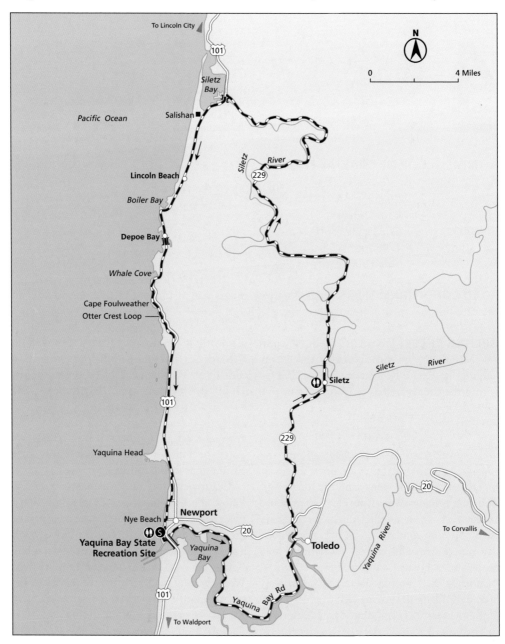

but definitely there when the passing lane arrives—taking you into the sleepy town of Siletz, which has a nice little store as well as a town park with a restroom. Out of town, the terrain changes to dense coastal forest, where the real fun begins. There's no shoulder, but it's good pavement with little traffic. Moss-draped boughs hang so low over the road you'll feel like ducking as you ride through the tree tunnel. It's a veritable Bike LeMans course: twisting, rising, falling, swooping, for miles. Stay in your lane, but ride like Steve McQueen.

Eventually you'll closely parallel the river and the homes perched on its banks, and then connect to US 101 after the water grows wide. Turning south on US 101, cross Siletz Bay—a wildlife preserve—before rolling through Salishan resort and spa (mani-pedi?). After a long, flat, and wide stretch through Lincoln Beach, get a quick taste of the more rugged coast at Boiler Bay and then check out the world's smallest harbor at famous Depoe Bay (more taffy opportunities). Climb up past picturesque Whale Cove and then drop down to the turnoff for the Otter Crest Loop, following the Coast Bike Route sign.

Otter Crest is flat-out one of my favorite pieces of riding in Oregon, even though the best part is maybe two miles long. That stretch, which comes after you cross the graceful arch of the Ben Jones Bridge, used to be closed to motor vehicles, and the forest was inexorably taking the road back—but now it's open to one-way vehicle traffic with a clearly marked, separate bike lane. It's the biggest climb of the day, but not a killer by any means. And the views, and the forest, and the. . . views. It's downright Zen-like. When you reach the Lookout Observatory, follow the bike route signs, drop down past the Inn at Otter Crest, stay straight at the next junction (no sign), and later rejoin US 101 at the bottom of Cape Foulweather—what you just climbed over.

Once back on the highway, drop low alongside two broad stretches of beach, with

A particularly fun stretch between Siletz and Kernville, on the inland leg of this route. You can't look at this road and not want to ride it.

the Yaquina Head lighthouse ahead and off to the right, before reaching the outskirts of Newport. Just past the golf course on the left, turn right onto Oceanview Drive—from here you'll be following the Oregon Coast Bike Route signs to the finish.

Oceanview lives up to its name: a narrow but slow-traffic beach boulevard that meanders along the water and through pleasant neighborhoods. Jog right and left according to the signs, passing through quaint Nye Beach and past the local performing arts center (excellent paved path down to the beach here) before passing a few hotels and arriving at the start-finish. Then go find a triple scoop to celebrate your ride.

0.0   From Yaquina Bay State Recreation Site, at SW Mark St. and SW Government St., go south into the park.
0.35 Bear right to go under US 101 bridge.
0.45 Right onto SW Naterlin Dr.
0.6   Left onto SW Bay Blvd.
2.05 Road becomes Yaquina Bay Rd.
13.75 Left onto US 20 business loop in Toledo.
14.6 Bear right at fork leading to US 20; go right of Dairy Queen.
14.7 Cross US 20; becomes Siletz Hwy. (SR 229).
22.0 Enter Siletz (restrooms).
45.75 Left onto US 101.
53.2 Cross bridge over Depoe Bay.
55.4 Right onto Otter Crest Loop (follow Oregon Coast Bike Route signs).
58.9 Right onto US 101.
64.3 Right onto NW Oceanview Dr. (follow Oregon Coast Bike Route signs to finish).
65.75 Left onto NW Spring St.
66.0 Right onto NW Eighth St.
66.05 Left onto NW Coast St.
66.45 Right onto W. Olive St.
66.6 Street becomes SW Elizabeth St. at left curve.
67.3 Right onto SW Government St.
67.35 Finish at Yaquina Bay State Recreation Site.

5   SWEET CREEK FALLS

A RIVER RIDE ON THE COAST, WITH MULTIPLE FALLS

Difficulty:	Moderate
Time:	3½ to 5 hours
Distance:	50.3 miles round-trip
Elevation Gain:	1050 feet
Best Seasons:	Year-round

ROAD CONDITIONS: SR 126, major highway with fast traffic, has wide shoulder with spotty pavement in first few miles. No shoulder—but also no traffic—on Sweet Creek Rd.; in 2011 a slide reduced road to one lane at about milepost 2, with traffic signal controlling traffic.

GETTING THERE: From US 101 in Florence, turn east on Eighth St. and then left (north) on Quince St., at intersection with SR 126. No parking at starting point, but it can be easily accessed from anywhere in the area.

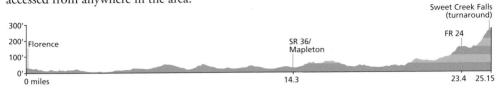

I don't know if this route is more about the ride or the destination, but sometimes that's just fine—one can be the reason and the other the bonus. This ride starts in a coastal town and ends up at an inland creek, but for the average rider, the route is far more pleasant to ride than one along the coast. The ride up Sweet Creek is quiet, pastoral, and enjoyable—and then you can explore a series of Eden-like waterfalls, all in a row. And a quick note: Wear walkable footwear and try to bring along some way to lock your bike, because you're going to want to explore on foot.

Start by heading east on State Route 126. Yes, this is a major coast-route highway, but for my money it's one of the easiest to pedal. While the shoulder pavement is a little spotty over the first few miles, it's consistently wide—and after the narrow spot in the road

identified as "Cushman," it broadens out and transitions to a velvety-smooth surface all the way to Mapleton. The traffic may be whizzing by, but it's far enough away that you don't feel claustrophobic, and besides, you're following the placid coastal stretch of the Siuslaw River. You're going upstream, but it's an easy spin that's just slightly uphill.

When you reach the beginnings of Mapleton, the shoulder narrows a bit, but it's only a short stretch to the turn for the bridge. Straight is SR 36; you want to turn right to stay on SR 126. Cross the Siuslaw and immediately look for the sign for Sweet Creek Road; turn right.

There's no appreciable shoulder here, but there's typically no appreciable traffic, either, and the surface is quite nice. The road backtracks along the Siuslaw for several miles, with

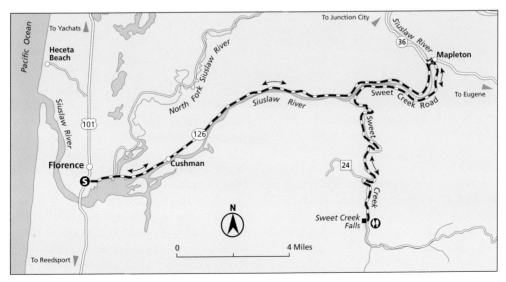

Sometimes it is about the destination: When you reach the turnaround point at Sweet Creek Falls, take the time to explore the trail and a series of picturesque falls.

the lush green vegetation of the coast forming a canopy overhead and ferns blanketing the hillside to the left. The last time I rode this, a slide had reduced the road to one lane at just about milepost 2, with a signal light controlling traffic.

After a sharp left turn, the road begins to follow Sweet Creek, which rises more sharply than the Siuslaw does (the majority of the climbing takes place in the last few miles to the falls). The road rolls and dips, veers and sweeps, with small farms and homesteads scattered on both sides. At 23.4 miles, Forest Road 24 veers down and away to the right; there's a sign indicating that the Sweet Creek Falls trailhead is 2 miles ahead.

It's actually a little less than 2 miles; when you reach the short road down to the trailhead parking lot, turn right and head in. There's a picnic table and a restroom here; if you want to explore, you can stash your bike in the bushes or lock it to the picnic table or something else handy.

And you really should explore. Sweet Creek tumbles through a series of at least five waterfalls in a very short stretch, and you can see all of them easily from the well-maintained trail. Even a short trek of a quarter mile will take you past several viewing benches, over a short bridge, and to a nice little falls.

When you've had your fill of the falls, turn around and head back. This time it's net downhill, and the road and shoulder are just as nice going back.

MILEAGE LOG

0.0	From SR 126 and Quince St. in Florence, just east of US 101, head east on SR 126.
14.3	Right to cross bridge on SR 126 at intersection with SR 36 in Mapleton.
14.5	Right onto Sweet Creek Rd. (CR 5036).
19.1	Bear left to stay on Sweet Creek Rd. (CR 5036) at intersection with Bernhardt Creek Rd. (CR 5034).
23.4	FR 24 on the right.
25.15	Reach Sweet Creek Falls access road; turnaround point. Retrace route to start.
50.3	Finish at SR 126 and Quince St. in Florence.

6 SIUSLAW AND SMITH RIVERS

UP ONE RIVER, DOWN ANOTHER, TO THE COAST

Difficulty:	Challenging
Time:	5 to 7 hours
Distance:	76.35 miles one way
Elevation Gain:	2408 feet
Best Seasons:	Year-round, unless Coast Range has significant snowfall

ROAD CONDITIONS: Uneven pavement surface on Siuslaw River Rd. worsens after 21 miles. Short bit of traffic on US 101 at end of ride.

GETTING THERE: From I-5, take exit 174 for Cottage Grove. Turn west off exit and then after 0.5 mile bear left at bottom of hill to merge with SR 99 (N. Ninth St.). Go 0.7 mile and turn right on W. Main St. Follow Main St. for about 1 mile and bear right at fork with Gowdyville Rd. onto Cottage Grove–Lorane Hwy. Follow it 11.4 miles to Territorial Hwy; bear left 0.1 mile to Siuslaw River Rd., the hub of Lorane. Local businesses are friendly about parking if you ask.

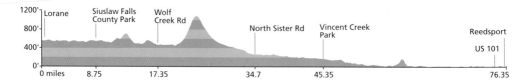

My notes from the last time I rode this route refer to "the chapel of the Coast Range"—a spot where spires of ash, maple, and alder form an arch above the road like the apse of a cathedral. And that snippet serves as a good summary of this route as a whole: It's like a hymn to the beauty of Oregon's forests and rivers. It's also a good way to ride to the coast that doesn't involve too much climbing. Note that this route is rated Challenging and not Epic; it's more about time in the saddle than overall exertion.

From Lorane, start out on good surface and flat terrain. After just a bit you'll be swallowed up by the forest, a mix of Willamette Valley and Coast Range at this point. At 8.75 miles is Siuslaw Falls County Park. The road wiggles up and down a bit, but the first time you really have to call on your hill-climbing

chops isn't until 13.2 miles. And that's just a shorty of less than a mile, with a yee-hah drop off the other side.

The big climb of the day starts at about 22 miles and lasts about 2.5 miles; the grade does reach into the 6 and 7 percent range for stretches. But it's nice and shady for the most part, and you can just find a good gear and go to your happy place.

The pavement surface gets worse as you ride, and it's fairly uneven through this section—so when you summit at 25.5 miles and start down, take it easy. It's 2.5 miles of pretty sharp descent, and then 5 or 6 miles of more gradual downhill—but with a lot of turns and the chattery pavement, make sure your hands and brake pads don't get overloaded.

Once it feels like the bottom, the good news is that it's not. Ahead are miles and miles of

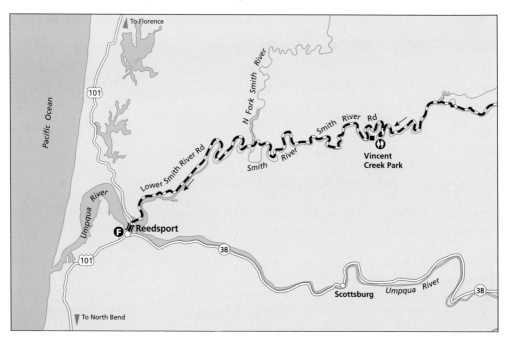

slightly declining grade, alongside a burbling creek. This is the part that evoked my "chapel" notes; light filters down to dot the road as you glide euphorically through the trees. At about 45.35 miles, Vincent Creek Park offers an idyllic setting for another break, including restrooms.

From here it's a pretty smooth run into Reedsport—a couple up-and-downs along the way, but mostly just meandering along with the Smith River as it grows wider and more placid. When you finally reach US 101, turn left and endure just under a mile of coast-highway traffic to reach the heart of town.

Route Variation: The ride from Cottage Grove to Lorane is also superlative—a smooth, forested alleyway. If you have time for 90 miles, consider starting in Cottage Grove.

The long stretch following the curves of the Smith River offers the easiest, most tranquil, and car-free route to the Oregon Coast.
Phil Bard/Cycle Oregon

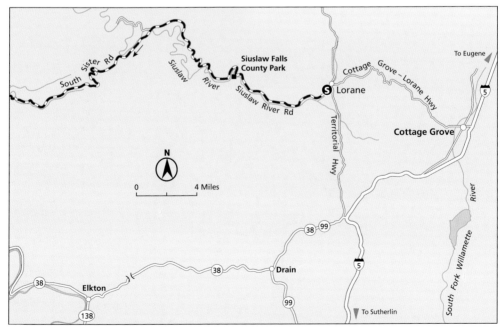

0.0	From Territorial Hwy. and Siuslaw River Rd. in Lorane, head southwest on Siuslaw River Rd.
8.75	Bear left at entrance to Siuslaw Falls County Park on right.
16.3	At five-way intersection, stay on Siuslaw River Rd.
17.35	Bear left to stay on Siuslaw River Rd. at intersection with Wolf Creek Rd.
19.05	Bear left onto South Sister Rd.
34.7	Bear left at intersection with North Sister Rd. as South Sister Rd. becomes Smith River Rd.
45.35	Stay right at entrance to Vincent Creek Park (restrooms) on left to stay on Smith River Rd., which becomes Lower Smith River Rd.
72.05	S. Smith River Rd. on left.
75.2	Left onto US 101.
75.45	Cross bridge over Umpqua River into Reedsport.
76.1	Left onto N. 10th St.
76.25	Left onto Greenwood Ave.
76.35	Finish at Triangle Park in Reedsport.

PORTLAND METRO

When you have something like 10,000 riders a day crossing a single bridge into downtown Portland, you know this is a place where people love to ride. Portland is renowned for its bicycle infrastructure—bike lanes, bike boulevards, right-turn boxes, route signage—and the riding options here are countless and varied. The West Hills, which rise above downtown, offer serious climbing; the eastside rolls out flat and broad. There are hundreds of common routes; beyond what's here, check out *Biking Portland: 55 Rides from the Willamette Valley to Vancouver,* written by Owen Wozniak for The Mountaineers Books.

7 BANKS–VERNONIA TRAIL

A STELLAR EXAMPLE OF RAILS-TO-TRAILS

Difficulty:	Easy to moderate, depending on length
Time:	1½ to 2½ hours, depending on stops
Distance:	20.65 miles one way
Elevation Gain:	938 feet
Best Seasons:	Year-round, unless snowfall levels get very low

GETTING THERE: From Portland, take US 26 west. At junction with SR 6 (Seaside or Tillamook), take SR 6. Just after crossing SR 47, take exit ramp for Banks (SR 47). Turn left off ramp into Banks. At north end of town, turn right on Banks Rd. and immediately left into Banks Trailhead parking area, which is clearly visible. Free parking; restrooms.

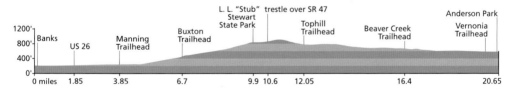

Whoever scratched his or her head one day and said, "Hmmm . . . why don't we turn that abandoned rail line into some kind of paved path?" was a very good friend to cyclists. (Apparently it was a Midwestern deal, in the mid-1960s, but I can't find any one person who is considered the originator.) Railroads have existing beds; they have nice, cleared-out right-of-ways; they often follow picturesque waterways; they rarely rise more than 1 or 2 percent in grade. Eureka!

The Banks–Vernonia Trail is one of the best examples of the benefits of this concept. Near a major metropolitan area, well designed and

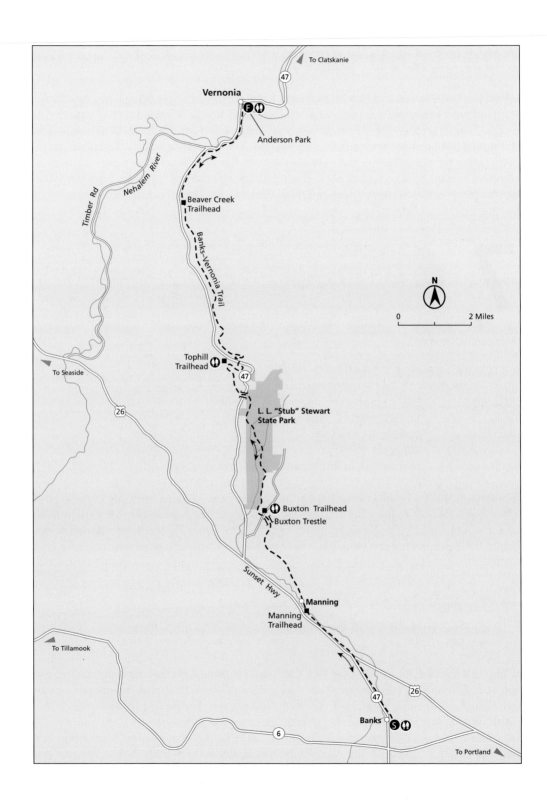

To Clatskanie

47

Vernonia

F

Anderson Park

Nehalem River

Timber Rd

Beaver Creek
Trailhead

Banks-Vernonia Trail

N

0   2 Miles

To Seaside

26

Tophill
Trailhead

47

L. L. "Stub" Stewart
State Park

Buxton Trailhead

Buxton Trestle

Sunset Hwy

Manning

Manning
Trailhead

To Tillamook

26

47

Banks   S

6

To Portland

built, passing through generally interesting terrain, it's a boon for casual riders, families who don't want to ride on streets, and many others. Although it can be busy on weekends, I'm frankly surprised it's not used more.

One of the beauties of the rail trail is that it's simple to do an out-and-back with the kids or friends—just head out and try to gauge when everyone's had half enough. If you don't want to climb much, that'll be about 5 miles from the Banks Trailhead.

The vast majority of users start at Banks, because it's closest to Portland. But while this rail trail peaks in the middle, it's far more uphill from the Banks side than the Vernonia side. Last time I rode it, with a friend and our two sons on tagalongs, we shuttled vehicles and started in Vernonia, and it was fantastic. The first 9 miles were slightly uphill, giving us a little workout, but the next 6 miles were a scream—we let the boys do all the pedaling and just concentrated on steering as we flew downhill through the forest at exhilarating-but-not-breakneck speeds. The shuttling was time-consuming, but it's worth considering.

You'll note on the mileage log that there are no actual turns or instructions; just follow the trail. From Banks, you start out riding through wide plains to the Manning Trailhead (most trailheads have restrooms); after that you swing away from the main roads and play in the woods for miles. Just before the Buxton Trailhead, after you've been climbing

(at an average grade of about 2.5 percent) for about 1.5 miles, is the Buxton Trestle, which is something you should see if you can: a long, graceful, curving wooden trestle that will make everyone say, "Wow."

After Buxton you're riding in wonderfully deep forest for the most part, passing through one of the newest state parks in Oregon, L. L. "Stub" Stewart State Park. After crossing over SR 47 on another, less-decorative trestle, there's a precipitous drop down to the Tophill Trailhead, adjacent to the highway. The trail on either side of the highway crossing is the most treacherous section by far, with grades of up to 11 percent. This might be a time to walk the bike.

Between Tophill and Beaver Creek trailheads is a stretch of new pavement that is just sublime. After the Tophill climb, it's basically downhill all the way to Vernonia—although it drops only 200 feet over 9 miles.

When you get to Vernonia, the trailhead as shown on the map is undeveloped as of 2011—just a gravel parking area, really. I suggest going another quarter mile or so to Anderson Park, which has restrooms and water. You can also keep going and make a loop around a large old log pond east of town if you want to extend the ride a mile or two.

Note: You can download a brochure that includes a map of the trail, with blowups of the trailheads, at the Oregon State Parks website: www.oregonstateparks.org/park_145.php.

MILEAGE LOG

0.0	From Banks Trailhead, at Nehalem Hwy. (SR 47) and NW Banks Rd., follow the rail trail.
1.85	Cross under Sunset Hwy. (US 26).
3.85	Reach Manning Trailhead.
5.05	Cross NW Pongratz Rd.
6.7	Reach Buxton Trailhead.
9.9	Intersect entrance road to L. L. "Stub" Stewart State Park.
10.6	Cross over SR 47.
10.9	Cross Nowakowski Rd.
12.05	Reach Tophill Trailhead.

Rails-to-trails conversions make for fantastic bike rides anyone can enjoy. On the Banks–Vernonia Trail, fall leaves beckon on a crisp autumn day. Oregon State Parks

12.1   Cross SR 47.
15.05   Cross McDonald Rd.
16.4   Reach Beaver Creek Trailhead.
18.75   Cross Adams Rd.
19.55   Cross Nehalem River.
20.15   Cross Lone Pine Rd.
20.45   Bear right at Vernonia Trailhead to follow bike path to right.
20.65   Finish at Anderson Park.

8 HAGG LAKE

A RURAL LAKE LOOP, CLOSE TO THE BIG CITY

Difficulty:	Moderate
Time:	2 to 2½ hours, with a few stops
Distance:	26.2 miles round-trip
Elevation Gain:	719 feet
Best Seasons:	Year-round

ROAD CONDITIONS: As you head out of Forest Grove on B St., called Nehalem Hwy. once you leave town, shoulders are decent, but there are a couple squeezes at bridge crossings. Beware of two fairly gnarly railroad crossings at beginning and end of Anderson Rd.

GETTING THERE: From Portland, head east on US 26 and take Glencoe Rd. exit. Turn left off ramp, cross over freeway, and turn right on Zion Church Rd., which becomes Cornelius–Schefflin Rd. At first roundabout, go left to stay on Cornelius–Schefflin. As you approach Cornelius, road becomes 10th St. Turn right onto SR 8 (Pacific Ave.) in Cornelius and follow it into Forest Grove. Turn left on Elm St. and go three blocks to Rogers Park, at corner of 17th Ave. Parking is on 17th Ave. on south side of park; portable restroom nearby.

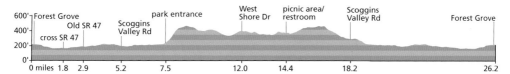

Maybe the most interesting tidbit here is that the loop around Hagg Lake is regularly used for cycling time trials. What does that tell you? Well, if you ride hard, this loop is a really good test of your fitness. But it's also a pleasant ride as more of a meander, with rolling hills, swooping curves, and some million-dollar views that aren't spoiled by sprawling McMansions. While you're just about 30 minutes from Portland, this is a very rural ride.

Hagg Lake was created by the US Bureau of Reclamation in the 1970s; a dam holds back Scoggins Creek, which comes down out of the Coast Range. The lake park features multiple picnic areas, two boat launches, and 15 miles of hiking-biking trails (there's some decent mountain-biking for the casual rider). The lake, which is stocked with rainbow trout, is popular with anglers.

The ride starts in Forest Grove, a bucolic college town whose name evokes its setting. It's not quite a small town and not quite a city; with a leafy campus and an old-fashioned downtown, it's a great place to hang around for an afternoon. Starting out from the city park, take a quick roll down 17th Avenue through a genteel neighborhood before you turn left on B Street and head out in the country. Right before you intersect the main

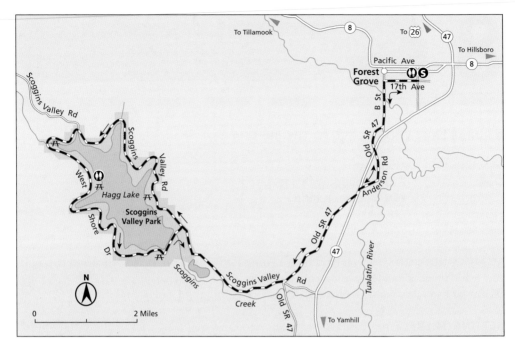

thoroughfare in these parts (State Route 47), turn right onto Old SR 47.

You'll be on the old highway for just 0.5 mile, with a herd of bison on your left and an orchard on your right, before crossing SR 47 onto Anderson Road. Anderson is more a country lane than a road, so expect little traffic. When Anderson ends back at the highway, take a quick left-right jog on SR 47 to get back onto Old SR 47.

Old SR 47 rolls past a vineyard and more orchards but has no shoulder at all. After 2.3 miles, you come to the intersection of Scoggins Valley Road, where there is a small grocery store and a parking lot that many cyclists use as a staging site. If you took the low-traffic route, your trip meter will be at about 5.2 miles.

Turn right onto Scoggins Valley Road and follow it to the entrance to Scoggins Valley Park at the foot of the dam. The shoulder here is wide and features a good surface, although it can be heavy with gravel and debris during the winter months. At 7.5 miles you'll reach the park entrance. There is no fee to ride your

bike into the park; if you drive in for a park-and-ride, you'll have to pay.

Once you pass the entrance, stay right on Scoggins Valley Road to begin the loop; you'll be greeted with a heart-starting climb that will alert you to the fact that the road around the lake is rarely—actually, more like never—flat. It's quite swoopy; short, low-gear climbs are rewarded with woo-hoo descents. You'll be afforded viewpoints at various places around the lake; at 9.9 miles, down to the left there's a panoramic view to the water.

The shoulders on the road around the lake are wide; the road-surface quality is uneven in places and gravel can accumulate on the edge, but generally you should feel safe with traffic.

When you reach the far end of the lake, at 12 miles, the road curls back to the left and becomes West Shore Drive. At 14.4 miles there's a picnic area with restrooms. When you get back to the dam, go left across the top and rejoin Scoggins Valley Road; take a right and retrace whichever route you took to get out here.

Route Variation: The route as mapped

crisscrosses and parallels the main SR 47 in an attempt to keep you off a busy highway, because Old SR 47 is flatter, has better pavement, and features very wide shoulders— however, it's your call. If you want to take the main highway, just follow it and turn right on Scoggins Valley Road to rejoin the route as mapped.

MILEAGE LOG

0.0	From Rogers Park, head west on 17th Ave.
0.5	Left onto B St.
1.3	Right onto Old SR 47.
1.8	Cross SR 47 to Anderson Rd.
2.8	Left onto SR 47.
2.9	Right onto Old SR 47.
5.2	Right onto Scoggins Valley Rd.
7.5	Entrance to Scoggins Valley Park; stay on Scoggins Valley Rd.
12.0	Bear left as road becomes West Shore Dr.
14.4	Picnic area (restrooms).
18.2	Right onto Scoggins Valley Rd.
18.7	Leave Scoggins Valley Park.
21.0	Left onto Old SR 47.
23.2	Left onto SR 47.
23.3	Right onto Andersen Rd.
24.3	Cross SR 47 onto Old SR 47.
24.8	Left onto B St.
25.7	Right onto 17th Ave.
26.2	Finish at Rogers Park.

Hagg Lake is a human-made body of water that draws anglers, hikers, and road and mountain bikers who enjoy its backcountry feel just a short distance from Portland.

9 BALD PEAK TWO WAYS

YOU LIKE DOWNHILL? EARN IT.

Difficulty:	Epic
Time:	3 to 5 hours
Distance:	45.1 miles round-trip
Elevation Gain:	2589 feet
Best Seasons:	Year-round, unless snow levels get very low

ROAD CONDITIONS: Near end of ride, where River Rd. intersects SR 8, use stoplight to cross highway onto SE 13th Ave., then go left on SE Maple St. to cross SR 8 again and loop around to parking lot.

GETTING THERE: From Portland, head east on US 26 and take Jackson School Rd. exit. Turn left off ramp, cross over freeway, and follow NW Jackson School Rd. south. At NW Evergreen Rd., jog right and then left to stay on (now NE) Jackson School Rd. Entering Hillsboro, Jackson School Rd. splits into one-way couplet; you'll be on NE Fifth St. Follow NE Fifth through town, across SR 8, to SE Walnut St. Turn left on Walnut and right on SE Eighth Ave. SE Eighth Ave. ends at parking lot for Shute Park. Free parking; restrooms. The ride begins across the park; follow bike path southeast through park to where SR 8 curves east, and start your odometer there.

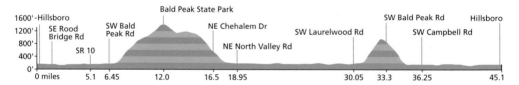

There's an ethos among hardcore backcountry skiing types: You can't go down anything you didn't climb up on your own. No chairlifts for these skiers. Well, you're going to get one of the fastest downhills in Oregon on this ride . . . but you're going to have to earn it by scaling one of the steepest pitches in this book.

Bald Peak is one of those local climbs everyone does at least once in a while to test themselves. The fun thing about it is that there are multiple ways to approach and climb it, each quite different in length, grade, and even

scenery. This particular lollipop route gives you the double bonus of climbing Bald Peak twice.

Leaving Hillsboro via River Road and Rood Bridge Road, you quickly get out of the urban ruckus and into the more pastoral aspects of Washington County—the reason so many riders gravitate in this direction. Enjoy the parks, pastures, and agricultural fields. After a brief stretch on State Route 10, jog to your left and catch Bald Peak Road. You've been afforded a pretty good shoulder to this point,

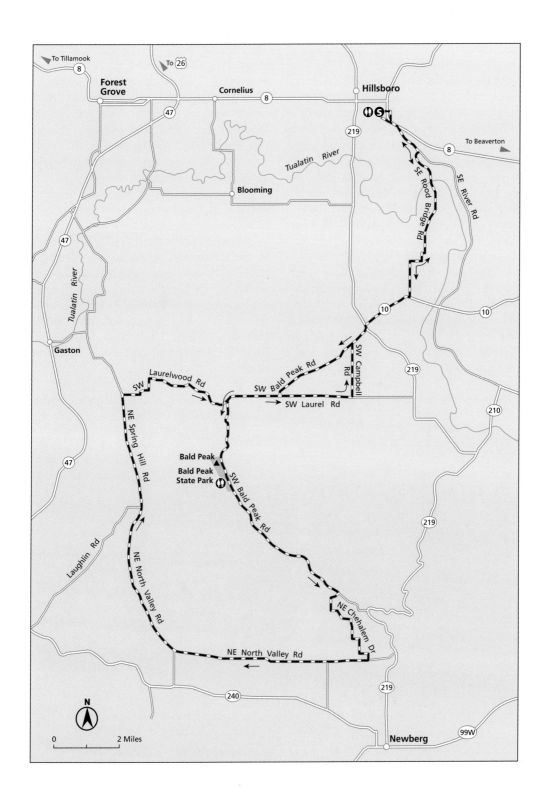

To Tillamook

Forest Grove

To 26

Cornelius

Hillsboro

To Beaverton

Tualatin River

Blooming

SE Rood Bridge Rd

SE River Rd

Tualatin River

Gaston

SW Laurelwood Rd

SW Bald Peak Rd

SW Campbell Rd

SW Laurel Rd

NE Spring Hill Rd

Bald Peak

Bald Peak State Park

SW Bald Peak Rd

Laughlin Rd

NE North Valley Rd

NE Chehalem Dr

NE North Valley Rd

Newberg

N

0   2 Miles

but it ends here—however, bikes are commonplace in these parts.

At the junction with Campbell Road, stay to the right; you'll be coming back through here later on Campbell. The first mile or so of Bald Peak is pretty flat, then it takes a definite turn for the up. Start a stair-step climb through orchards, going through an S curve as you join Laurel Road. At what looks like the top (but it's not), turn left to begin the loop around Bald Peak. Just around the corner, if you'd like a little preview of what's ahead, look down Laurelwood Road and note the steep-grade warning sign.

You're not done climbing *this* climb, though—not even close. The ascent started at about 7.5 miles, and it's a full 5 miles long. When you see the antennas and radio towers, you know the top lies near. Stop in at Bald Peak State Park for restrooms, water, and a breather—if you need any of those.

The descent from here offers spectacular views of the Tualatin Valley, the Coast Range, even Hagg Lake (Ride 8) in the distance. After passing Kings Grade on the right, you have a bit more to climb. Soon you can see Ribbon Ridge, full of high-end vineyards, as you resume your winding descent. This road is popular with motorcycles, which tells you about the curves; there are occasional patches of rough surface. Take a right on Chehalem Drive at 16.5 miles—don't miss it—as a cut-off to North Valley Road.

When you reach North Valley Road, revel in the smoothness of the surface, pedaling through rollers amid orchards and more wineries than you can count. Bear right at the intersection of Ribbon Ridge Road; the road you're on eventually becomes Spring Hill Road. Turn right onto Laurelwood Road at 30 miles and take a deep breath or three.

Climbing does have its rewards: The backside of Bald Peak offers views out over the Tualatin Valley, including Hagg Lake (Ride 8) in the distance.

After four 90-degree turns, keep twisting until you pass the big school on the right. When you pass Parmele Road about 2 miles into Laurelwood Road, prepare for the pain. It's only 2 miles, but the incline maxes out at around 18 percent. Climb up to the sharp right turn, get a tiny breather, resume suffering, get one more tiny flat spot, resume suffering. When you can see the stop sign, it'll all be over soon.

At the top, turn left and retrace around the corner on Bald Peak Road. Now it's a carnival slide, straight down with a few dips, serving up views of the entire Tualatin Valley. Let 'er rip as you dare—riders can hit 50-plus miles per hour here—staying straight all the way down to a slight uphill that looks like a bobsled-track runout. Turn left at Campbell, rejoin Bald Peak Road, and retrace back to the start as the adrenaline gradually reabsorbs.

MILEAGE LOG

0.0	From Shute Park, head east on SR 8.
0.25	Right onto SE River Rd.
1.4	Right onto SE Rood Bridge Rd.
1.6	Bear left to remain on SE Rood Bridge Rd.
5.1	Right onto SW Farmington Rd. (SR 10).
6.4	Left onto SR 219.
6.45	Right onto SW Bald Peak Rd.
6.95	Bear right at fork with SW Campbell Rd.
9.15	Bear right to remain on SW Bald Peak Rd. at intersection of SW Laurel Rd.
10.35	Bear left at 90-degree turn to remain on SW Bald Peak Rd.
12.0	Entrance to Bald Peak State Park (restrooms).
16.5	Right onto NE Chehalem Dr.
16.75	Bear left to stay on NE Chehalem Dr.
18.95	Right onto NE North Valley Rd.
23.5	Bear right at stop sign at intersection of NE Ribbon Ridge Rd. to stay on NE North Valley Rd.
27.3	Road becomes NE Spring Hill Rd. at intersection with NE Laughlin Rd. on left.
30.05	Right onto SW Laurelwood Rd.
33.3	Left onto SW Bald Peak Rd.
34.5	Continue straight as road becomes SW Laurel Rd.
36.25	Left onto SW Campbell Rd.
37.5	Bear right onto SW Bald Peak Rd.
38.0	Left onto SR 219.
38.05	Right onto SW Farmington Rd. (SR 10).
39.35	Left onto SE Rood Bridge Rd.
42.85	Bear right to stay on SE Rood Bridge Rd.
43.8	Left onto SE River Rd.
44.2	Cross SR 8, which becomes SE 13th Ave.
44.55	Left onto SE Maple St.
44.8	Cross SR 8.
44.95	Left onto SE Eighth Ave.
45.1	Left to finish at Shute Park.

10 WINE COUNTRY TOUR

VENI . . . VELO . . . VINO

Difficulty:	Moderate
Time:	3 to 5 hours
Distance:	50.05 miles round-trip
Elevation Gain:	1122 feet
Best Seasons:	Year-round

GETTING THERE: From Portland, head east on US 26 and take Glencoe Rd. exit. Turn left off ramp, cross over freeway, and turn right on Zion Church Rd., which becomes Cornelius–Schefflin Rd. At first roundabout, go left to stay on Cornelius–Schefflin. As you approach Cornelius, road becomes 10th St. Turn right onto SR 8 (Pacific Ave.) in Cornelius and follow it into Forest Grove. Turn left on Elm St. and go three blocks to Rogers Park, at corner of 17th Ave. Parking is on 17th Ave. on south side of park; portable restroom nearby.

People love driving through wine country. The rolling hills, the winding back roads, the verdant vineyards with their orderly rows contouring the hillsides, the quaint towns and stately homes . . . and the tasting rooms.

Hey, sounds like a good ride (although you might want to refrain from the tasting rooms while you're on the bike). This route meanders through and past pretty much everything described above.

Starting in Forest Grove, head out of town via Fern Hill Road and then Spring Hill Road; it doesn't take long to get out in the country here. The roads follow valleys; for the first 11 miles there's naught but a few tiny bumps in the elevation. In fact, only three sections can even be considered climbs—and the largest of them rises 150 feet.

So we'll not talk about climbs, because you're here for the ambience. This is the kind of ride you can easily take at a leisurely pace, even if you're accustomed to pushing it. Take the time to notice the angles of an interesting fence line, see if you can coax a horse over to you so you can rub its muzzle, wonder at the architecture of the hilltop wineries, try to identify the scents riding the air currents . . . it's that kind of ride.

The route is a classic lollipop; early in the loop section, you'll pass through Carlton, which is fast becoming one of those little towns that tons of people consider to be their charming little secret (quick, tell someone about it before *everyone* knows). There's a store and a peaceful little spot in town at the railway station for some shade. After some

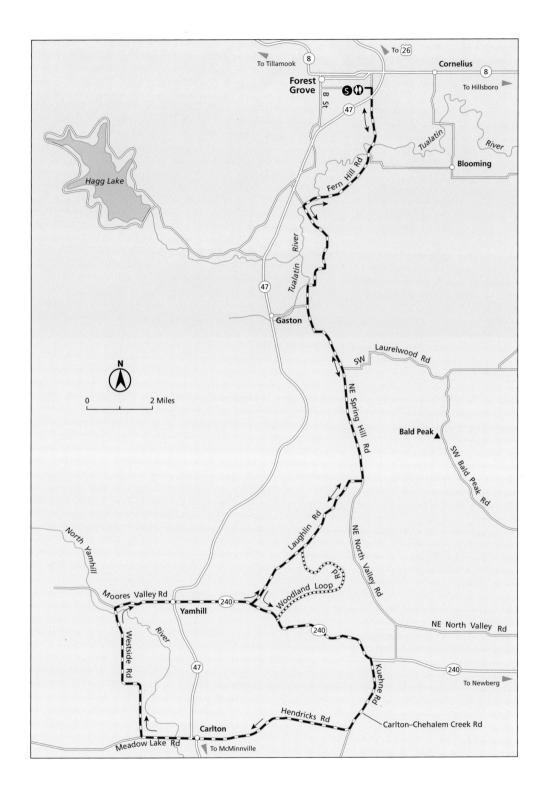

To Tillamook

8

To 26

Cornelius 8

To Hillsboro

Forest Grove

S

B St

47

Blooming

Tualatin River

Fern Hill Rd

Tualatin River

Hagg Lake

47

Gaston

SW Laurelwood Rd

N

0   2 Miles

NE Spring Hill Rd

Bald Peak ▲

SW Bald Peak Rd

Laughlin Rd

Woodland Loop Rd

NE North Valley Rd

North Yamhill

Moores Valley Rd

240

Yamhill

NE North Valley Rd

Westside Rd

River

47

240

240

To Newberg

Kuehne Rd

Hendricks Rd

Carlton–Chehalem Creek Rd

Carlton

Meadow Lake Rd

To McMinnville

The swelling hills and fertile land of wine country offer scenes of natural beauty everywhere you look. Phil Bard

more back-road exploration, the loop brings you through Yamhill, another authentic old burg with a pretty cool general store.

At 33.75 miles, turn from State Route 240 onto Laughlin Road and head back the way you came. And if you're an oenophile, or at least an intelligent one, you'll have left some time to drive back to some of those wineries for a little sample.

Route Variation: Oh, OK, we'll talk about climbing just a little bit. If you feel the need to add about 350 feet of elevation, take a left at 14.4 miles onto Woodland Loop Road; you'll get a stout climb that eventually drops back down to SR 240, a bit east of the main route; just take a left onto SR 240, and you'll soon be back on the main track.

MILEAGE LOG

0.0	From Rogers Park, head north on Elm St.
0.1	Right onto 18th Ave.
0.65	Right onto Maple St.
1.0	Cross SR 47; becomes Fern Hill Rd.
4.6	Left onto Spring Hill Rd.
12.0	Right onto Laughlin Rd.
14.4	**Variation:** Left on Woodland Loop Rd. for extra climb.
16.25	Left onto SR 240.
19.95	Right onto Kuehne Rd.
20.55	Bear right as road becomes Carlton–Chehalem Creek Rd.
21.7	Bear right as Carlton–Chehalem Creek Rd. becomes Hendricks Rd.
25.0	Road becomes Main St.

25.3	Enter Carlton.
25.7	Road becomes Meadow Lake Rd.
26.9	Right onto Westside Rd.
29.9	Cross Old Railroad Grade Rd.
30.2	Road becomes Moores Valley Rd.
30.4	Bear right to stay on Moores Valley Rd.
32.0	Enter Yamhill; stay straight as road becomes SR 240.
33.75	Left onto Laughlin Rd.
38.0	Left onto Spring Hill Rd.
45.45	Right onto Fern Hill Rd.
49.05	Cross SR 47; road becomes Maple St.
49.4	Left onto 18th Ave.
49.95	Left onto Elm St.
50.05	Finish at Rogers Park.

11 SAUVIE ISLAND

SPLENDID SOLITUDE ON A BOUNTIFUL ISLAND

Difficulty:	Moderate
Time:	2 to 3 hours
Distance:	31.9 miles round-trip (Variation: 12.6-mile loop)
Elevation Gain:	581 feet
Best Seasons:	Year-round

ROAD CONDITIONS: In crossing St. Johns Bridge, you have two options: Sidewalk is wide enough to accommodate bikes, and it keeps you out of traffic; four-lane bridge roadway has no shoulders. If you take the sidewalk, yield to walkers, and be aware that at bridge's two giant support pillars, sidewalk takes a quick jog around girders. If you ride the road, stay right and pedal fast.

GETTING THERE: In north Portland, go to Peninsula Park at corner of N. Ainsworth St. and Albina St. Parking on perimeter streets; park has public restrooms. As noted below, you can also easily start this ride on Sauvie Island at parking lot just below bridge.

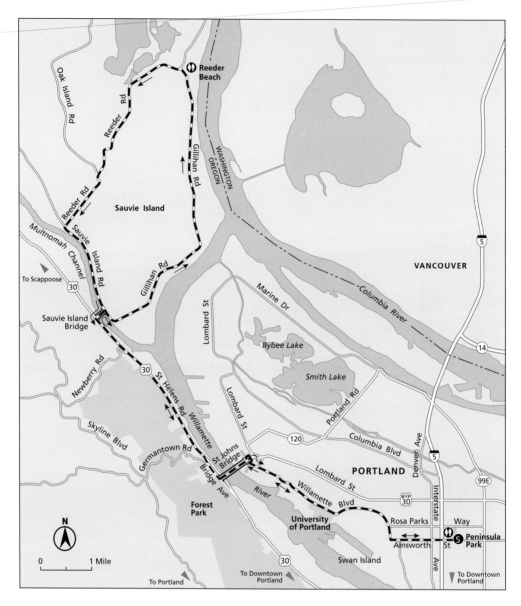

As you're pedaling around pastoral Sauvie Island, with its wide-open expanses of farm fields, lakes, and wildlife habitat, consider that the island itself is almost exactly the size and shape of Manhattan. But only about 1000 people live on this island—and that's why you're riding here. This ride is very popular with those who want a leisurely, flat ride that covers some ground and isn't too impacted by traffic.

The full ride starts from Peninsula Park in Portland, site of the city's first formal rose garden. It's a great place to stroll around, with its multitude of rose varieties, graceful fountain in the center, and gazebo and playing fields beyond.

Roll west down Ainsworth until it ends at Willamette Boulevard; take a right and follow the curving road. When you come to the intersection of Rosa Parks Way (formerly Portland Avenue), there's a special crossing marked for bikes, but be prudent—there's no signal to stop cars here.

Once you're onto Willamette, there's a nice bike lane for several miles. You're riding along a bluff above the Swan Island industrial area; the downtown Portland skyline is over your left shoulder, and directly across the Willamette River is heavily wooded Forest Park, one of the largest city parks in the world.

At 2.6 miles the road takes a sharp right, and the bike lane ends at around 4 miles. You're entering the St. Johns neighborhood, passing by two giant water towers. Just past the second, at 4.5 miles, is the intersection of Willamette Boulevard and Richmond Avenue; go straight, but be careful here—cars coming from the right do not have to stop.

Pass directly underneath the majestic St.

The Sauvie Island Bridge is the only way on or off the island other than by boat. Once you get on the island, it feels a long way from Portland even though it's not.

Johns Bridge, then turn right immediately on the other side of it and go up a narrow one-way street that parallels the bridge roadway. At the top, circle right to get on the bridge.

Coming off the bridge, turn right down the hill to the intersection of US Highway 30. You'll pass by the turnoff for Germantown Road, one of the main ways up to Skyline Boulevard (Ride 12). At the stoplight for US 30, turn left and ride on the wide shoulder.

At 9.7 miles you reach the Sauvie Island Bridge. Turn right and cross the bridge, taking time if you can to scan the horizon ahead for mountains; on a clear day you can see both Adams and St. Helens, and sometimes Rainier far in the distance.

The island loop can be ridden in either direction; this ride takes you counterclockwise. Loop around to the left under the bridge, following Gillihan Road. There are no shoulders here, but there's not much traffic, either. You'll pass everything from pumpkin patches to cattle farms to small tree nurseries.

As the road gradually loops around to the left, at 16 miles you'll intersect Reeder Road. If you go to the right, the road stays paved for about 4 miles, leading to a series of beaches, some clothing-optional; turn left to stay on the main loop. At 16.8 miles a pullout has informational signs and a portable restroom. At 18.7 miles Oak Island Road takes off to the right; it goes about 4 miles (3 miles of it paved) before dead-ending; some beautiful protected wildlife areas lie down this road.

At 20.4 miles the road comes to a T at Sauvie Island Road; go left. Sauvie Island Road brings you back to the bridge—if you haven't noticed, it's the only way on or off the island by bike or car—at 22.3 miles.

From here, backtrack over the bridge, along US 30, and up and over the St. Johns Bridge. Follow the mileage log to get back to Willamette and then retrace your route back to the start.

Route Variation: On the island side of the Sauvie Island Bridge is a parking lot—a great place to park if you'd like to skip the bridges and highways and just ride the island loop. A small store is adjacent.

MILEAGE LOG

0.0	From Peninsula Park, head west on N. Ainsworth St.
1.1	Right onto Willamette Blvd.
1.4	Cross Rosa Parks Way; jog left and join bike lane on Willamette Blvd.
2.6	Bear right to stay on Willamette Blvd.
4.5	Cross Richmond Ave. (cross traffic does not stop).
4.8	Right turn, immediately after passing under bridge.
4.9	Right onto St. Johns Bridge (choose sidewalk or roadway).
5.6	Right onto Bridge Ave. at end of bridge.
6.0	Left onto US 30.
9.7	Right onto Sauvie Island Bridge.
10.1	Left onto Gillihan Rd. (go under bridge).
16.0	Left onto Reeder Rd.
16.8	Pullout with informational signs and portable restroom.
18.7	Pass Oak Island Rd. on right.
19.05	Bear left to stay on Reeder Rd.
20.4	Left onto Sauvie Island Rd.
22.3	Cross Sauvie Island Bridge.
22.4	Left onto US 30.

26.0	Bear right onto Bridge Ave.
26.4	Left onto St. Johns Bridge.
27.1	Right onto Syracuse St. (at end of bridge).
27.1	Right onto Burlington Ave.
27.15	Left onto Willamette Blvd.
27.4	Cross Richmond Ave. (cross traffic does not stop).
29.2	Bear left to stay on Willamette Blvd.
30.5	Right to stay on Willamette Blvd. at Rosa Parks Way (turn for bikes only).
30.8	Left onto N. Ainsworth St.
31.9	Finish at Peninsula Park.

12 SKYLINE BOULEVARD TRAVERSE

A ROLLER-COASTER RIDE ABOVE THE CITY

Difficulty:	Challenging
Time:	1½ to 2 hours
Distance:	20.3 miles one way; many variations possible
Elevation Gain:	1283 feet
Best Seasons:	Year-round, although Skyline gets occasional snow and freezing rain in winter

ROAD CONDITIONS: No bike lane and really no shoulder. Stay off main Cornelius Pass Rd.; it's not safe for bikes.

GETTING THERE: From Portland, take US 26 west. Take Sylvan exit 71B; Skyline begins at end of off-ramp to right. Turn right off ramp, then right on Westgate, and right again on Canyon Court, to come back up to a cul-de-sac abutting Skyline; park here. By bike from the south, connect to start via Humphrey Blvd., *not* Scholls Ferry Rd., which has heavy traffic and no shoulder.

If the downtown Esplanade is where you'll find every casual rider in Portland on a sunny day, Skyline Boulevard is where you'll see every serious one. This is the backbone of

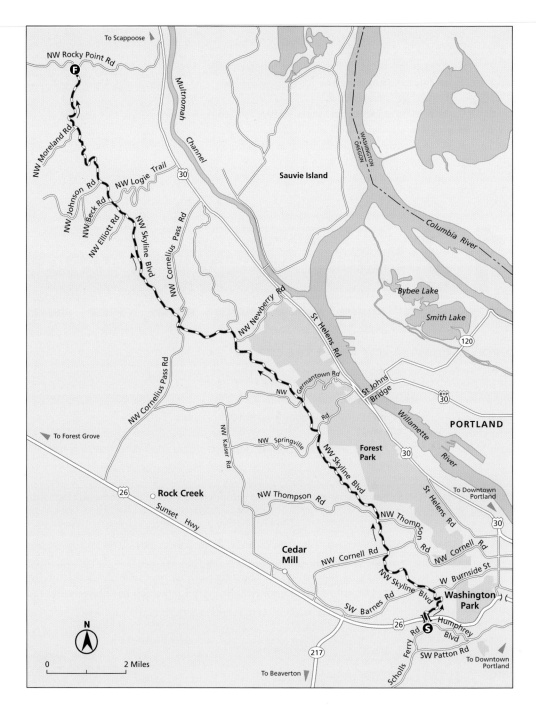

riding routes in the city—the place everyone ends up when they're looking for hill work, views, or both.

Why is it so popular? In a word: versatility. Although the entire length of Skyline runs just 20 miles, it's intersected by so many good

This ride earns its name, as it rides the tall ridge between the Columbia River drainage to the north (shown here) and the Tualatin Valley to the south.

riding roads that the possible route combinations are nearly infinite. You can create a ride of any length and difficulty (well, not an easy one) with Skyline as its core. And that's what most local riders do.

Skyline itself doesn't involve an inordinate amount of climbing—just under 1300 feet over 20 miles. It's getting *to* it that requires some work. It's called Skyline for a reason: It basically follows a knife's-edge ridge of the West Hills, which separate Portland and its river basins from the sprawling Tualatin Valley. All the ways to get to Skyline require hundreds of feet of ascent, so once you're there the boulevard itself can seem relatively easy.

So let's say you're getting to know Skyline for the first time, and you decide to ride it end to end. Here are a few things you should

know about it. First, it's never really flat. Aside from one stretch late in the ride, everything is pretty much going up or down. And also know that because there's no bike lane and really no shoulder, you have to be alert at all times, but so many riders use this road that most local drivers know to expect you. And as you ride farther northwest away from the city, traffic gets appreciably thinner. Use good road manners and play nice with the cars, and they're typically courteous in return.

Skyline officially starts at the end of Scholls Ferry Road; the actual transition point is the Sylvan overpass above US Highway 26. That's where this route description starts, although there's no obvious starting point or parking area.

Skyline starts with a lung-awakening climb

of just over 1 mile at between 3 and 5 percent. You're climbing through an almost tunnel-like canopy of trees, past some of the pricier real estate in town. After you briefly join W. Burnside Street (turn left onto Burnside and then split back off to the right to follow Skyline), the road stair-steps up at the same grade for another mile; at 1.7 miles there's a great view of Mount St. Helens framed by trees. At 2.3 miles you get relief in the form of a long downhill with gentle speed bumps.

Just about 3 miles in, start a gentle roller coaster for about 5 miles. Catch majestic views to both the east and west and pass the venerable Skyline Drive-In, the Skyline Memorial Gardens (a tomb with a view?), and the rustic Skyline Tavern. Along the way the roadside homes transition to more spread-out "horse properties," and later you'll see barns, orchards, and Christmas tree farms.

Somewhere on this ride you're likely to tune in to the joy of Skyline: that sense of being on an amusement park ride—it twists and turns, it lifts and drops, and there's always something interesting to see around you.

At 12.1 miles, drop down a steep slope to Cornelius Pass Road, a main connecting road across the West Hills. There's a tricky little crossing—go straight across and then right at the stop sign to stay on Skyline.

Here is where the real work starts. Cornelius Pass is the low-elevation point of the ride; now you're heading for the high point, at the very end. That means it's pretty much uphill for the last 8 miles. But, with the exception of the first 0.75 mile past Cornelius Pass Road and a couple short gut-busting climbs, it's generally 1 to 3 percent—manageable. There's a very nice section of serpentine, nearly flat road between 16.5 and 18 miles. The homes get more interesting and the views even better on this stretch, and traffic becomes almost a memory.

When you reach Rocky Point Road, Skyline is finished. Here you face a choice: You can turn around and backtrack to the start; you can take Rocky Point down to US 30 and follow the four-lane "river highway" back to Portland; or you can choose a turnoff road and explore.

Route Variations: The roads that intersect Skyline fall away toward either the Columbia River (roughly east) or the Tualatin Valley (roughly west). You can connect these roads in many ways—down one and then up another—along the length of Skyline. Possibilities include NW Cornell Road, NW Thompson Road, NW Springville Road, NW Germantown Road, NW Newberry Road, NW McNamee Road, NW Elliott Road, NW Logie Trail–Beck Road, NW Johnson Road, NW Moreland Road, and NW Rocky Point Road. The best approach is to map out different options and routes, then check out variations until you get to know them all.

MILEAGE LOG

0.0	From Skyline Blvd. at US 26, head north on SW Skyline.
1.3	Left onto W. Burnside St.
1.5	Bear right onto NW Skyline Blvd.
3.1	Cross NW Cornell Rd.
4.1	Cross NW Thompson Rd.
7.95	Cross NW Germantown Rd.
12.1	Cross NW Cornelius Pass Rd., then bear right to stay on NW Skyline Blvd.
15.9	Cross NW Logie Trail–NW Beck Rd.
20.3	Finish at NW Skyline Blvd. and NW Rocky Point Rd.

13 MARINE DRIVE PATH

A SMOOTH LITTLE BIKE PATH, DOWN ALONG THE RIVER

Difficulty:	Easy
Time:	30 to 45 minutes
Distance:	8.3 miles one way
Elevation Gain:	79 feet
Best Seasons:	Year-round

ROAD CONDITIONS: Traffic can be fast and thick on NE Marine Dr. itself, but shoulder is ample. Bike path east of NE 122nd Blvd. is mossy.

GETTING THERE: Find your way to NE 33rd Dr. and head north until it ends at NE Marine Dr. Right before you reach NE Marine Dr., take angled left into driveway to small parking lot. Bike path starts at underpass beneath NE 33rd. If you're pedaling to the start, NE 33rd Dr. has a good bike lane once you get past NE Columbia Blvd., but interchange with Columbia is pretty dicey and not recommended for kids or inexperienced riders. If this is a family ride, drive to the start.

Portland's NE Marine Drive bike path offers something every city should have: a flat, wide, paved bikeway with a nice view—a path that stretches out for miles so you can ride separately from traffic, pedaling in segregated bliss. If you want a place to ride without taxing yourself, a spot to take the whole family menagerie of bikes, or just a quick, easy ride to clear your head on a weekday afternoon, this is a great choice.

The path has only 79 feet of elevation gain over 8-plus miles, so you won't need your climbing lungs here; the strongest force you'll fight is likely to be wind. A voice of experience: As you head east, you may be under the impression that you're feeling particularly

frisky today; it may even feel downright effortless. But . . . be prepared for windy reality when you turn around.

The route starts from the parking lot adjacent to NE 33rd Drive. You start by going under 33rd, emerging onto a broad, smooth path. The pavement is 10 to 12 feet wide here, a great start to your ride. To your left is the dike that NE Marine Drive runs atop; to the right is land owned by Portland International Airport. In fact, on this section you're directly below some common flight paths; you may get the thrill of a large passenger jet directly overhead.

At 0.9 mile, use the crosswalk signal at NE Marine Drive, then swing right to stay on the

The Marine Drive path offers a smooth riverside ride, sheltered from the wind (sometimes) and the airport on the other side of the dike.

path. Now you're riding atop the dike; the Columbia River is below to your left, with some sandy river beach showing.

And if you're riding on a pleasant summer weekend, there will be traffic of all kinds; plenty of people like to take advantage of this resource. In addition, you're likely to see sailboats, personal watercraft, beach rompers, fishermen, and wildlife.

At 2.2 miles, you'll pass through a pair of posts adjacent to the Sea Scout Base; shortly thereafter go through another set and drop down closer to the river. At 4.1 miles there's a fork that heads up toward the road; ignore it and continue straight. At 4.6 miles you'll rise up to road level (passing more posts) and then drop back down to go under the Interstate 205 bridge. Just on the other side of the bridge, at 4.9 miles the path ends at a crosswalk. Here you have several choices.

While this route goes farther, you can turn around here and backtrack for a nice ride of roughly 10 miles. You can cross NE Marine Drive and connect to the I-205 Bike Path, which heads south for miles and miles. Or, for the route mapped here, turn left, ride a short stretch on the shoulder of NE Marine Drive, and connect to more bike path to extend your ride on the river.

If you choose to continue on this route,

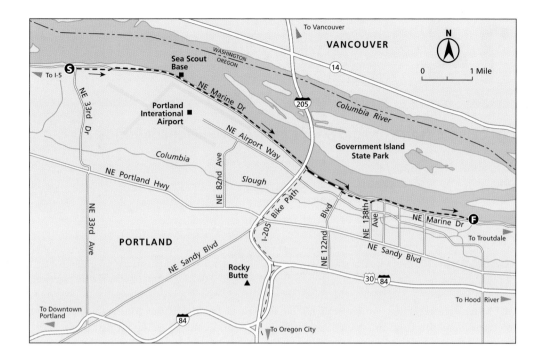

cross NE Marine Drive using the signal and pick up the ample right shoulder—consistently 5 or 6 feet wide. You'll ride about 0.75 mile on the shoulder; traffic can be fast and thick, but you have more room than in many bike lanes.

Just after crossing the intersection of NE 122nd Boulevard, catch a bike path on the right side of the road and follow it for just over 0.5 mile. This path doesn't get too much sun and can get quite mossy; don't make any sudden moves on the bike. Or you could just skip this part of the path and stay up on the shoulder of Marine Drive a little while longer.

After a quick crossing of NE 138th Avenue and a very short road segment, the path crosses NE Marine Drive again at 6.4 miles; there's no crossing signal. Once you join the path here, it's a nice roll of nearly 2 miles to the end of the line, where the path rises back up to NE Marine Drive and terminates near a group of houseboats.

MILEAGE LOG

0.0	From parking lot off NE 33rd Dr. at NE Marine Dr., head east on bike path.
0.9	Cross NE Marine Dr.
4.1	Stay straight at fork.
4.7	Cross under I-205.
4.9	Cross NE Marine Dr.—join bike lane.
5.7	Bear right to rejoin bike path on right across NE 122nd Blvd.
6.2	Cross NE 138th Ave.
6.4	Cross NE Marine Dr.
8.3	Finish at end of bike path at NE Marine Dr.

14 EASTSIDE NEIGHBORHOODS

EXPLORING A SERIES OF PORTLAND'S REVITALIZED NEIGHBORHOODS

Difficulty:	Moderate
Time:	2 to 3 hours, plus stops
Distance:	27.3 miles round-trip
Elevation Gain:	554 feet
Best Seasons:	Year-round

ROAD CONDITIONS: NE Alberta St. is not too bike-friendly, although there are plenty of riders. It's narrow and busy; you may prefer to follow the parallel Going St. greenway for this section.

GETTING THERE: Find your way to Holladay Park in Lloyd District (there are many ways to access the park). Park on streets surrounding the park, in large parking lot east of the park, or even in Lloyd Center shopping mall lots. Three of Portland's Tri-Met light-rail MAX lines (Blue, Green, and Red) stop directly at park; bikes are allowed on trains.

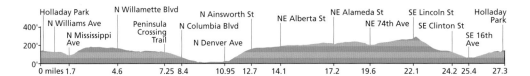

One of the endearing characteristics of Portland is that it's really a bunch of distinct neighborhoods that together make up a vibrant city. And many of them historically featured individual commercial districts at their core—which a steady procession of redevelopment efforts have re-created: bustling, neighborly pockets of restaurants, boutiques, and other shops. And each neighborhood retains a certain individuality in its flavor.

This route winds all over the place, generally making a figure eight joining two loops, so it might be a good idea to carry a cue sheet—although much of it follows established bike routes the City of Portland has thoughtfully signed.

After a couple of jogs coming out of the park, you're riding up a wide, well-marked bike lane on Williams Avenue, one of the heaviest bike-commuter routes in Portland. This fact has not been lost on developers, who have begun building a chic commercial district along the heart of Williams.

But that's farther up Williams; you're going to scoot over to Mississippi Avenue, which exploded some years before Williams. After a strenuous but short climb, emerge along Mississippi to find a funky collection of restaurants and businesses.

At the top of Mississippi, jog left at the S curve to hop over to Michigan, which parallels Interstate 5. After a left on N. Ainsworth Street, come to a T at N. Willamette Boulevard,

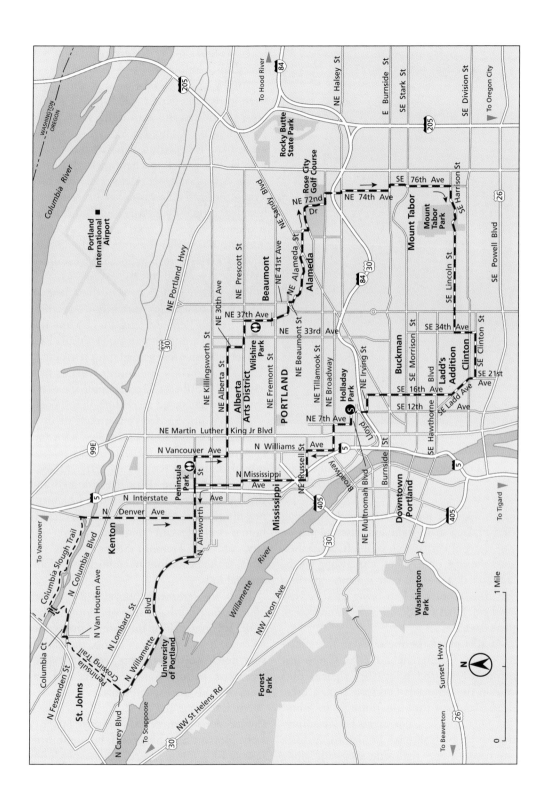

If you want something to define your neighborhood, build it big… very big. Paul Bunyan towers over the Kenton neighborhood in North Portland.

which hugs the top of a bluff with sweeping views; take a sharp right and pass the private University of Portland on your left. Soon after, enter the edge of St. Johns, a sprawling neighborhood that was its own separate city into the 20th century before being absorbed by Portland. It has a rebounding downtown scene these days, too.

At this point the route leaves the streets for a bit. Turning right on N. Carey just before the railroad bridge (it's signed) puts you on the Peninsula Crossing Trail, a bike-pedestrian path that cuts through St. Johns, crossing a couple major streets before emptying out on N. Columbia Boulevard. A quick jaunt down the right-side sidewalk along Columbia gets you to N. Van Houten, where

you can cross Columbia, turn right, and connect to the Columbia Slough Trail.

After a lovely section of trail through a treed park (take either way when it forks), cross the bridge and turn right. Here you're paralleling the Columbia Slough, riding up on a dike. This section is paved but rough, with a few gravel patches; pick your way along. At Interstate–N. Denver Avenue, take a right turn and follow over two bridges (wide bike lane), then take a right at Paul Bunyan (trust me, you'll see him) onto Denver and into the blue-collar Kenton neighborhood, another example of how locals have worked to create a core of shops and businesses.

Follow Denver and its good bike lane all the way south back to Ainsworth (look familiar?), turning left and crossing I-5 on this broad boulevard, then passing Peninsula Park and its expansive rose garden (plus restrooms). After a jog down N. Vancouver Avenue, turn left onto NE Alberta Street to enter one of the city's most celebrated revived neighborhoods.

Alberta, once a decrepit stretch of drug houses and boarded-up businesses, has come back to life as an arts district with an eclectic mix of shops and restaurants. After Alberta, roll past Wilshire Park (restrooms) and through the genteel Beaumont and Alameda neighborhoods. Alameda Ridge offers stately homes and pleasant views south over the city, and NE Fremont Street, which you cross, is the Beaumont neighborhood's commercial hub.

End up crossing above I-84 before approaching the back side of Mount Tabor Park. This route skirts the base of the extinct volcano; if you feel like a climb, the park is very much worth exploring, with its expansive views, pastoral water reservoirs, and network of roads, paths, and trails.

After passing the park, head back west toward downtown on SE Lincoln Street, a leafy, pleasant bike boulevard, before shifting over to SE Clinton Street and another funky little neighborhood core. From there angle across the unique X-shaped street layout of handsome Ladd's Addition.

From there it's a straight shot up SE 16th Avenue through the Buckman neighborhood, across I-84 again, and back to Holladay Park.

In just over 27 miles, you've passed through or touched on at least eight different neighborhoods featuring their own commercial districts; hopefully you've found time to explore a few of them in more depth.

MILEAGE LOG

0.0	From Holladay Park, head west on NE Multnomah Blvd.
0.2	Right onto NE Seventh Ave.
0.4	Left onto NE Broadway.
0.8	Right onto N. Williams Ave.
1.3	Left onto Russell St. N.
1.7	Right onto N. Mississippi Ave.
2.85	Left onto N. Prescott St.
2.9	Right onto N. Michigan Ave.
3.6	Left onto N. Ainsworth St.
4.6	Right onto N. Willamette Blvd.
6.1	Bear right to stay on N. Willamette Blvd.
7.2	Right onto N. Carey Blvd.
7.25	Join Peninsula Crossing Trail path.
7.6	Cross N. Lombard St.
8.1	Cross N. Fessenden St.
8.4	Right onto N. Columbia Blvd.—on sidewalk.
8.5	Left onto N. Van Houten Ave.; cross N. Columbia Blvd.
8.55	Right onto Columbia Court.
8.8	Left to cross railroad tracks onto bike path.
9.3	Cross Columbia Slough.
9.35	After bridge, right onto bike path.
10.95	Right onto N. Denver Ave.
11.4	Bear right to stay on N. Denver Ave.
11.95	Jog right to cross N. Lombard St.
12.7	Left onto N. Ainsworth St.
13.2	Pass Peninsula Park (restrooms) on left.
13.5	Right onto N. Vancouver Ave.
14.1	Left onto NE Alberta St.
15.7	Right onto NE 30th Ave.
16.0	Left onto NE Prescott St.
16.2	Jog right to cross NE 33rd Ave.
16.4	Right onto NE 37th Ave.
16.5	Pass Wilshire Park (restrooms) on right.
16.9	Jog left, then right, onto NE 38th Ave.; cross NE Fremont St.
17.0	Bear right to stay on NE 38th Ave.
17.2	Bear left onto NE Alameda St.
17.3	Cross NE 41st Ave.
18.3	Cross NE Sandy Blvd.; stay on Alameda.

18.6	Right onto NE 62nd Ave.
18.7	Left onto NE Sacramento St.
19.05	Bear right onto NE 72nd Dr. (down hill).
19.5	Left onto NE Tillamook St.
19.6	Right onto NE 74th Ave.
19.9	Jog left crossing NE Halsey St.; stay on NE 74th Ave.
20.65	Left onto E. Burnside St.
20.7	Right onto SE 76th Ave.
20.95	Jog right crossing SE Stark St.; stay on 76th.
21.7	Right onto SE Harrison St.
22.1	Bear left as Harrison becomes SE Lincoln St.
22.2	Jog left to stay on SE Lincoln St.
23.9	Left onto SE 34th Ave.
24.2	Right onto SE Clinton St.
24.7	Jog left to stay on SE Clinton St.
24.95	Right onto SE 21st Ave.
25.0	Jog left onto SE Division St.; take diagonal onto SE Ladd Ave.
25.4	Bear right onto SE 16th Ave. at traffic circle.
25.5	Stay on SE 16th Ave. at traffic diamond.
25.7	Jog left to stay on SE 16th Ave. crossing SE Hawthorne Blvd.
26.85	Left onto NE Irving St.
27.0	Right onto NE 12th Ave.
27.0	Cross I-84.
27.05	Jog left onto NE 11th Ave. crossing NE Lloyd Blvd.
27.3	Finish at Holladay Park.

15 DOUBLE VOLCANO

ONE RIDE, TWO EXTINCT VOLCANOES

Difficulty:	Moderate
Time:	1 to 2 hours
Distance:	18.1 miles round-trip
Elevation Gain:	778 feet
Best Seasons:	Year-round, although if it snows in Portland these are two of the higher points

ROAD CONDITIONS: Watch for gravel in corners descending Rocky Butte. Roads on Mount Tabor are a bit of a maze.

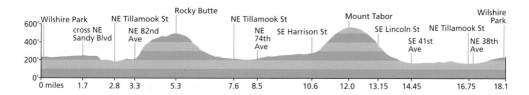

		Rocky Butte				Mount Tabor				Wilshire

Wilshire Park · cross NE Sandy Blvd · NE Tillamook St · NE 82nd Ave · NE Tillamook St · NE 74th Ave · SE Harrison St · Mount Tabor · SE Lincoln St · SE 41st Ave · NE Tillamook St · NE 38th Ave · Wilshire Park

600' — 400' — 200' — 0'

0 miles   1.7   2.8 3.3   5.3   7.6 8.5   10.6   12.0 13.15 14.45   16.75   18.1

GETTING THERE: Find your way to Wilshire Park in Northeast Portland, corner of NE Skidmore St. and NE 37th Ave. (easily reached by car or bike from any direction). Free parking along NE Skidmore; restrooms and water in center of park.

Sure, one's a "mountain" and one's a butte—but the cool thing is that Mount Tabor and Rocky Butte are both actually extinct volcanic cones. How often can you say you rode to the top of two volcanoes in one short ride, right in the middle of a city? And while there's a moderate amount of climbing involved—all of it compacted into a 1.25-mile climb and a 1.5-mile one—you'll be paid off with splendid, panoramic views over the city to rivers and mountains.

Note: This ride is best done with your map and turn-by-turn mileage log handy; there are far more turns than miles. Much of it is on established bike routes, and their green signs will be helpful on many of the little jogs and turns.

Start at Wilshire Park in northeast Portland; zigzag a bit to cross NE Fremont Street and then follow the curving Alameda Ridge, with stately homes perched to capitalize on the best views. After crossing the five-way intersection at NE Sandy Boulevard—shoot pretty much straight across the angle to stay on Alameda—take a few more zigs and zags, including a drop down onto a street that bisects the Rose City municipal golf course.

NE Tillamook Street takes you east to the

Cars are prohibited on the curving road to the top of Mount Tabor, providing a quiet climb up to expansive views over Portland and out to the West Hills.

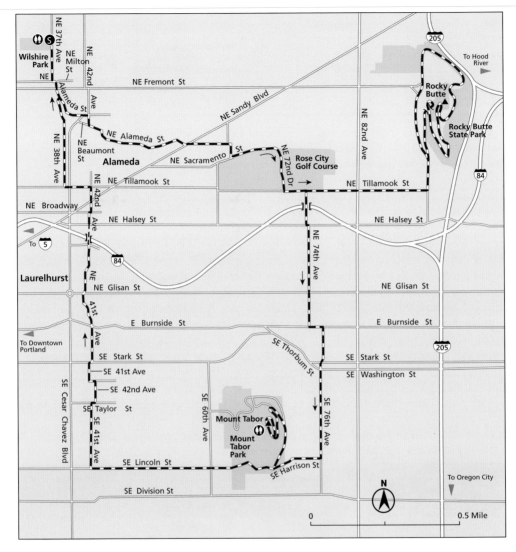

base of Rocky Butte State Park. The climb here is steady at 4 or 5 percent, punctuated by a figure eight that includes a tunnel with a center curb just like Disneyland's Autopia. There's a false summit at a sweeping left curve, with one last bit of uphill business right before the summit. At the top, make a counterclockwise loop to enjoy the views of more imposing (and more recently active) volcanic peaks to the north. Then enjoy the road back down; watch for any gravel in the corners.

It takes a bit more urban maneuvering to make your way south to Mount Tabor Park. When you turn from SE 76th Avenue onto SE Harrison Street, take a good look at your map and directions to try to orient yourself; the roads on Tabor are a bit of a maze: sharp right, left fork, sharp left, loop at the top (restrooms); retrace down. About 300 feet of gain, and again the views are impressive, especially to the west toward downtown and the West Hills.

A point of interest: Mount Tabor is the site of weekly Wednesday night road races in the summer, with riders completing multiple laps that are basically up-down-and-nothing-in-between. It's fun to watch, and anyone can race.

After a westward shot down SE Lincoln Street, a nice bike boulevard, cut north for more slightly wiggly navigation back to the start at Wilshire Park.

MILEAGE LOG

0.0	From Wilshire Park, at NE Skidmore St. and NE 37th Ave., head south on NE 37th Ave.
0.3	Jog left and immediately right onto NE Alameda St., up to NE Fremont St.
0.4	Cross NE Fremont St.
0.75	Cross NE 41st Ave.
0.8	Bear right at first intersection to stay on NE Alameda St.
1.7	Go straight across NE Sandy Blvd. to stay on NE Alameda St.
2.1	Right onto NE 65th Ave.
2.15	Left onto NE Sacramento St.
2.4	Bear right down hill onto NE 72nd Dr. (through golf course).
2.8	Left onto NE Tillamook St.
3.3	Cross NE 82nd Ave.
3.8	Left onto NE 92nd Ave.
4.05	Bear right at fork to go up NE Rocky Butte Rd.
4.4	Enter tunnel.
5.3	Right at top of climb and loop around top of butte.
5.65	Pass the road you came up on, then bear right down hill on NE Rocky Butte Rd.
6.75	Go straight at stop sign at intersection with NE Fremont St. to take NE 92nd Ave. south.
7.6	Right onto NE Tillamook St.
8.1	Cross NE 82nd Ave.
8.5	Left onto NE 74th Ave.
8.75	Jog left at NE Halsey St. to stay on NE 74th Ave.
9.25	Cross NE Glisan St.
9.5	Left onto E Burnside St.
9.6	Right onto SE 76th Ave.
9.85	Jog right crossing SE Stark St. and SE Washington St. couplet to stay on SE 76th Ave.
10.6	Right onto SE Harrison St.
11.0	Sharp right up hill onto SE East Tabor Dr.
11.45	Bear left at fork onto SE North Tabor Dr.
11.65	Sharp left up hill past barriers onto SE Tabor Summit Dr.
12.0	Bear right at top of climb for one-way loop around summit.
12.3	Bear right down hill, retracing route on SE Tabor Summit Dr., SE North Tabor Dr., and SE East Tabor Dr.
13.15	Bear right onto SE Lincoln St. at junction with SE Harrison St.
13.3	Bear left to stay on SE Lincoln St.
14.45	Right onto SE 41st Ave.
14.95	Jog right onto SE 42nd Ave. at crossing of SE Taylor St.
15.15	Left onto SE Morrison, then jog right onto SE 41st Ave.

15.35	Jog right at crossing of SE Stark St. to stay on SE 41st Ave.
15.65	Cross E. Burnside St.
15.9	Cross NE Glisan St.
16.3	Bear right onto NE 42nd Ave. to cross I-84 on bike-pedestrian overpass.
16.4	Cross NE Halsey St.
16.55	Jog right at NE Broadway to stay on NE 42nd Ave.
16.6	Cross NE Sandy Blvd.
16.75	Left onto NE Tillamook St.
16.9	Right onto NE 38th Ave.
17.55	Jog right, then left onto NE Alameda St.
17.7	Cross NE Fremont Ave.
17.75	Jog left, then right onto NE 37th Ave.
18.1	Finish at Wilshire Park.

16 WEST HILLS HIGHLIGHTS

PARKS AND GARDENS AND ZOOS . . . AND HILLS

Difficulty:	Challenging
Time:	1 to 1½ hours, plus stops
Distance:	15.9-mile loop
Elevation Gain:	1115 feet
Best Seasons:	Year-round, although if it snows, West Hills include highest points in Portland

ROAD CONDITIONS: Fairmount and Hewett are twisty with virtually no shoulders, but traffic is very low. Road surface on Kingston Dr. can be rough; also a few blind corners. Madison Dr. bike path is steep and slightly rough.

GETTING THERE: Find your way to Salmon Springs Fountain on downtown Portland's waterfront, accessible by bike from Eastbank Esplanade river loop or any of numerous bike lanes and bridges that converge on downtown. Buses and MAX trains get you very close as well. Park downtown at meters (often scarce) or in garages.

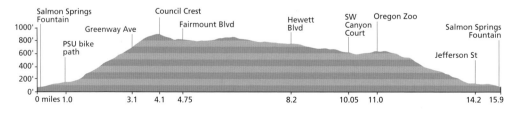

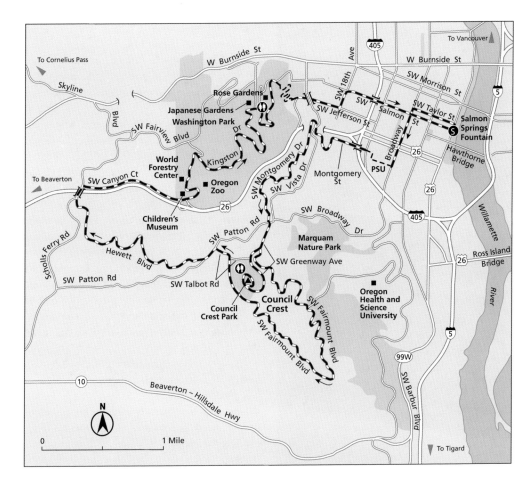

It took me a long time to get used to the feeling of getting in a grueling hill-climbing workout in Portland's West Hills and then noticing on the way home that I logged only 22 miles. But that's an advantage of the topography here: You can get some serious hill work in a short time, leaving from just about anywhere in the city.

This route brings two separate benefits: a vigorous workout, and plenty of beauty along the way: gorgeous leafy streets, impressive residential architecture, and views to the horizon in all directions. It also takes you by some of the city's highlights, including the Oregon Zoo and the renowned rose and Japanese gardens of Washington Park.

Start at the Salmon Springs Fountain, where kids gravitate when the sun is out. Take a quick jaunt north up SW Naito Parkway and turn left on SW Taylor Street. This ride begins and ends with a jolt of urban adrenaline, which serves as a nice contrast to some of the tranquil residential roads in the middle.

At 0.4 mile, turn left onto SW Broadway, into the well-marked bike lane heading up the hill through downtown. When you get to the campus of Portland State University, turn right at SW Harrison (1 mile) onto a bike-pedestrian path. Follow it until you have to turn, then jog right and left, staying on the path. Cross SW 12th Avenue at the signal and continue on Montgomery Street over Interstate 405.

The West Hills Highlights route starts from the Salmon Street Springs, a popular spot alongside the river in downtown Portland.

At 1.5 miles, Montgomery curves sharply left, and the climbing begins. All the pain is really concentrated in the next 2.5 miles; the grade starts at a brisk 7 percent and maintains between 5 and 6 percent pretty much all the way to the top. But it's a pleasant climb for the eyes: interesting houses, a sinuous roadway, low traffic, and views as you rise above the city.

At 1.9 miles make an offset crossing, turning right very briefly at SW Vista Avenue and then left back onto Montgomery Drive. At 3.1 miles, intersect SW Patton Road, crossing with a slight left jog onto Greenway Avenue.

Follow Greenway as it curves left at Talbot (3.6 miles) and then right as it begins the last rise to Council Crest Park (restrooms). Enter Council Crest's hilltop loop (at 4 miles) and go right. About halfway around, stop to take in the view north.

Continue your loop and exit the park where you came in, then backtrack down Greenway. Just after passing Talbot, which is the first road to the left, take a sharp right at 4.75 – then you'll be faced with two streets; take the right one, which is Fairmount, even though it has no street sign. (Don't be confused by the next direction in the log being about Talbot; you'll intersect it again in a few miles.) Fairmount is a twisty, serene road with virtually no shoulders but very low vehicle traffic and very high cyclist-runner-walker traffic. You'll make a large arc to the southwest and then come back around the other side of Council Crest.

At 8.05 miles turn left on Talbot and follow it a short distance to the stop sign at SW Patton Road (8.1 miles). Turn left onto Patton and then quickly take the second right onto Hewett Boulevard (go past Humphrey). Hewett is another version of Fairmount: a smooth, winding back road (no shoulders) that rolls past hillside houses on stilts and induces you to swoop through the curves just to feel the centrifugal force.

When Hewett ends, intersecting Humphrey (10 miles), shoot straight across to the curb cut that will take you up on the US Highway 26 overpass. Cross over the freeway and look for the sidewalk to the right down to the cul-de-sac. This is SW Canyon Court. Follow it down the hill to the entrance to the Oregon Zoo (11 miles.). Stay left, climbing up and around the zoo parking lot. At 11.4 miles, turn right onto Kingston Drive, a local delicacy of a road that winds through the forest of Washington Park. The road surface can be rough here; be cautious going around a few blind corners.

Drop down to an intersection at 13 miles.

To explore the International Rose Test Gardens (free) or the Zen-like Japanese Garden (not free), go left. There's also an amphitheater and a great kids' playground here (and restrooms). To continue the route, at the intersection at 13 miles turn right and wind down past the city water reservoir.

At the stop (13.9 miles), turn right onto the one-way road and follow it for just 0.1 mile, looking for the bike path marked "Madison Court." This switchback path (caution) takes you down through a gate; turn right and connect to Jefferson Street. Carefully follow the left-hand sidewalk to the traffic circle (14.7 miles) then make the equivalent of a left onto SW 18th Avenue. Pay careful attention to the MAX tracks through here. Turn right at SW Salmon Street (14.95 miles) and follow it back through downtown and down to the river and your starting point.

MILEAGE LOG

0.0	From Salmon Springs Fountain, head northeast on SW Naito Pkwy.
0.05	Left onto SW Taylor St.
0.4	Left onto SW Broadway.
1.0	Right onto SW Harrison St. (campus path).
1.1	Jog right onto SW 11th Ave. (campus path).
1.15	Jog left onto SW Montgomery St.
1.2	Cross I-405.
1.9	Right onto SW Vista Ave. (briefly join Vista and then bear left to stay on Montgomery).
2.0	Bear left to stay on SW Montgomery Dr.
2.2	Jog right, then left, then right, to stay on SW Montgomery Dr.
3.1	Jog left at SW Patton Rd. to join SW Greenway Ave.
3.6	Bear left at SW Talbot to stay on SW Greenway Ave.
3.9	Bear right on SW Council Crest Dr.
4.0	Bear right to enter Council Crest Park (restrooms) loop counterclockwise.
4.2	Bear right to exit Council Crest park loop.
4.3	Bear left onto SW Greenway Ave.
4.75	Sharp right on SW Fairmount Blvd. (unsigned), just past SW Talbot on the left.
8.05	Bear left onto SW Talbot Rd.
8.1	Left onto SW Patton Rd.
8.2	Bear right onto SW Hewett Blvd.
10.0	Cross SW Humphrey Blvd. (cross to sidewalk, then take sidewalk to freeway crossing).
10.05	Right onto sidewalk to connect to SW Canyon Court cul-de-sac.
11.0	Bear left onto SW Knights Blvd. (Oregon Zoo entry); stay left.
11.4	Right onto SW Kingston Dr.
13.0	Right at stop sign onto SW Kingston Ave., entrance to Washington Park (restrooms).
13.3	Bear left as road becomes SW Sherwood Blvd.
13.9	Right onto SW Washington Way.
13.95	Right onto Madison Court (path), through gate and to right.
14.2	Left onto sidewalk on SW Jefferson St.
14.7	Left onto SW 18th Ave. at traffic circle.
14.95	Right onto SW Salmon St.
15.9	Finish at Salmon Springs Fountain.

17 EASTBANK ESPLANADE

A RIVER'S-EDGE VIEW OF THE HEART OF PORTLAND

Difficulty:	Easy
Time:	15 to 30 minutes, depending on stops
Distance:	3-mile loop
Elevation Gain:	108 feet
Best Seasons:	Year-round

GETTING THERE: This loop can be accessed from any number of points, but for this route, find your way to intersection of NE Lloyd Blvd. and NE Oregon St. Park along NE Lloyd Blvd. (other possibilities are near SE Salmon and SE Water, where you can easily access Esplanade, and any parking spot near SW Naito Pkwy. on downtown side). You can take your bike on MAX light-rail system to Rose Garden stop on east side of Willamette River, one block from start of this route.

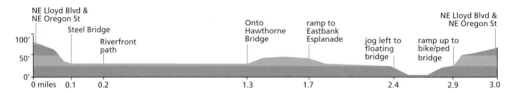

This is a route everyone who lives in or visits Portland should ride, run, walk, or spin in a wheelchair. It provides a wonderful, easy excursion as well as an unusual angle on downtown Portland; instead of seeing the cityscape from above—via Washington Park in the West Hills, a 30th-floor restaurant, or Interstate 5 heading north over the Marquam Bridge—on the Esplanade you're looking up, but with some splendid foreground for perspective. When the cherry trees on the west bank are in bloom, it's breathtaking.

The Vera Katz Eastbank Esplanade (the official name of the east half of the loop) is an audacious tribute to Portland's vision for itself. Decades ago, forward thinkers transformed the west bank of the Willamette River, eliminating the freeway-choked barrier between downtown and the river in favor of a public-park waterfront that has been wildly successful—but the east side of the river remained mostly an ugly industrial area huddling in the shadow of I-5 overpasses—until Portland leaders decided in the late 1980s that the city needed a park, and a loop. With the strong support of Mayor Katz during the final stages of planning and financing, the Esplanade was completed in May 2001.

Upon its opening, and ever since, the Esplanade has become a very popular place

A unique feature of the Eastbank Esplanade is the floating-bridge walkway. It rises and falls with river levels, but always provides a stellar view across to downtown Portland. >

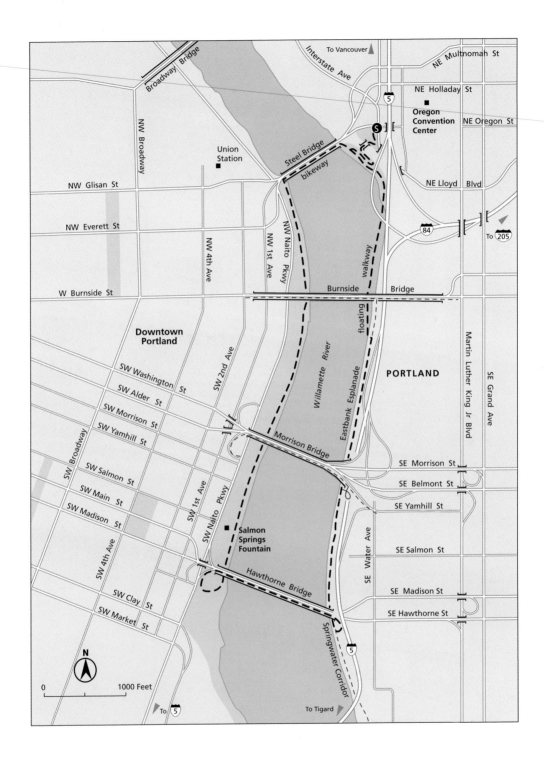

To Vancouver

Interstate Ave

NE Multnomah St

NE Holladay St

Oregon Convention Center

NE Oregon St

NE Lloyd Blvd

NW Broadway

NW Glisan St

NW Everett St

Union Station

Steel Bridge

bikeway

NW Naito Pkwy

NW 1st Ave

NW 4th Ave

walkway

84

To 205

W Burnside St

Burnside Bridge

Downtown Portland

SW 2nd Ave

floating

Willamette River

Eastbank Esplanade

PORTLAND

Martin Luther King Jr Blvd

SE Grand Ave

SW Washington St

SW Alder St

SW Morrison St

SW Yamhill St

SW Broadway

SW Salmon St

SW Main St

SW Madison St

SW 1st Ave

SW Naito Pkwy

Morrison Bridge

SE Morrison St

SE Belmont St

SE Yamhill St

SE Water Ave

SE Salmon St

SW 4th Ave

■ **Salmon Springs Fountain**

SW Clay St

SW Market St

Hawthorne Bridge

SE Madison St

SE Hawthorne St

5

N

0   1000 Feet

Springwater Corridor

To 5

To Tigard

0.0	From trailhead at SE Fourth Ave. and SE Ivon St., head south on trail.
2.0	Oaks Bottom Wildlife Refuge.
3.0	Cross SE Tacoma St.
3.1	Left onto SE Umatilla St.
3.8	Cross SE 17th Ave.
3.9	Right onto SE 19th Ave.
4.2	Sharp left onto trail.
5.0	Cross SE 32nd Ave.
5.1	Enter Tideman Johnson Nature Park (restrooms).
5.6	Cross SE Johnson Creek Blvd.
6.9	Cross SE Bell Ave. and SE Johnson Creek Blvd.; jog right onto trail.
7.8	Cross SE 82nd Ave.
8.2	Cross SE Flavel St.
8.7	Cross I-205.
9.2	Cross SE Foster Rd.
9.5	Cross SE 111th Ave.
10.1	Cross SE 122nd Ave.
10.9	Cross SE 136th Ave.
11.4	Pass Powell Butte Nature Park on left.
12.9	Cross SE Jenne Rd.
13.4	Cross SW Highland Dr.; pass Linneman Stn. (restrooms) on right.
14.7	Cross Eastman Pkwy.
16.4	Cross SE Regner Rd.; enter Gresham.
17.0	Cross SE Hogan Rd.
18.9	Finish at SE 267th Ave. and SE Rugg Rd.—pavement ends.

19 LAKE OSWEGO LOLLIPOP

A DOUBLE-LOLLIPOP RIDE AROUND OREGON'S MOST EXCLUSIVE LAKE

Difficulty:	Challenging
Time:	2 to 3 hours, plus stops
Distance:	27.6-mile loop
Elevation Gain:	1430 feet
Best Seasons:	Year-round, unless snowfall levels get very low

GETTING THERE: Find your way to Pioneer Courthouse Square, bordered by SW Broadway, SW Sixth Avenue, SW Taylor St., and SW Yamhill St. Street parking is predictably scarce;

garage parking is a bit expensive. By bike, take a MAX train from any station in Portland area; the square is a major light-rail hub.

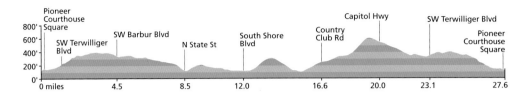

Another of the attractions of riding in Portland—which is either a pretty small city or a really big town, depending on whom you ask—is that you can ride from the heart of downtown and access all sorts of interesting scenery and places in just a few hours. This ride is another example: In fewer than 30 miles you'll cover a lot of ground both physically and socioeconomically. Lake Oswego has traditionally been Portland's wealthiest suburb—

hey, the lake itself is accessible only to residents, if that tells you anything.

The ride starts at Pioneer Courthouse Square, often referred to as "Portland's living room," smack-dab in the heart of downtown and a vibrant, eclectic place that reflects what the city is all about. The downtown bike-lane system is good enough to provide some comfort as you wheel along next to traffic.

Climb up SW Broadway through Portland

The Lake Oswego Lollipop ride features a circuit around the namesake lake. This view is from one of the bridges over fingers of the lake.

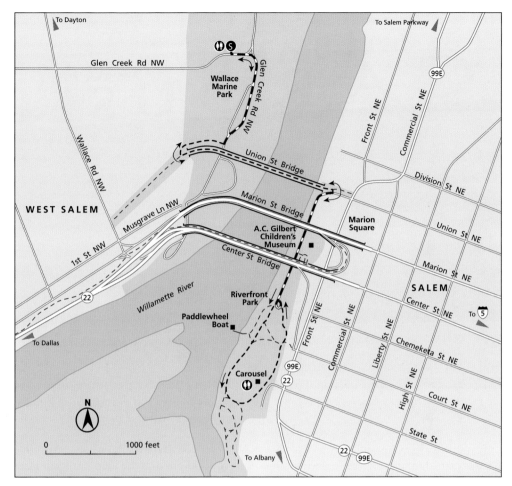

Just before you come to the Union Street bike-pedestrian bridge (if you stay straight you'll pass under it), jog right onto the sidewalk to access the ramp up to the bridge overpass. At the top of the ramp, turn left onto the bridge—first watch for traffic in both directions, though.

Crossing the bridge, take a minute to stop and look up- and downriver, noting the paddleboat anchored upriver. At the end of the bridge, look for a curb cut to your right and use it to get onto Water Street NE. Follow Water Street NE south along a pleasant stretch of river, with a wide sidewalk and benches strung along the way.

At about 0.7 mile, on your left is a pair of brightly painted Victorian houses, along with several other buildings. This is the A. C. Gilbert Children's Museum, named for the inventor of the Erector Set (also known as the "Man Who Saved Christmas"). You'll know you're at the right place when you see the giant rocking chair on the porch, plus the statue of the playful young girl on the lawn. The museum is definitely worth a stop.

Just past the museum, pass under the Center Street Bridge overhead, and then burst out into the open space of Riverfront Park. Stay to your right to access a bike-pedestrian path that parallels the river; follow this until you can see the paddlewheel boat below—also worth a look-see.

The Riverfront Carousel is a highlight of Salem's Waterfront Park and this ride, along with the paddlewheel boat and the children's museum.

From there, loop around counterclockwise on the path, heading for the large building across the park. This structure houses a wonderful carousel that still operates regularly; restrooms are nearby.

As you continue your circle around the park, you can stop at one of several covered pavilions with picnic tables, or you can just sprawl out on the large grassy expanses.

Whatever you decide to do, when you're done just continue around the loop until you meet up with Water Street NE again, turn right, and retrace your path back to the start.

One last note: When you take the off-ramp from the Union Street Bridge back down toward Glen Creek Road NW, be careful with your speed, and remember that there are posts at the bottom of the ramp.

MILEAGE LOG

0.0   From Wallace Marine Park's parking area, head south on Glen Creek Rd. NW.
0.2   Right onto bike-pedestrian path to access Union St. pedestrian bridge.
0.3   Left onto Union St. Bridge.
0.5   Right onto Water St. NE.
0.7   A. C. Gilbert Children's Museum on the left.
0.8   Bear right to stay on Water St. NE at intersection and parking area for Riverfront Park Loop.

0.95	Bear left to access Riverfront Park (restrooms) loop bike path; follow it counterclockwise.
1.1	Bear left at fork in bike path to complete the loop.
1.15	Right, back onto Water St. NE.
1.5	Left onto sidewalk for Union Street pedestrian bridge.
1.75	Right onto descent ramp from bridge.
1.8	Left onto Glen Creek Rd. NW.
2.05	Finish at Wallace Marine Park parking lot.

21 SILVER FALLS

RIDE TO THE PARK, WALK TO WATERFALLS

Difficulty:	Challenging
Time:	2 to 3½ hours
Distance:	34.05-mile loop
Elevation Gain:	2133 feet
Best Seasons:	Spring through fall; possibly winter

GETTING THERE: From I-5 take exit 271 for Woodburn–SR 214, heading east into Woodburn on SR 214. Turn right at intersection with SR 99 and then left just under 1 mile later to stay on SR 214. Follow SR 214 through Mount Angel and into Silverton, turning right on C St., left on N. Water St., and right on E. Main St. Cross bridge to small municipal park; parking lot is on left, on W. Main St. a half-block west of Silver Creek, which bisects downtown. Free parking; restrooms.

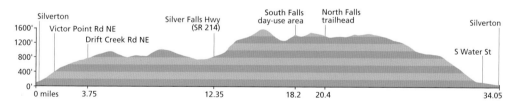

Sometimes a ride is just a ride . . . and sometimes it's a trip. Here's a route you should make a day of.

Silverton itself is a lovely little town with an interesting historic core with good restaurants, shopping, and a lot of cool old houses. The town is also home of the Oregon Garden, a superlative collection of plant life that's worth a stop anytime you're near. Plan to spend some time in Silver Falls State Park in the middle of the ride, whether just for a snack or lunch or to do some hiking. And

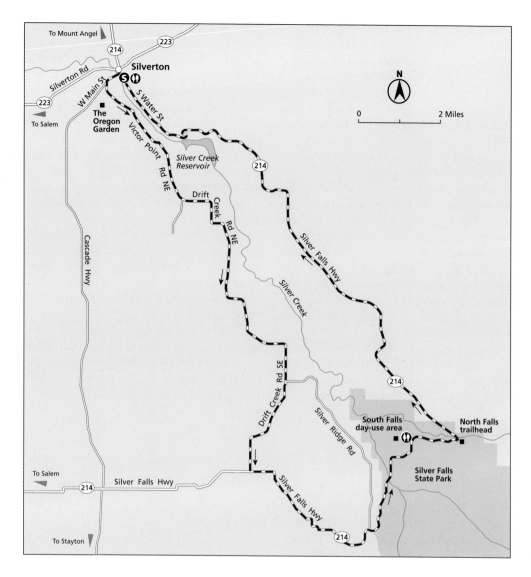

if you pass through Mount Angel coming or going, stop to check out the Benedictine Abbey, with its pleasing architecture and hilltop views.

But you're here to ride . . . and this is a fun one. It's only 34 miles long, so I'm tempted to rate it Moderate, but there's more than a modicum of climbing involved here. However,

there's something about rising out of town, looking out over the Willamette Valley, rolling through the forest and the park, and then cruising the long downhill back into town that just feels satisfying every time.

Start right in Silverton's downtown core, heading southwest briefly on W. Main Street before angling off on Eureka Avenue, which

< The Silver Falls ride takes you past numerous waterfalls—some easily viewed and some a little more secluded along wooded trails. Phil Bard

becomes Victor Point Road NE. After 0.5 mile of leg-stretching, start a bit of work on the first of two significant climbs for the day. This one is nearly 5 miles, on Drift Creek Road NE, but the grade is generally a comfortable 3 to 5 percent, and it affords some broad views of the agricultural bounty of the valley to the west.

The next 6 miles or so travel through the swelling rollers of the Cascades foothills. The land here is still open and cultivated, up against the mountain forests. When you turn left onto Silver Falls Highway (State Route 214), soon enough you get to know a little more about the mountains, as you embark on the stiffest climbing of the day. After a stretch of mild ascent, at around 13.5 miles you get a mile of solid 6 percent. But, as so often happens, it's through scenery that compensates for the struggle.

And between miles 16 and 17, when you hit the boundary of Silver Falls State Park, you'll see why this is a special enclave of nature. The road winds and plunges through the deep forest,

and it feels far more primitive than riding on a numbered state highway should. When you get to the South Falls day-use area on the left, it's worth riding to the far end of the lot and walking the short trail to the falls there. There's also picnicking here, as well as restrooms.

Equally worth a stop a bit later is the North Falls trailhead, on the sharp left curve over the bridge. A short traipse shows you one set of falls, and you can also hook up to the Trail of Ten Falls (pretty self-explanatory).

When you leave the park, you've already done most of the work. A few gradual slopes keep you alert, but in general it's a peaceful backcountry glide. And then, because you've already eaten your veggies, you've earned something sinfully delicious to finish with: a blissful 7-mile drop back to town, at a pitch you can pedal or coast.

Once you reach the outskirts of town, the road flattens out as it follows the path of Silver Creek back into downtown, where the highway is named S. Water Street and old-town bistros and creekside cafés await.

MILEAGE LOG

0.0	From parking lot at W. Main St. and Fiske St. in Silverton, head southwest on W. Main St.
0.3	Left onto Eureka Ave.
1.35	Road becomes Victor Point Rd. NE.
3.75	Bear left as road becomes Drift Creek Rd. NE.
7.5	Road becomes Drift Creek Rd. SE.
12.35	Left onto Silver Falls Hwy. (SR 214).
18.15	Pass main entrance to Silver Falls State Park.
18.2	Pass South Falls day-use area (restrooms) on left.
20.4	Pass North Falls trailhead on right.
32.2	SR 214 becomes S. Water St.
33.85	Right onto Lewis St.
33.9	Left onto S. First St.
33.95	Left onto E. Main St.
34.05	Finish at parking lot at W. Main St. and Fiske St. in Silverton.

22 COVERED BRIDGES RIDE

FIVE HISTORIC BRIDGES, AND A PASTORAL RIDE TO BOOT

Difficulty:	Moderate
Time:	3½ to 5 hours, with a few stops
Distance:	49.1 miles round-trip
Elevation Gain:	1112 feet
Best Seasons:	Year-round

ROAD CONDITIONS: No shoulder on Ridge Dr. Traffic on Hannah Bridge. Use caution crossing railroad tracks past Hoffman Bridge and past Gilkey Bridge.

GETTING THERE: From I-5, take exit 238 for Jefferson. Turn left off ramp and drive into Jefferson. Just across bridge entering town, turn right at stoplight onto Jefferson–Scio Dr. Follow that road into Scio. As you approach town, shortly after you go through an S curve, turn right at stop sign onto Main St. Go three blocks to NW First and turn left to the small city park just past the Depot Museum. Small gravel strip for free parking.

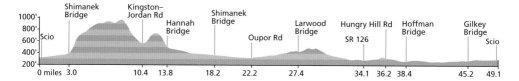

Bridges are pretty much just a way to get across something; most of us don't think twice about them generally. But an old covered bridge? That's just cool, and people will flock to see it.

This ride starts in Scio (pronounced like "silo" without the "l") and offers five different covered bridges, one of which you get to cross twice. The route is kind of a drunken figure eight—it takes a little conniving to get you to all these bridges on one ride.

Start at the little park in Scio, just past the Depot Museum. Go back to Main Street and turn left, and at the end of town take another left (east) on State Route 226, which has a narrow shoulder and a decent surface.

Richardson Gap Road (no shoulder, low traffic) takes you to your first quarry: Shimanek Bridge. Originally built in 1891 and rebuilt in 1966, this may be the most photogenic bridge of the day, with its barn-red paint and white trim.

Continuing on the same road, get ready for a nasty little climb that curves up a ridge for 0.5 mile. At the top, bear right onto Ridge Drive as your heart and lungs recover. The scenery compensates for the fact that there's no shoulder on this chip-seal road.

The next section features gently rolling hills followed by a steep, dippy descent of 1.5 miles on Valley View Drive, which does, indeed, provide valley views.

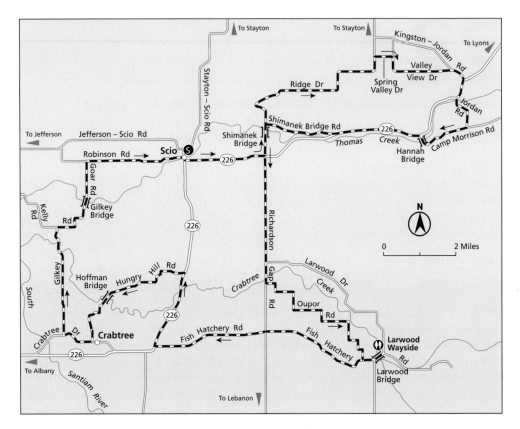

At the bottom, turn right onto Kingston–Jordan Road and then 0.5 mile later right onto SR 226. In another 0.5 mile, turn left on Jordan Road, crossing an uncovered bridge over Thomas Creek; check out the shallow, tumbling falls to the left—and gear down for steep-nasty climb number two. The good news: It levels off after the first half. At the top, at 12.4 miles, turn right onto Camp Morrison Road.

Soon you'll enjoy a pitched, curvy downhill of 0.75 mile to Hannah Bridge, a white, open-sided one-lane bridge—be cautious of traffic. On the other side of the bridge, turn left on SR 226 and follow it just over 2 miles before veering to the right onto Shimanek Bridge Road.

This pleasant stretch follows the winding path of Thomas Creek, bringing you back to the Shimanek Bridge again. Once back on SR 226, enjoy the luxury of a good shoulder as you ride flat and straight onto Richardson Gap Road to Oupor Road, which makes a series of 90-degree turns before ending at Fish Hatchery Road.

Turn left here and continue to a stop sign; go straight onto Meridian Road, and around the corner you'll find Larwood Bridge, at the alliterative junction of Crabtree Creek and the Roaring River. Ride through the bridge and find the Larwood Wayside around to the left, which has restrooms, picnic tables, and photogenic views back to the bridge.

Retrace your tracks onto Fish Hatchery Road and follow it through a quick rise and a few rollers, but mostly this is flat spinning, with a reminder of why this area calls itself the Grass Seed Capital of the World.

Turn right onto SR 226 again, going across Crabtree Creek to Hungry Hill Road, a lovely

The handsome riverfront park in Corvallis is the starting point for this ride, which features bike paths and low-traffic roads for an easy loop around town.

you. At 9 miles, turn right onto the straight-arrow path, downhill, passing through a gate into the Benton County Fairgrounds.

After crossing NW 53rd, jog left to connect to the Midge Cramer Bike Path, a smooth and wide lane taking you past llamas and small barns. As the path turns left, take the right fork to go through the covered bridge.

After the bridge, pass cow and sheep barns associated with Oregon State University's agricultural programs; local families flock here in the spring to watch lambs being born. At 10.95 miles, cross SW 35th Street onto Campus Way to cut directly through campus, passing under a bridge archway early on. Wend your way through the bucolic campus.

At SW 14th Street, stay straight into a curving linear parking lot, and continue onto SW Madison Avenue, eventually crossing stone pavers with Central Park to your left and the eclectic arts center to your right. Turn right on SW Seventh Street and left on SW Jefferson Avenue. As you hit the downtown core, carefully make your way down to SW First Street, turn left, and glide back to Waterfront Park.

MILEAGE LOG

0.0	From Waterfront Park at SW First St. and Monroe Ave., head south along First.
0.45	Cross under highway overpass.
0.5	Bear right at fork in path.
1.2	Cross SW 15th St.
1.5	Cross Brooklane Dr.
2.0	Cross SW 35th St.
2.1	Bear left at sharp bend in path.

2.4	Bear right at fork in path.
2.5	Cross SW Research Way.
2.9	Cross SW 45th St.
3.5	Cross SW 53rd St.
3.7	Jog left at Barley Hill Rd.; path switches to other side of road.
4.7	Enter Philomath.
5.05	Cross James St.
5.3	Right onto Applegate St.
5.85	Bear left to stay on Applegate St.
6.0	Right onto S. 19th St.
6.05	Cross US 20–SR 34 in Philomath; road becomes N. 19th St.
7.15	Bear right as road becomes SW West Hills Rd.
8.2	Bear left as road becomes SW Reservoir Rd.
8.6	Left into Bald Hill Natural Area.
9.0	Right onto bike path.
9.8	Jog left across NW 53rd St. and connect to Midge Cramer Bike Path.
10.95	Cross SW 35th St.
11.8	Cross SW 14th St.; follow curve to right and continue onto SW Madison Ave.
12.2	Right onto SW Seventh St.
12.2	Left onto SW Jefferson Ave.
12.6	Left onto SW First St.
12.75	Finish at Waterfront Park at SW First St. and Monroe Ave.

24 KINGS VALLEY

WIDE-OPEN FIELDS, THEN SECLUDED VALLEYS

Difficulty:	Challenging
Time:	4 to 6 hours
Distance:	65.9-mile loop
Elevation Gain:	1998 feet
Best Seasons:	Spring through fall; possibly winter

ROAD CONDITIONS: Heavy traffic on SR 99. Rough surface on Helmick Rd.

GETTING THERE: From I-5 take exit 228 and head west on SR 34. Entering Corvallis, cross over Willamette River on Harrison St. Bridge. Turn left on Fourth St. and right on SW Monroe Ave. Central Park is between SW Sixth and Eighth streets and SW Monroe and Madison avenues. Metered street parking on park perimeter; restrooms in park.

One of the things I enjoyed about living in the bucolic university town of Corvallis is that it's easy to get out of quickly on a bike. There's plenty of good road and mountain biking starting from town, and the Kings Valley route is just one good example. This ride is a mix of wide-open Willamette Valley and forested Coast Range, with some good up-and-down and a few tiny hamlets along the way for interest.

From the north side of the park, head west a couple blocks, then north on NW 10th Street, following a bike lane through town. After a jog through heavy traffic over to State Route 99 and 1.5 miles on the wide-shouldered highway, head off the beaten path with a series of turns that lead to a long stretch north on Independence Highway. Traffic is pretty light here in the country. Pass sheep farms, Christmas-tree farms, horse pastures, and agricultural lowland—classic Willamette Valley countryside. Enter Polk County, seeing why it's renowned for smooth pavement.

At just under 18 miles, a quick jog back onto and off of SR 99 puts you on Helmick Road; pass green, leafy Sarah Helmick State Park (restrooms, picnic tables) before a short, steep S turn climb through a tunnel of trees and then out into the rolling landscape. Helmick Road is not one of the county's trophy roads—it's pretty rough in spots. Pass picturesque Fircrest Cemetery on the way into Monmouth, an even smaller university town. The city park on Main Street has restrooms; Western Oregon University borders Main.

A left turn on Whitman leads out of Monmouth, becoming the Falls City Highway (SR 194)—more buttery Polk County road. A couple rollers will warm your legs up, followed by one more too big to call a roller. The peak yields an exhilarating mile-long descent, followed by another 0.75-mile climb and another fun descent.

Right before you hit 33 miles, turn left onto Kings Valley Highway (SR 223) and cross the Little Luckiamute River. There's a stout 1-mile climb at around 5 percent; at 39.8 miles at the intersection with Maple Grove Road, take a right to stay on the highway. Roll up and down through tiny Pedee and later past its historic schoolhouse. At 44 miles, the pristine white Ritter Creek Bridge parallels the road; there's a small wayside here.

When you reach Kings Valley, it may not live up to its regal name; there's nothing particularly palatial here, but there is a store, as well as a barn that's older than the state of Oregon, and you cross the Luckiamute River (the big one, apparently). Soldier on through a series of climbs over the next 8 miles; their saving grace is that the descents are steeper than the ascents.

The last big drop brings you through the spread-out "town" of Wren, past a couple wineries, across the Marys River, and to an intersection where you join US Highway 20, a fairly major route to the coast. It has a pretty good shoulder as you initially climb for 1 mile.

Just before reaching the town of Philomath, SR 34, another coastal route, joins in. Follow US 20/SR 34 into town, where the road splits into a one-way couplet. There are stores and other services aplenty here. Just after the couplets rejoin, turn left at the stoplight at N. 19th Street, which offers the comfort of an ample bike lane. Stay with the bike lane through a right and a left curve as the road

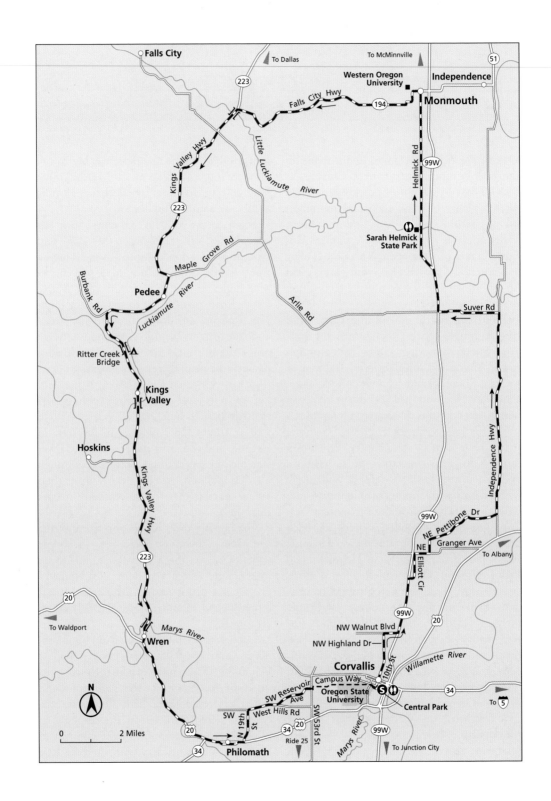

Falls City

To Dallas

To McMinnville

Western Oregon University

Independence

51

223

194

Monmouth

Kings Valley Hwy

Little Luckiamute River

Helmick Rd

99W

223

Maple Grove Rd

Sarah Helmick State Park

Burbank Rd

Pedee

Luckiamute River

Arlie Rd

Suver Rd

Ritter Creek Bridge

Kings Valley

Hoskins

Kings Valley Hwy

223

Independence Hwy

20

To Waldport

Marys River

Wren

99W

NE Pettibone Dr

NE Granger Ave

To Albany

Elliott Cir

99W

20

NW Walnut Blvd

NW Highland Dr

Corvallis

10th St

Willamette River

34

SW Reservoir Ave

Campus Way

Oregon State University

Central Park

To 5

SW West Hills Rd

SW 19th St

SW 53rd St

Marys River

99W

20

34

Ride 25

To Junction City

N

0   2 Miles

34

Philomath

becomes SW Reservoir Avenue, which spills out onto NW 53rd Street at the county fairgrounds. Take a quick jog left on the bike path paralleling the street and then cross at the stoplight to the Midge Cramer Bike Path, a wide, smooth ribbon of asphalt. At an S curve you have the option of riding through a covered bridge—of course you should—and then you enter the campus of Oregon State University.

You're now on Campus Way, which takes you straight through the vibrant campus. At SW 14th Street, Campus Way curves to the right as a parking lot–throughway; stay with it and at SW 11th Street it becomes SW Madison, which leads right back to Central Park.

This route explores the west edge of the Willamette Valley and the lower reaches of the Coast Range. Greg Lee/Cycle Oregon

MILEAGE LOG

0.0	From Central Park, at NW Seventh and NW Monroe in Corvallis, head west on Monroe.
0.15	Right onto 10th St.
1.05	At traffic circle, 10th becomes NW Highland Dr.
1.8	Cross Circle Blvd.
2.15	Right onto Walnut Blvd.
2.65	Cross NW Ninth St., then move to left lane for next turn.
2.7	Left onto SR 99.
4.35	Right onto NE Elliott Circle.
5.35	Right onto NE Granger Ave.
5.9	Left onto NE Pettibone Dr.
8.9	Left onto Independence Hwy.
13.4	Bear left at intersection with NW Springhill Dr. to stay on Independence Hwy.
15.65	Left onto Suver Rd.
16.85	Cross railroad tracks—rough surface.
17.75	Right onto SR 99.
18.2	Left onto Helmick Rd.
21.2	Bear left at intersection with Old Fort Rd. to stay on Helmick Rd.
25.0	Enter Monmouth.
25.5	Bear left onto Warren St.
25.75	Left onto Main St.
26.0	Left onto Whitman St. (SR 194).
32.95	Left onto Kings Valley Hwy. (SR 223).
39.8	Bear right at Maple Grove Rd. to stay on SR 223.
40.3	Enter Pedee.
42.65	Bear left at intersection with Burbank Rd. to stay on SR 223.

44.0	Pass Ritter Creek Bridge and wayside.
45.7	Enter Kings Valley.
54.1	Enter Wren.
54.4	Left onto US 20.
58.55	Enter Philomath; stay straight on US 20–SR 34.
58.7	Bear right as highway becomes one-way couplet.
59.9	Left onto N. 19th St.
61.0	Bear right as 19th becomes West Hills Rd.
62.0	Bear left as road becomes SW Reservoir Ave.
63.25	Left onto bike path paralleling SW 53rd St.
63.5	Right to cross SW 53rd St. onto Campus Way bike path.
64.6	Cross SW 35th St.
65.5	Cross SW 14th St.; follow Campus Way to right around curve.
65.65	Campus Way becomes SW Madison Ave. at SW 11th St.
65.9	Finish at Central Park.

25 ALSEA FALLS

VALLEYS AND FORESTS . . . AND ONE GREAT WATERFALL STOP

Difficulty:	Challenging
Time:	4 to 6 hours
Distance:	58.9 miles round-trip
Elevation Gain:	2474 feet
Best Seasons:	Spring through fall

ROAD CONDITIONS: South Fork Rd. less smooth after Alsea Falls. Traffic on SR 34; down-hill curves after Marys Peak Rd.

GETTING THERE: From I-5, take exit 228 and turn west, following SR 34 for 10 miles to Corvallis. Just before crossing Willamette River to enter town, turn left at stoplight for SR 34 bypass for the coast. Follow bypass past OSU campus and turn left at SW 35th St., then right onto SW Country Club Dr. Sunset Park is on right at SW 45th St. Free parking; restrooms.

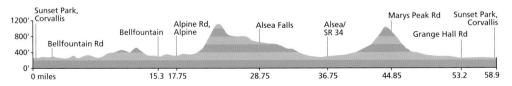

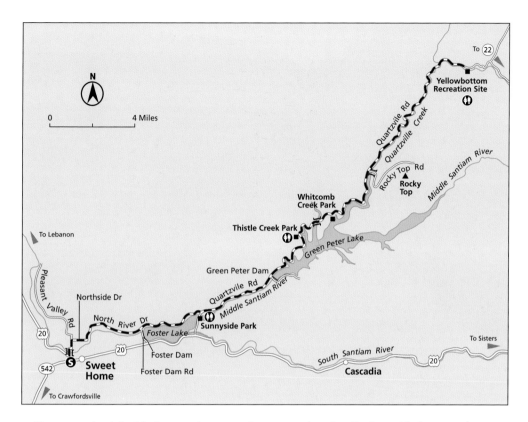

For a good while it's just a pleasant valley ride without a lot of up-close interaction with water—but that changes when you pass Foster Dam, which gathers water from both the Middle and South forks of the Santiam River. Say what you want about dams, but they do create a nice shoreline to ride along. (And if they make you grumpy, you'll get plenty of wild-river views later.) Other than a couple short stretches and some spots where the vegetation narrows the edges, there's a bit of shoulder through here as you skirt the edges of Foster Lake.

At the east end of Foster Lake, a left turn puts you on Quartzville Road, which you'll be on for a very long time—no more turns. Right away you drop down along Sunnyside Park, a large and well-appointed facility (restrooms).

After this, the road winds along a stretch of the Middle Fork that runs through a marvelous little rock canyon between dams; a little

more than 3 miles later, it's dam number two, Green Peter. I don't know who Peter was, but I know where the first word came from: the water in both the river canyon and the lake is an amazingly deep shade of green—hard to capture with a tourist camera but startling to the eye.

About at the dam road, there's a sign that says "Winding road next 8 miles," so you know what you're in for. It dips and swoops and touches on the lake; you make three small climbs on the way up (and remember, you're going upriver here, so it's net uphill). At just past 18 miles, the road crosses a lake finger, and from here the river transitions first to wide and then narrower and more tumbly.

There are plenty of campgrounds, both formal and informal, along the way, many with restrooms available; among them are Thistle Creek Park (restrooms), Whitcomb Creek Park, and Yellowbottom Recreation Site

As Quartzville Creek begins to transition to Green Peter Lake, it's wide and placid. Farther up it becomes narrow and more wild.

(restrooms). You're way back in the country here; Yellowbottom makes a good turnaround point. Of course, the thing about an out-and-back route is that as soon as it feels like halfway, you just turn around. And if you hear a faint echo of banjoes, it's time.

MILEAGE LOG

0.0	From White's Park on Pleasant Valley Rd. just off US 20, head north on Pleasant Valley Rd.
0.7	Right onto Northside Dr.
1.45	Bear left at 90-degree turn; road becomes N. River Dr.
4.75	Continue straight; Foster Dam Rd. to right.
7.9	Left onto Quartzville Rd.; Sunnyside Park (restrooms) to right.
11.85	Pass Green Peter Dam road on right.
16.25	Pass Thistle Creek boat launch on right; park on left has restrooms.
17.95	Pass Whitcomb Creek Park.
21.95	Bear left at Rocky Top Rd. bridge on right.
30.5	Reach Yellowbottom Recreation Site (restrooms)—turnaround point; retrace route back to start.
61.0	Finish at White's Park.

27 EUGENE BIKE PATHS

A WORLD-CLASS NETWORK OF PAVED PATHS—AND THE CROWDS TO PROVE IT

Difficulty:	Easy
Time:	30 minutes to 1½ hours
Distance:	11.9-mile loop
Elevation Gain:	92 feet
Best Seasons:	Year-round

ROAD CONDITIONS: Heavy bike and pedestrian traffic in places on path; some uneven, bumpy, and chip-seal surfaces.

GETTING THERE: From I-5, take I-105 west, taking exit 2 for Autzen Stadium–Coburg Rd. in Eugene. Follow signs for Autzen Stadium, which puts you on Country Club Rd. as it circles around beneath I-105 and Coburg Rd. At first right after passing under Coburg Rd., turn into Alton Baker Park. Plenty of free parking; roomy restrooms.

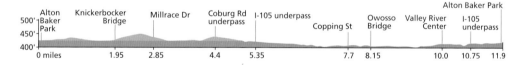

Eugene occupies its own little universe: a place where aging hippies live alongside fresh-faced college kids; a town where the natural-food co-op may be busier than the chain grocery, but the local university has built a juggernaut of an athletic program with extensive funding from the world's largest sneaker company. And on this ride you get to see it all—most of it up close and personal, because in one lap around this superb network of bike-pedestrian paths you'll encounter a complete cross-section of the local population. You'll also enjoy cool, leafy corridors, plus breezes off the river and plenty of spots to pull off and just relax amid natural beauty, right in the middle of the city.

Starting in Alton Baker Park, follow

what used to be an actual road—Day Island Road—and in the first mile pass a slide show of Eugene: the park, a permanent homeless camp, a co-op garden, a dog park, the world-famous Pre's Trail running network, and Autzen Stadium, home of the University of Oregon Ducks football team.

The road surface is uneven initially, but at 1.25 miles fork to the right onto a smoother surface. Follow the gentle contours of the path along the Willamette River and cross over the Knickerbocker Bridge to the other bank. The path is wider here but has more root-bumps and other spots to be wary of. After a very short section along the sidewalk of Franklin Boulevard, a sign points you onto Walnut Street, which becomes Garden Avenue, a quiet section of street on the fringes of the

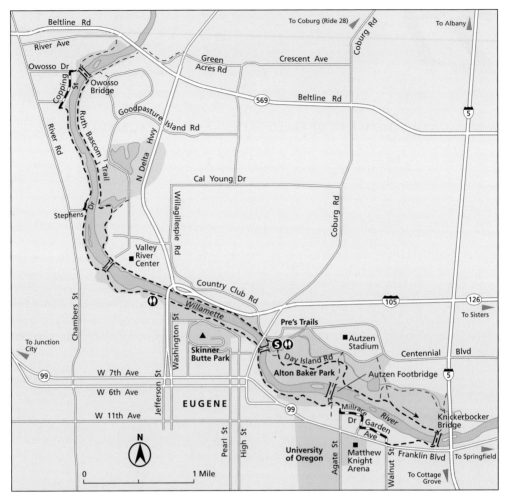

U of O campus (the new Matthew Knight Arena looms off to your left).

Take a right at the bike path sign onto Millrace Drive, then follow it around and turn right again to rejoin the dedicated path. Pass by the turnoff to the Autzen Stadium footbridge, going by a soccer field and then the old and new versions of the local electricity plant. Pass under a graceful pedestrian bridge and then Coburg Road. Just after, take the right fork toward the river and enter a lovely section that snakes through lush foliage alongside Skinner Butte Park. Here the crowds can be thick, so temper your speed and be polite.

As you cross under I-105, a community rose garden on the left also offers public restrooms. At about 6 miles a bridge heads across the river to the right, to the Valley River shopping center. Most foot and bike traffic turns off here, so the next section offers a bit more seclusion. However, the surface is chip seal, not as smooth as before.

At 6.5 miles there's a short segment along a street, and then at 7.7 miles a longer section through a quiet neighborhood before a sharp right turn puts you back onto the path. Soon after, take the right fork and cross the Owosso Bridge; at the bottom of the off-ramp, turn left to head back along the other side of the river toward the start in Alton Baker Park.

The highlight of the next section is an elevated "causeway" above a section of the river that has been diverted into a sort of nature-preserve slough where turtles bask on logs and songbirds abound. Later, pass the sprawling shopping center and then follow the riverbank directly across from Skinner Butte Park where you were earlier.

To finish, go under I-105, Coburg Road, and the pedestrian bridge in succession. Just after the last, cross a small footbridge and take a careful left to wind back through the heart of the park to the parking area.

MILEAGE LOG

0.0	From north end of Alton Baker Park parking lot, off Day Island Rd., head south on Day Island Rd.
0.7	Cross footpath to Autzen Stadium.
1.25	Bear right at fork to stay next to river.
1.95	Right to cross Knickerbocker Bridge.
2.1	Right at end of bridge.
2.4	Bear right to join sidewalk on Franklin Blvd.
2.55	Right onto Walnut St.
2.6	Bear left at 90-degree turn; street becomes Garden Ave.
2.85	Right onto Millrace Dr.
3.15	Right at sign for Riverfront Pkwy. (past barricades) onto bike path.
3.3	Bear left at intersection, then jog left and immediately right (Autzen Stadium bridge to right).
4.4	Pass under Coburg Rd.; take fork to right just after.
5.35	Pass under I-105; community rose garden (restrooms) to left.
6.05	Bear left at bridge to Valley River Center on right.

Eugene's bike path system gets plenty of use, with multiple access points and parks along the way, including this stretch near Skinner Butte Park.

6.5	Bear right on short section of street, then back on path.
7.7	Right onto Copping St.
8.05	Right onto Owosso Dr. to rejoin bike path.
8.15	Right to cross bridge over river.
8.25	Left at end of bridge off-ramp, to head south on bike path.
10.0	Pass perimeter of Valley River Center.
10.15	Go straight at bridge to right.
10.75	Pass under I-105.
11.7	Pass under Coburg Rd. and pedestrian bridge.
11.75	Left onto bike path across Alton Baker Park toward parking lot.
11.9	Finish at Alton Baker Park parking lot.

28 McKENZIE VIEW

A LOCAL RIDE WITH A VIEW

Difficulty:	Moderate
Time:	2 to 3 hours
Distance:	38.4 miles round-trip
Elevation Gain:	525 feet
Best Seasons:	Year-round

ROAD CONDITIONS: Traffic on Coburg Rd.; narrow shoulders beyond town.

GETTING THERE: From I-5, take I-105 west, taking exit 2 for Autzen Stadium–Coburg Rd. in Eugene. Follow signs for Autzen Stadium, which puts you on Country Club Rd. as it circles around beneath I-105 and Coburg Rd. At first right after passing under Coburg Rd., turn into Alton Baker Park. Plenty of free parking; roomy restrooms.

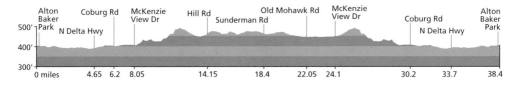

Not every ride has to be epic—sometimes you can find satisfaction in a good "local ride." Because I have friends and relatives in the Eugene area, I find myself riding McKenzie View Drive fairly often, and it's always a pleasant ride—nothing earth-shattering, but also one I don't get tired of. The nice bike path system in town, the peaceful meanderings

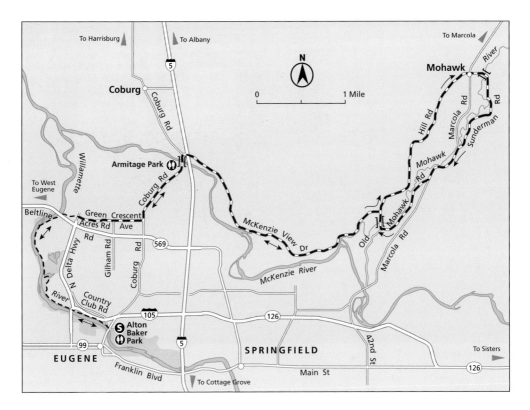

of McKenzie View Drive itself, with views of the legendary McKenzie River—placid through here—and quiet back roads through the Mohawk Valley . . . it's a great ride for conversation and just enjoying being out.

From the Alton Baker Park lot, ride past the restrooms and across the ponds—play nice; this is not a dedicated bike path—to access the path proper and scoot under the cool pedestrian bridge. Travel along the banks of the Willamette on the popular Ruth Bascom trail system's North Bank section, past riverside brewpubs and hotels and then a shopping mall (really, it's not so bad; look left and you'll hardly notice it's there). Continue on the path as it follows the river; for one stretch you're on an elevated causeway above what used to be a sluggish slough; local officials diverted a channel of the river through this section and created a thriving wildlife area.

When the bike path finally peters out at 4.65 miles, use the crossing signal to go kitty-corner across N. Delta Highway and into the bike lane on Green Acres Road. Wind through a generic commercial district and then follow the bike lane through neighborhoods, as the road name changes to Crescent Avenue, until you turn left onto busy Coburg Road. This route saves you from the worst of Coburg Road, however; it's less than 2 miles on this thoroughfare, with a generous bike lane, and you're leaving the city.

Just before you cross the McKenzie River on Coburg Road, to your left is Armitage Park, a nice place for a snack stop on your way back and a good place for restrooms in either direction. Turn right onto McKenzie View Drive just past 8 miles, twist under a couple overpasses, and emerge into the countryside.

This is probably the best stretch of the ride; there's a reason everyone calls this route McKenzie View: Enjoy glimpses of the river to your right as you parallel the water. There

My riding buddy, Pat, looks like he's going really fast on this leafy stretch of Sunderman Road, part of the McKenzie View route, a local favorite.

are some dips and bumps, enough to get you running through a few gears, but nothing that should make you want to die. A note: While there's no wide shoulder, locals are pretty used to seeing us out here.

Right around 14 miles, try to determine if the humongous log home to your left is cool or a blight; I can't decide. Then turn left on Hill Road and follow it past small farms and mobile-home country estates; again, there's some up-and-down, but it's reasonable. Just past 18 miles there's a nice country store where the folks are friendly and the drinks are cold.

Cross over Marcola Road, the local highway, and enjoy a quiet sojourn along Sunderman Road, with several sublime stretches of twisting curves through leafy canopies, as well as views of a decent golf course. At the end of Sunderman, jog left onto Marcola Road for just under 1 mile, then branch off onto Old Mohawk Road.

Near the end of Old Mohawk, encounter Hill Road again; take a right for just 0.3 mile to get back to McKenzie View Drive. From here it's a retrace, with slightly different views of the river from the other direction.

MILEAGE LOG

0.0	From parking lot in Alton Baker Park, head west on path through park.
0.15	Right to join main bike path; go under pedestrian bridge.
1.15	Cross under I-105.
4.2	Cross under Beltline Rd. (SR 569).
4.65	Go straight at end of bike path; cross N. Delta Hwy. kitty-corner to access bike lane on Green Acres Rd.
5.55	Cross Gilham Rd.; Green Acres becomes Crescent Ave.

GETTING THERE: From I-5, take exit 174 and head west on overpass, dropping down onto SR 99, which curves around and becomes Ninth St. in Cottage Grove. At intersection with Main St., turn left; Row River trailhead is on your left, at E. 10th St. Free street parking.

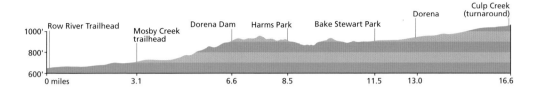

One of the big benefits of the rails-to-trails movement—beyond, of course, scenic pathways with gentle slopes—is that an old railroad bed typically has some good tales to tell. In the case of Cottage Grove's Row River Trail, you're traveling along the same path as the town's economy over the last 150 years.

The first real boom in the area was mining—gold and more—and a railroad was built to bring the goods down from the mountains. When the mining played out (although it still hangs on in isolated spots), the railroad was convenient for hauling the timber Cottage Grove came to rely on, down to the five local mills. But timber has gone the way of mining, and today people are more likely to enjoy Cottage Grove for its sylvan setting and outdoor recreation opportunities—like the Row River Trail.

One last interesting bit of background: "Row" rhymes with "cow" in this case—the river was named for a fight between two early settlers over grazing rights, a fight that ended with a murder. Yikes.

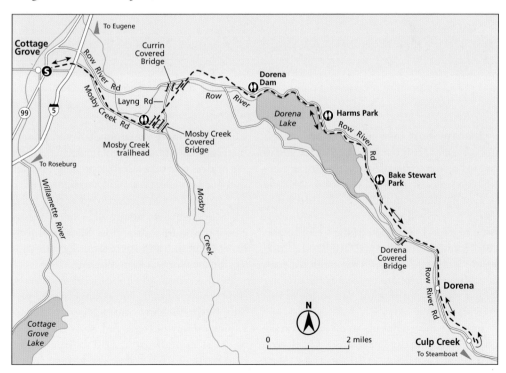

The Row River Trail, a wonderful rails-to-trails conversion, skirts the shores of Dorena Lake in the foothills of the Cascades. Greg Lee

The trail starts right in downtown, and it doesn't really get interesting until after you've crossed a couple streets, gone under the freeway, and passed the Walmart and the lone remaining timber mill. The path is decent—about 8 feet wide, with only a few bumps from tree roots. Right about the 1-mile mark, you'll join up with Mosby Creek Road, riding beside it to the Mosby Creek trailhead park at 3.1 miles. There are restrooms here, along with a parking lot if you'd like to make this your start point.

Just past this trailhead, you'll cross a trail-only bridge, with the 1920 Mosby Creek covered bridge paralleling it to the right (Lane

County has more remaining covered bridges than any county west of Appalachia). After the bridge, ride beneath trees arching over the trail—a neat effect on a long straight stretch. At 3.8 miles, cross Layng Road with a butte on your right. At about 4.5 miles, before crossing Oak Road, the Row River, and Row River Road in quick succession, look to your left for the Currin covered bridge.

At this point you'll begin to notice the climb; most railroad grades don't exceed 2 percent, but you'll know you're going up. There's a thick canopy of trees, and moss encroaches on the sides of the path. At 6 miles, cross the road again. At 6.6 miles, the Dorena Dam, built to control seasonal flooding, is accessible via a short walk up a gravel road; there's also a small park with picnic tables and restrooms. The view from the dam takes in the sweep of Dorena Lake and the Cascades beyond.

The grade flattens out here. There are several large bumps in the pavement through this section, but they're well marked with paint. The trail meanders peacefully, following the contours of the lake, and you can enjoy periodic views of the water on your right. At 8.5 miles, Harms Park offers more restrooms and benches, along with a bit of cinematic history: The trestle bridge here was used in films as varied as *The General* (1926, Buster Keaton), *Emperor of the North* (1973, Ernest Borgnine), and, perhaps more familiarly, *Stand By Me* (1986, River Phoenix).

Around 10.2 miles, the trail breaks out of the trees into a valley, more closely paralleling Row River Road. If you're not wanting to put in the full 30-plus miles, this is a good place to turn around; you've seen the majority of the good scenery.

At 11.5 miles, Bake Stewart Park offers restrooms. At 13 miles you can turn right and backtrack just a bit to see your third covered bridge of the day, Dorena. There's a small store near Dorena for some refreshments.

After passing Hawley Butte on your left, the trail ends at 16.6 miles at Culp Creek, which once was a bustling timber town but today sits sleepily along the river. Now it's time to turn around and see everything from the opposite side on your way back.

MILEAGE LOG

0.0	From trailhead at E. 10th St. and E. Main St., head east on trail.
0.3	Cross 16th St.
0.5	Cross Gateway Blvd.
0.95	Cross Thornton Lane.
1.6	Cross Row River Rd. (by weigh station).
3.1	Pass Mosby Creek trailhead (restrooms); view southeast to covered bridge.
3.8	Cross Layng Rd.
4.7	Cross Oak Rd. and Row River; view west to Currin covered bridge.
4.8	Cross Row River Rd.
6.0	Cross Row River Rd.
6.6	Pass Dorena Dam (restrooms).
8.5	Pass Harms Park (restrooms).
10.2	Turnaround option for shorter ride.
11.5	Pass Bake Stewart Park (restrooms).
13.0	Enter Dorena; view of covered bridge nearby.
16.6	Enter Culp Creek; end of trail—reverse route to return.
33.25	Finish at trailhead at E. 10th St. and E. Main St.

SOUTHERN OREGON

Southern Oregon has a distinct flavor—no better represented than by the fact that the entire area tried to secede and form its own state in 1941, until World War II pulled everyone together. The country here is a little more untamed, the terrain a little more rugged, the people a little more independent. While refined towns like Ashland soothe the senses, there are also plenty of out-of-the-way spots to take your bike for some back-road fun. And as these routes attest, there are lots of hills.

31 TOUR DE FRONDS

CLIMBING UP TO EDEN

Difficulty:	Epic
Time:	5 to 7 hours
Distance:	69.7 miles one way
Elevation Gain:	5466 feet
Best Seasons:	Late spring to early fall

ROAD CONDITIONS: Road narrows after Daphne Grove; chip-seal and rough pavement through Eden Valley. No shoulders until last few miles.

GETTING THERE: From I-5, take exit 119 for Winston and Dillard; turn west off exit and follow SR 99–42. When SR 42 splits off just more than 3 miles later, bear right on it. Follow highway for 46.5 miles (and pass through town called Remote) to junction with SR 542; turn left and take SR 542 south roughly 19 miles to Powers. This route could start anywhere in Powers, but I picked Fourth Ave. and Hemlock. Plentiful free parking in town.

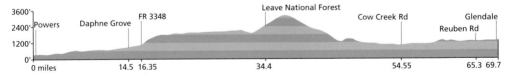

When I first heard of an event called the Tour de Fronds, a tough ride on some kind of designated bike route no one had ever heard of down in southern Oregon, I was intrigued. So I rode it with a friend and was struck by the small-town hospitality: The ride benefits the tiny end-point towns of Powers and Glendale, and rest stops tend toward "look for the pickup camper pulled over on the road." The people were gracious and enthusiastic, and, with only

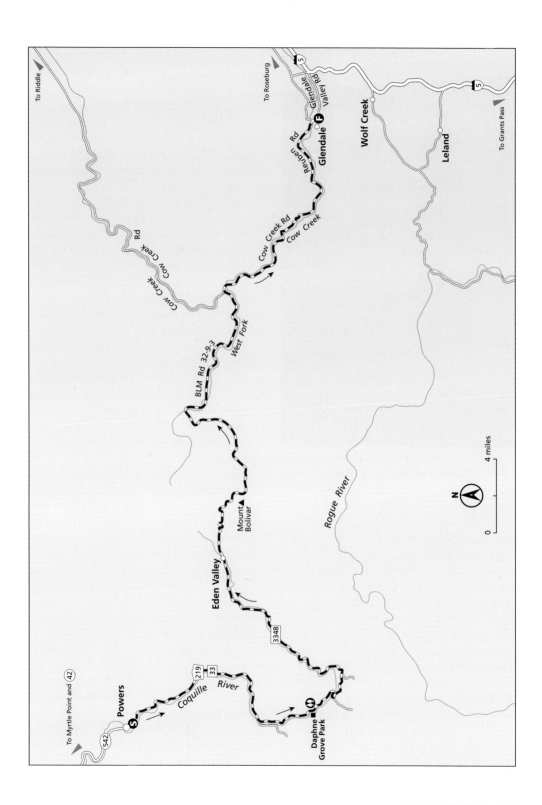

To Riddle

To Roseburg

5

Glendale Valley Rd

5

To Grants Pass

F

Glendale

Wolf Creek

Leland

Rauben Rd

Cow Creek Rd

Cow Creek

Cow Creek Rd

Cow Creek Rd

West Fork

BLM Rd 32-9-3

Rogue River

N

0   4 miles

Mount Bolivar

Eden Valley

3348

To Myrtle Point and 42

Powers

219

33

Coquille River

542

S

Daphne Grove Park

This shot gives you a sense of the splendid isolation of this route, winding its way through towering trees on a lightly traveled road.
Phil Bard/Cycle Oregon

a few dozen riders on our route, the event felt like a little secret.

But the course didn't make much of an impression on me. I remember thinking, "This is OK—just like any ride through any forest in Oregon." I'm a little competitive with that buddy, so we went hard and it hurt. But I didn't remember that much about it. I figured, "Did it—probably won't do it again."

Then I rode it again on Cycle Oregon. And this time I was awakened to the pleasures of the route. The remoteness and the hospitality were still impressive, but so was the beauty. And it wasn't as hard this time. (But it was still darned hard.)

If you get a chance to do the event, check it out. Having support and fellow riders on roads this remote is reassuring, and it helps a couple towns that can use it. But you can also gather a group of hardy friends and shuttle this route to Glendale, 4 miles west of Interstate 5 from near exit 80. The Powers-to-Glendale direction has more climbing but has you finish closer to the freeway, which is why I've mapped it this way.

Leaving Powers, spin easily out of town along the South Fork of the Coquille River, a lovely boulder-strewn stream. It's a gradual and steady climb for miles, and the road is draped with a mix of maple, Douglas fir, alder, madrone, and white cedar. There's a nice little park at Daphne Grove, at 14.5 miles, for a quick break (restrooms)—because the route is going to get harder.

The road heads up and away from the river, starting a 3.5-mile climb that winds upward at a grade of 6 to 8 percent past small waterfalls and hillsides exploding with ferns. But then it flattens out and hangs around 1 percent for 12 miles, passing through paradisiacal Eden Valley, which offers several good spots to pull off for lunch.

Right about 31 miles, drop into a thrilling, serpentine, smooth plummet for 1 mile (an 8 percent grade—careful), but then pay the piper in a big way. The next 5 miles are a true grind of an ascent—a granny-gear, "glad I have (or: wish I had) a triple ring" kind of effort as you rise up next to Mount Bolivar, which delivers a cruel false summit.

When you finally reach the crest at about 37.5 miles, catch your breath and then drop off the top like you're on a black-diamond ski run—one that happens to be 8 miles long. It's sharply down, then a little milder, then sharp again.

Aside from two nasty little uphills to remind you that the road is in charge, it's basically a flat ride for the last 25 miles. As you follow Cow Creek into the town of Glendale, enjoy the pastoral scenery at the conclusion of your ride.

MILEAGE LOG

0.0	From Fourth Ave. and Hemlock St. in Powers, head south on Fourth Ave., which becomes CR 219 (FR 33).
14.5	Reach Daphne Grove Park (restrooms).
16.35	Left onto FR 3348.
18.0	Enter Eden Valley.
34.4	Leave national forest; road becomes BLM Rd. 32-9-3.
54.55	Bear right onto Cow Creek Rd.
65.3	Road becomes Reuben Rd.
69.7	End at intersection with Brown Rd. in Glendale.

32 ROGUE RIVER RAMBLE

WILD AND SCENIC—AND A LITTLE GHOSTLY

Difficulty:	Challenging
Time:	4 to 6 hours
Distance:	61.3 miles round-trip
Elevation Gain:	3127 feet
Best Seasons:	Spring through fall; possibly winter

ROAD CONDITIONS: Merlin–Galice Rd. a little rough beyond Galice; river-rafting traffic. Lower Graves Creek Rd. narrows to one lane in places, but traffic is light.

GETTING THERE: From I-5, take exit 66 for Merlin. Turn west off exit ramp, onto Monument Dr., and follow it 2.2 miles to a right turn onto Pleasant Valley Rd. About 2.7 miles later, bear right onto Merlin–Galice Rd. and follow it 7 miles (a spectacular drive) to Indian Mary County Park on the right, on Rogue River. Free parking; restrooms.

Riding in Oregon, it's easy to get caught up in different ideals of beauty: craggy mountains draped in white, seemingly bottomless deep-blue lakes, rugged coastal headlands. But I think I'd rather ride alongside a stream than anything else. The sound of running water is so soothing, plus there's usually a nice leafy canopy above and the road is rarely straight.

The Rogue River is a superlative waterway. It was one of the original group of eight rivers nationally that were designated as Wild and Scenic in 1968, and it remains a bucket-list rafting trip for anyone who loves the outdoors. This ride gives you a tantalizing taste of it.

Even the drive to the start of this route is exceptional, with a viewpoint down into a deep and rugged canyon between Merlin and the start. Once you set out on the road, it

parallels the river for miles, serving up a succession of picture-worthy views. Just before Galice, pass Bear Camp Road, a truly epic suffer-fest climb up and over to the coast (can't put *every* great ride in this book). Galice has a store and riverfront-deck dining.

Pass by numerous small resorts and parks, all taking advantage of proximity to the river. The road here is wide but a little rough; you may encounter a lot of rafting shuttle-van traffic for the first 12 miles in the summer. The reason the traffic ends at 12 miles is because you cross and head away from the river, right

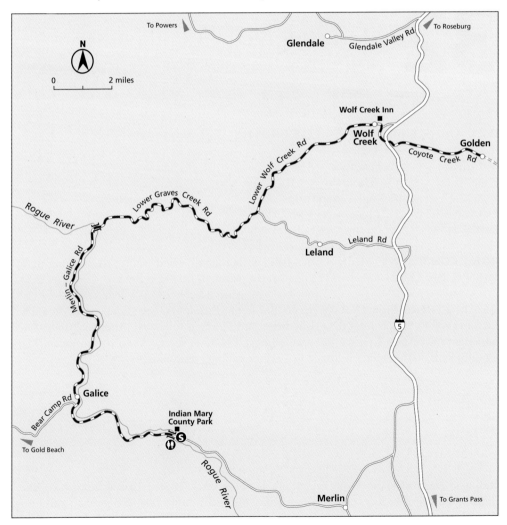

You don't have to all dress alike when you ride with friends, but it does look cool. The Rogue River Ramble is nearly continuously beside rushing water. Greg Lee/Cycle Oregon

where the Wild and Scenic section begins—no paved roads connect to the river for many, many miles.

But as you turn away, don't despair; the riding actually gets prettier, if that's possible. Now you're following Lower Graves Creek, and the section between here and the town of Wolf Creek is a paradise of twisting, climbing, dropping, and swooping through deep forest alongside the rushing water. The road occasionally narrows to the equivalent of one lane, but traffic is very light. There are plenty of small climbs, but only two are sustained, each about a mile. This is simply a superb stretch of riding.

Just after 26 miles, you quite suddenly emerge in Wolf Creek, like someone who's been lost out in the woods and stumbled upon civilization. About the first thing you see is the historic Wolf Creek Inn, the oldest continuously operated hotel in Oregon. Built in 1883, it's now actually a state park, but you can stay here or have lunch here.

And now for something completely different: Follow the mileage log to get across Interstate 5 and connect to Coyote Creek Road. A little bit less than 4 miles up the road (and, yes, it's up—but, again, not too strenuous) you'll find the ghost town of Golden. This is one of the best-preserved ghost towns in the state; you can go inside the fully intact church, peer in the store windows, and read several fascinating interpretive signs covering mining and community history. It's a good spot for a picnic before heading back (since the road turns to gravel here).

MILEAGE LOG

0.0   From entrance to Indian Mary County Park, head west on Merlin–Galice Rd.
4.5   Pass Bear Camp Rd. on left.
4.75   Enter Galice.

11.9	Cross Rogue River and bear right; road becomes Lower Graves Creek Rd.
20.8	Bear left onto Lower Wolf Creek Rd.
26.45	Right onto Front St. in Wolf Creek.
26.6	Right onto Old SR 99.
27.0	Left to cross under I-5.
27.1	Bear right onto Coyote Creek Rd.
30.65	Reach Golden, turnaround point; retrace route back to start.
61.3	Finish at Indian Mary County Park.

33 CEDAR FLAT LOOP

THE MOST MISLEADING NAME EVER

Difficulty:	Epic
Time:	4½ to 7½ hours
Distance:	72.6 miles round-trip
Elevation Gain:	4334 feet
Best Seasons:	Late spring through fall

ROAD CONDITIONS: Rough pavement on Williams Hwy. Cedar Flat Rd. narrows to one lane in places; possibly gravel, boulders, even small trees in road on descent.

GETTING THERE: From I-5 at Grants Pass, take exit 58 for SR 99–US 199 (Redwood Hwy.). Follow N. Sixth St. (SR 99 S) and after 3 miles follow signs for SR 238. Follow this highway for 18 miles to Applegate; ride starts and ends at Applegate Store. Ample parking; owners are bike-friendly (of course, buy a drink or something more).

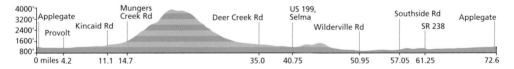

If you pin me down and ask me what I think is the toughest climb in this book, it might sound silly if I say "Cedar Flat," but that's just what I might say. Because this road—and this route—is gloriously misnamed.

Actually, this is more like two rides; just look at the elevation profile. It's basically a no-sweat jaunt through the pastoral Applegate Valley—punctuated by scaling a sheer wall in the woods. This route is not for those afflicted with vertigo or anyone who doesn't harbor the sick notion that the steeper a hill is, the better you feel about it after you climb it.

The ride starts at the Applegate Store, the kind of local hub where if you hang out all day you'll see almost everyone who lives in

35 BEAR CREEK GREENWAY

A SCENIC BIKE FREEWAY THROUGH SOUTHERN OREGON

Difficulty: Easy
Time: 1½ to 2½ hours
Distance: 17.7 miles one way (easy to hop on and off)
Elevation Gain: 20 feet
Best Seasons: Year-round

ROAD CONDITIONS: Path has occasional (marked) root-bumps; surface worse near Talent. Some sharp turns.

GETTING THERE: From I-5, take exit 19 for Ashland. Turn west off exit ramp, go to SR 99 and turn left, and follow SR 99 into town for roughly 1.5 miles. Turn left on W. Hersey St., go around right-hand curve, and then take second left, onto Helman St. Follow Helman until it ends just past intersection with W. Nevada St., at Ashland Dog Park. Free parking; restrooms.

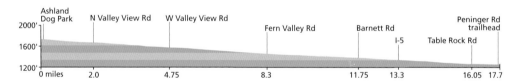

While they're not typically a beauty to behold, freeways come from a good concept: an unfettered transportation corridor right through town that you can get on and off at regular intervals. Well, the good folks of Jackson County have created a bike-pedestrian equivalent with the Bear Creek Greenway, a nifty bike freeway that stretches almost 18 miles and connects no fewer than five communities, from Ashland to Central Point. It's a great resource, one that gets used a lot.

I've mapped this ride to start at the southern end of the trail, where most tourists are anyway: Ashland. Plus it's downhill all the way in this direction—check out the elevation gain (and I think that's all on one overpass).

Start at the Ashland Dog Park at the end of Helman Street, which becomes one lane right before the parking lot—keep going. It's a clean and pleasant trailhead, to be sure. And the greenway itself starts out like a paved nature trail: You're tucked between town and Interstate 5, but all you hear is running water and birdsong. Cross a creek twice, note the llamas and then the small rock cairns on the right, and pass by a boutique vineyard. Parallel State Route 99 for a bit, then it's back into the wild. The trail is smooth but has occasional root-bumps, which are helpfully marked with spray paint.

After a park (covered picnic tables, restrooms) at 4.75 miles, the charm factor drops considerably once you cross W. Valley View

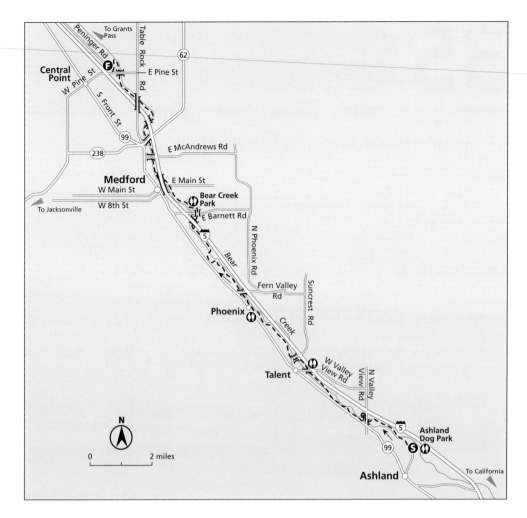

Road. This appears to be the ghetto section of the trail, and everything about the trail reflects it, including pavement. But then at 5.4 miles, with a jog to the left over a bridge, you're movin' on up—to a broad and smooth path that passes an orchard. At 7.6 miles there's a park with a nice spot for kids to stop and play.

You'll see all kinds and ages on this path; the true test of a project like this is who uses it, and on a sunny Sunday it's walkers, joggers, moms with strollers, old guys on motorized wheelchairs, fishing buddies on bikes, cycling couples, and the occasional jersey-wearing bike nut.

Along this stretch you pass first through the town of Talent and then Phoenix. At 8.3 miles, stay right to go under a bridge—this is a tight, blind corner, so be careful. And at 9.9 miles take a very sharp right, even though it appears the main path goes straight. Ride a street through a softball complex and then reconnect to the path, now entering Medford.

Here you're in the literal shadow of the freeway for a stretch, first beside it and then under it. At 11.75 miles, take the left up onto the overpass and drop down next to the dog park; take the right even though the straight looks better. This takes you into the verdant

The Bear Creek Greenway is more than a convenient way to connect five towns without riding with automobile traffic—it also offers some inviting Southern Oregon panoramas. Alex Georgevitch

paradise of Bear Creek Park (restrooms), and you then follow the creek through a maze of underpasses and another park.

At 15 miles the path gets a little sketchy; at 15.3 miles cross under I-5 and take the sharp right loop—stay to the right over the wood-railed bridge; the surface is very bad on the bridge. But from here it's wide, smooth sail-ing to the end of the trail in Central Point. Unfortunately, the end is a decidedly unglam-orous gravel parking lot with no facilities at all. Plans are afoot to improve this end point eventually.

You can access or exit the greenway in many, many places along the route; go to www.bear-creekgreenway.com for a detailed map.

MILEAGE LOG

0.0	From Ashland Dog Park, head northwest on bike path.
0.25	Bear left at end of Oak St. to stay on bike path; cross bridge.
1.5	Parallel Eagle Mill Rd.
2.0	Cross under N. Valley View Rd.—loop around to right.
2.8	Right to continue on bike path.
4.75	Cross under W. Valley View Rd.; park with restrooms near Talent.
5.4	Left onto Suncrest Rd. just after bridge.
5.45	Right turn back onto bike path.
7.6	Pass park (restrooms) near Phoenix.
8.3	Bear right at fork to cross under Fern Valley Rd.
9.9	Bear right to stay on main path.
10.2	Right onto unnamed street through ballpark near Medford.
10.3	Rejoin path.
11.3	Cross under I-5.
11.5	Cross under Highland Dr.

11.75	Bear left to cross above E. Barnett Rd. near dog park.
11.8	Bear right at intersection in path into Bear Creek Park (restrooms).
12.0	Bear left at fork in path.
12.85	Cross under Cottage St.
12.9	Cross under E. 10th St.
13.15	Cross under E. Eighth St. (E. Main St.) in Medford.
13.3	Cross under I-5.
14.2	Cross under E. McAndrews Rd.
14.8	Cross under SR 62.
14.9	Bear right at intersection in path.
15.3	Cross under I-5; make loop to right to cross bridge and continue on path.
16.05	Cross under Table Rock Rd.
17.5	Cross under E. Pine St.
17.7	Finish at Peninger Rd. trailhead in Central Point.

36 OLD SISKIYOU HIGHWAY

THE JOY OF TAKING THE SLOW ROUTE

Difficulty:	Challenging
Time:	2 to 3½ hours
Distance:	29.45 miles round-trip
Elevation Gain:	2146 feet
Best Seasons:	Spring through fall

GETTING THERE: From I-5, take exit 19 for Ashland. Turn west off exit ramp, go to SR 99 and turn left, and follow SR 99 into town. Lithia Park is on the right just as you enter downtown core. Turn right at triangle-shaped plaza and follow Winburn Way to find free parking; restrooms in several places in park.

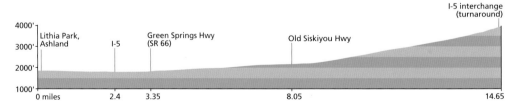

Sometimes you pick a ride for the views, for the challenge, or because it's handy to where you are. And sometimes you pick it just because you feel good while you're riding it. For some reason, riding up Old Siskiyou Highway has given me a slightly goofy sense of euphoria every time I've ridden it. (OK, it happened the first time, and I've just replicated.)

If you've ever driven Interstate 5 south of Ashland, you know there's a humongous pass that rises into the sky, and unless you've got a big honkin' engine, it's a strain to get up it—plus all the semis crawling along . . . This route actually takes you up to the top of Siskiyou Pass the old way—and it's stunningly tranquil and satisfying in comparison.

I start you in Lithia Park not because it's

the most convenient access to the route, but because it's one of the best city parks in the state, hands down. A tumbling stream, wandering paths, shady spots, and abundant garden patches . . . spend some time hanging out there, pre- or postride.

So you have to make your way through downtown at the start, but since traffic is pretty congested here, it at least moves slowly. Veer over onto E. Main Street and get a nice bike lane for a long while. Cross over I-5 and start heading out of town with the large patchwork hills looming to the east.

Join up with State Route 66 for a few

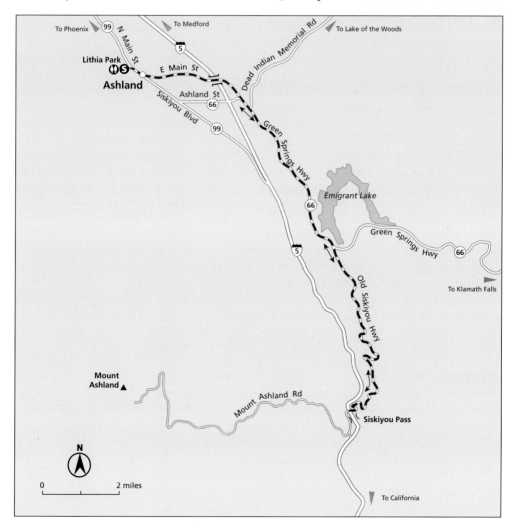

Between Ashland and the turnoff to Old Siskiyou Highway is sparkling Emigrant Lake, a recreation haven for all of southern Oregon.

miles—practically a bike boulevard in these parts, what with those heading up Dead Indian Memorial Road or Green Springs Highway (see Ride 37, The Lakes Loop) and those joining you on your route.

When you turn off onto Old Siskiyou Highway, the first stretch is not much of a strain, as you pass by a few open spaces, the stray bed-and-breakfast, and some small ranches. But once you start ascending and the trees stretch overhead, the highway becomes a slice of paradise. A mix of oak, cedar, and fir creates a leafy ceiling of shade as the road twists upward. This is one of the places where I learned the joy of spinning a hill instead of attacking it—this is 6 miles of up, but the incline is pretty steady at an average grade of 5

percent, which is perfect for finding a low gear and just enjoying.

Follow a series of lefts and rights, always going higher, until you emerge at—oh, that's right—the top of the I-5 climb. There's a restaurant-resort here—and choices. You can turn around and go back the way you came, cross over I-5 and continue on the old highway for a while into California (eventually it merges with the freeway), or go a little farther and then turn right on Mount Ashland Road to do some serious ascending up to the ski area.

Whichever you choose, you'll get to glide back down that glorious stretch of Old Siskiyou Highway—and I hope you feel a little euphoric too.

MILEAGE LOG

0.0	From Lithia Park in Ashland, along Winburn Way, head north on Winburn Way.
0.1	Bear right in downtown plaza to connect to Main St.
0.45	Get in left lane and take left fork for E. Main St.
2.4	Cross over I-5.
3.35	Left at stop sign to join Green Springs Hwy (SR 66).
6.2	Pass Emigrant Lake recreation area on left.
8.05	Right onto Old Siskiyou Hwy. (old SR 99).

14.65	Reach I-5 interchange—turnaround point; retrace route back to Ashland.
28.85	Bear right where E. Main St. joins SR 99 in town and splits into couplet, onto Lithia Way.
29.25	Left onto Water St., just before crossing Lithia Creek; pass under SR 99 onto Calle Guanajuato.
29.45	Finish at Lithia Park.

37 THE LAKES LOOP

THE BEST OF SOUTHERN OREGON, ALL IN ONE RIDE

Difficulty:	Epic
Time:	4 to 5½ hours
Distance:	51.35-mile loop
Elevation Gain:	4229 feet
Best Seasons:	Late spring through fall

ROAD CONDITIONS: Fast traffic on SR 66. Road surface a little worse on E. Hyatt Lake Rd.

GETTING THERE: From I-5, take exit 14 at Ashland. Turn west onto Ashland St. (SR 66), go roughly 1 mile, and turn right on Siskiyou Blvd., the main drag. Then take the fourth right, at Garfield St., and follow it several blocks north to Garfield Park. Free street parking; restrooms.

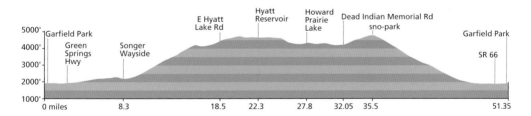

Ashland is an enchanting town in an idyllic setting, and it's surrounded by some great bike riding. I like this route because it touches on all the best elements of this part of the state: grassy hills, verdant valleys, still forests, alpine lakes, broad meadows . . . it takes you past it all.

When you head east out of Ashland, you have two choices, and both present a long, tall challenge: Dead Indian Memorial Road and Green Springs Highway (State Route 66). All the locals have their opinion about which they prefer to go up and which they'd rather go down. I've ridden up both, and for my money Green Springs is the better climb. While the road can be narrower and a

The ascent up Green Springs Highway is sinuous, relentless, and exposed—but the views are comforting.

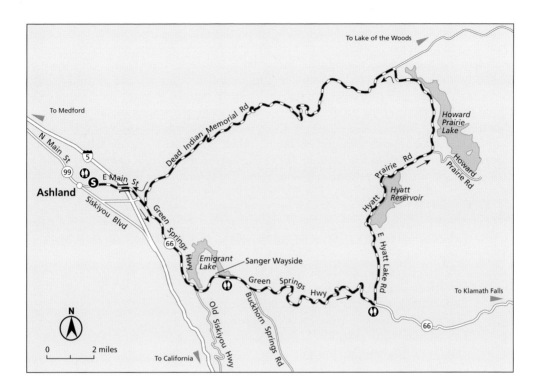

little rough in spots, the climb seems steadier somehow, and it seems as though you can more easily get into a rhythm. Dead Indian gets much steeper in the second half, which can be hard to deal with mentally. So this route goes up Green Springs.

Leaving Garfield Park, you get a bike lane from the start as you cross over Interstate 5 and then join Green Springs Highway (SR 66). Once you're clear of town, the riding is wide open, with towering brown hillsides above you on the left. On Green Springs, unfortunately, the road is smooth and the shoulder is chip seal; be careful with the temptation to ride in the car lane, because the traffic is typically light but fast.

Skirt the horseshoe-shaped Emigrant Lake from miles 5 through 9. After you pass the turnoff for the Old Siskiyou Highway (old SR 99) (Ride 36) at about 7 miles, there's one initial warm-up rise followed by a drop down to the lakeshore. The Sanger Wayside at 8.3 miles offers restrooms.

At 9.6 miles, when you pass Buckhorn Springs Road, the ascent begins for real—about 7 miles at a steady 5 to 7 percent grade. The road snakes upward, delivering panoramic views back toward town and off to Mount Ashland to the west at several points. It's a long piece of work, but it's never boring.

At around 16 miles, crest and head for the junction of E. Hyatt Lake Road, a couple miles ahead. A resort-restaurant at the junction offers good food and friendly service. Once you're on E. Hyatt Lake Road, the surface is less nice, and it starts off with a couple miles of climbing; after that, it's basically flat or downhill for miles and miles.

Here you're pedaling through prairies; the wildflowers in season are a profusion of brilliance. The road hugs the shore of first Hyatt Reservoir and then Howard Prairie Lake; services are available at several "resorts" along the way. It's carefree riding—a nice piece of punctuation between the big up and the big down.

At 32 miles, turn left at the junction with Dead Indian Memorial Road. It starts relatively flat, but you do have to negotiate one more climb, a little grinder of a couple miles. At the top you can take a breather at a pullout on the left before setting off on the long glide down.

And it is a long one—12 miles, give or take a couple flatter sections, to the bottom. The decline is as much as 11 percent at points near the top, with sections of sustained 7 and 8 percent. It's not terribly technical—you might need your brakes only three or four times if you're an avid downhiller. But it's fairly exposed through the bottom two-thirds, making it susceptible to strong headwinds, especially in the afternoon.

Once you reconnect to Green Springs Highway in the flatlands, it's an easy cruise as you retrace your route back into town.

MILEAGE LOG

0.0	From Garfield Park, at E. Main St. and Garfield St. in Ashland, head east on E. Main St.
1.3	Cross over I-5.
2.2	Left at stop sign to join Green Springs Hwy. (SR 66).
6.95	Stay left at Old Siskiyou Hwy. (old SR 99) on right.
8.3	Entrance to Sanger Wayside (restrooms) on left.
9.6	Stay left at intersection with Buckhorn Springs Rd.
18.5	Left onto E. Hyatt Lake Rd.
22.3	Pass Hyatt Reservoir, to the right.
27.15	Bear left at intersection with Howard Prairie Rd.
27.8	Pass Howard Prairie Lake, to the right.
32.05	Left onto Dead Indian Memorial Rd.
35.5	Pass sno-park pullout on right before descent.
49.15	Right onto Green Springs Hwy. (SR 66).
49.35	Bear right onto E. Main St.
50.2	Cross over I-5.
51.35	Finish at Garfield Park.

38 PROSPECT TO ASHLAND

THE LONG AND WINDING ROAD

Difficulty:	Epic
Time:	5 to 7½ hours
Distance:	76 miles one way
Elevation Gain:	4436 feet
Best Seasons:	Late spring through fall

GETTING THERE: From I-5 in Medford, take exit 30 onto SR 62 north to turnoff for Prospect; turn south on Mill Creek Dr. and follow it a short while until Red Blanket Rd. (Butte Falls–Prospect Rd.) branches left. Prospect State Park is a little farther up on Mill Creek Dr. (parking, restrooms). Ride starts at corner of Mill Creek Dr. and Butte Falls–Prospect Rd., next to Prospect State Park.

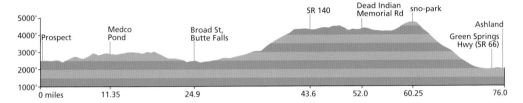

If you like variety in your rides and you've got all day to ride—and you'd like to maybe start in a very small town and end up in a highly cultured small city—this route is a winner. First of all, it connects directly to Crater Lake Up-and-Over (Ride 56), connecting the varied attractions of Crater Lake and Ashland. It also showcases a diverse blend of topography and flora. And, of course, there's some climbing and descending involved.

Leaving Prospect, the road starts flat and then bucks up and down a bit, dropping sharply down to cross a rushing creek, then heading up a nice grade—kind of a three-stair-step up to 11 miles, topping out at Medco Pond, a small body of water surrounded by high-mountain beauty.

From there it's plateau riding in the forest and meadows, with just a few elevation bumps. Then, when you see a sign for "Curves Ahead," in this case that means uphill curves—but not for long, and right afterward comes a snaky, grin-worthy descent through every possible shade of green.

At 24 miles, turn right to head the short distance into Butte Falls, a tidy little town centered around a sylvan community park. There's a store and a couple restaurants here, and the well-tended park (restrooms) is a nice shady spot to have a break. Then retrace back out to the junction, going straight this time.

Follow a pleasant creek for a while, with nothing too up or too down. Eventually begin a steady 1 percent climb for a long stretch, and then at 36 miles comes the real work of the day: a 5.5-mile ascent. You'll rise 1000 feet in less than 3 miles; the pitch reaches 7 percent, with a few stretches of semi-relief at 2 to 3 percent. It's not so much a stair-step climb; it's more a case of the needle on the pain meter swinging back and forth a bit.

When you reach State Route 140, take a quick right-left jog to access Forest Road 37 (Big Elk Road), a less refined surface, for about 8 miles. Riding through here is like body-surfing large waves: crest, trough, crest, trough—including a couple of screaming-deep troughs.

At Dead Indian Memorial Road (52 miles), turn right; about 1 mile later the pavement changes settings to "magic carpet ride" for a while. Bisect high-prairie meadows, and a riot of wildflowers when they're in season, and go past the turnoff for Hyatt and Howard Prairie lakes.

You have one last piece of business to deal with on this day: 3 miles of up-grade. The first 0.5 mile lets you acquaint yourself with the hill, then it's a regular 4 percent; find your gear and turn it. The grade relents at about 60 miles, then slaps you one last time for the last 0.25 mile to the sno-park at the summit.

I'd advise a break here; while you have a lot of downhill ahead, it can actually be a little wearing. Dead Indian drops for 12 miles; it's long and winding, with a few flatter bits scat-

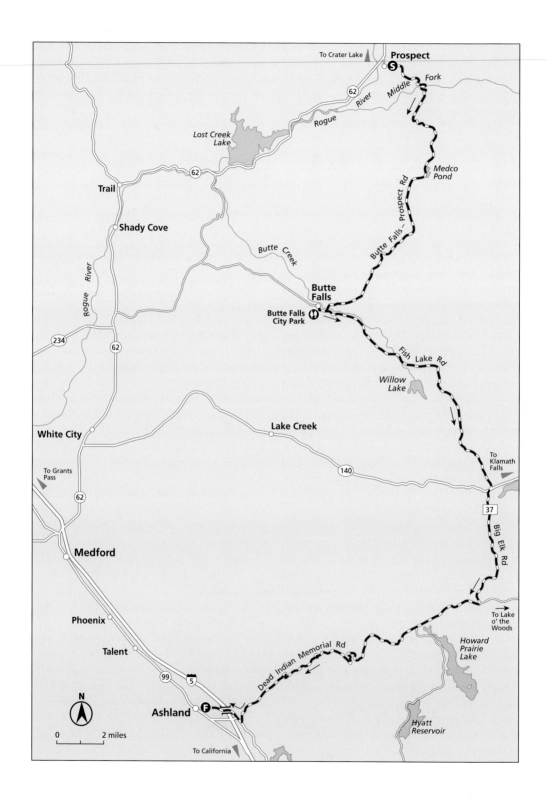

To Crater Lake

Prospect Ⓢ

Middle Fork

62

Rogue River

Lost Creek Lake

Butte Falls–Prospect Rd

Medco Pond

62

Trail

Shady Cove

Butte Creek

Rogue River

Butte Falls

Butte Falls City Park Ⓗ

Fish Lake Rd

Willow Lake

234

62

Lake Creek

140

To Klamath Falls

White City

To Grants Pass

62

37

Big Elk Rd

Medford

Phoenix

To Lake o' the Woods

Howard Prairie Lake

Talent

Dead Indian Memorial Rd

99 5

N

Ashland Ⓕ

Hyatt Reservoir

0   2 miles

To California

The beginning of the long and winding swoop down Dead Indian Memorial Road—a 12-mile descent into the charming city of Ashland. Phil Bard/Cycle Oregon

tered in—it averages out to about 6 percent. There tends to be a strong headwind in the afternoons here, which you'll probably face, and also probably curse.

The last section of this road is relatively flat, as is the ride into Ashland, where bike-friendly brewpubs, countless haute cuisine choices, and live Shakespearean performances await.

MILEAGE LOG

0.0	From corner of Mill Creek Dr. and Red Blanket Rd. (Butte Falls–Prospect Rd.) in Prospect, head east on Red Blanket Rd. (Butte Falls–Prospect Rd.).
1.05	Bear right to stay on Butte Falls–Prospect Rd.
11.35	Pass Medco Pond.
24.0	Right at T intersection onto Fish Lake Rd. for short detour to Butte Falls.
24.65	Bear right onto Laurel Ave. in Butte Falls.
24.9	Left onto Broad St. to reach city park (restrooms).
25.0	Left onto Fir Ave.
25.15	Left onto South St.
25.3	Right onto Laurel Ave. to leave Butte Falls.
25.4	Left onto Fish Lake Rd.
26.05	Continue straight on Fish Lake Rd at intersection with Butte Falls–Prospect Rd.
43.6	Right onto SR 140 (Lake of the Woods Hwy.).
43.8	Left onto FR 37 (Big Elk Rd.).
48.9	Bear right to stay on FR 37 (Big Elk Rd.).
52.0	Right onto Dead Indian Memorial Rd.
60.25	Pass sno-park pullout on right before descent.
73.6	Right onto Green Springs Hwy. (SR 66).
73.85	Bear right onto E. Main St.
74.7	Cross I-5 on overpass.
76.0	Finish at Garfield Park in Ashland.

MOUNT HOOD AND THE COLUMBIA GORGE

Three natural landscapes define Oregon for most people: Crater Lake, Mount Hood, and the Columbia Gorge. The latter two of these are located in direct proximity, together forming an outdoor playground unrivaled in the country. When people in Hood River say they skied in the morning and windsurfed in the afternoon, they're not kidding. With plenty of land and water managed as recreation areas in this region, outdoor activities abound.

39 SANDY RIVER ROLLER COASTER

THREE RIVER CROSSINGS, WITH PLUNGES AND CLIMBS ON EITHER SIDE

Difficulty:	Challenging
Time:	2½ to 3½ hours
Distance:	32.8-mile loop
Elevation Gain:	2011 feet
Best Seasons:	Spring through fall; possibly winter

ROAD CONDITIONS: First bridge narrow, no shoulder; Historic Columbia River Hwy. shoulder disappears before Springdale. Gordon Creek Rd. has some rough patches. Chip-seal surface begins at Clackamas County line.

GETTING THERE: From I-84 east of Portland, take exit 17 for Marine Dr. Continue straight on frontage road past truck stops and fast-food joints, turn right at stoplight onto 257th Ave., and go uphill. At next stoplight, turn left onto Historic Columbia River Hwy. and into Troutdale's downtown. Park anywhere along street. By bike, you can access this route from Portland several ways—most likely via Marine Dr. or NE Halsey St.

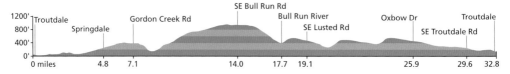

Last time I rode this route, my buddy called it "a perfect Oregon river ride." I had to agree—this has all the elements we love: a rushing river with burbling tributaries feeding in, mossy forest roads, dramatic plunges from bluff lands to riverbeds, and the attendant climbs back

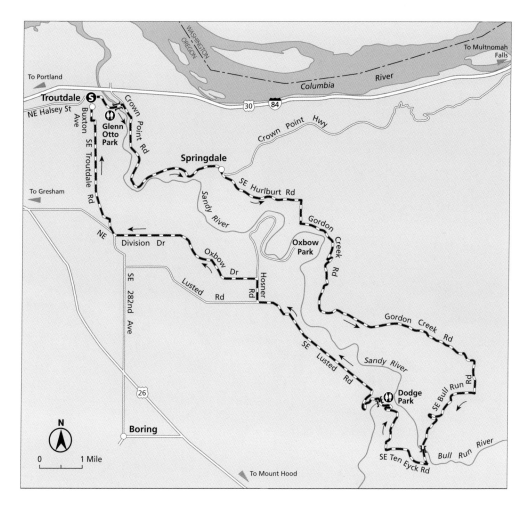

out. This medium-length loop route crosses river bridges three different times and features enough climbing that it'll feel like well more than the listed 2000 feet of gain. There's a reason it's called "roller coaster": every thrilling downhill means you've got to work your way back up for the next one.

The ride starts in downtown Troutdale, a quaint, historic town whose main street serves as the gateway to the Historic Columbia River Highway. Head east on the main drag, with a nice bike lane (it's the last one you'll see). Cruise down the hill past Glenn Otto Park (restrooms available south of parking lot). Here's your first river crossing, of the Sandy.

This narrow bridge has no shoulder, so check traffic before you take the lane. Turn right after the bridge onto Crown Point Road, which is still the historic highway.

For a while you parallel the Sandy, just as with the Multnomah Falls Out-and-Back (Ride 41). You're on a slight incline, which is good to get your heart and lungs ready for what's to come. As the grade increases a bit, the shoulder disappears; keep an ear out for traffic and stay as far right as you can. At 4.8 miles come to Springdale, a small town with a store.

Soon after Springdale, fork to the right onto SE Hurlburt Road, which continues

Any of the river crossings on the Sandy River Roller Coaster will beckon you to stop and take in the beauty of your surroundings. Plus, river crossings are usually right before climbs.

climbing, with some rollers. At 7.1 miles there's a four-way stop; turn right on Gordon Creek Road. From here the road has some rough patches; keep an eye on the pavement. After a quick dip and rise, the road drops down to where Buck Creek joins the Sandy. This is a good spot for a view; across the Sandy is Oxbow Park, and you'll often see anglers in the river.

And here comes the first serious climb. The initial section is steep, with two switchbacks. When you think you've topped out, you haven't, really—everything's still uphill for a good while, although less painfully so. You climb past moss-laden trees and a sun-dappled road (on the right day), so at least the ambience is uplifting.

The climbing—for now—ends at the Clackamas County line, where (unfortunately) the surface changes to chip seal. Don't miss the vista to the southwest from right at the county line. Along here the road becomes SE Bull Run Road; at about 15 miles turn right to stay on it and get ready to have the wind in your face and a smile on it, as you ride a delicious 1-mile descent to the next bridge, at 17.7 miles. This crossing is of the Bull Run River, an outfall of the two protected reservoirs that supply Portland's water.

The climb out from this canyon is mercifully brief. Spill out onto SE Ten Eyck Road at 18.2 miles, taking a right. Ten Eyck comes to a T at SE Lusted Road at 19.1 miles; go right. At roughly 20 miles, start another winding descent, this time back down to the Sandy,

passing by Dodge Park (restrooms) just before the bridge at 20.9 miles.

This third climb up from a river is a notch easier, with a more reasonable grade on which you can get a nice spin going. Look back down through the lush forest for views of the road and the river below. Follow Lusted down a long, straight stretch of relatively flat ground before tackling the last climb of the day: one last fairly steep rise of about 0.5 mile back up top.

The plateau you're on is some extremely fertile land—you'll see a profusion of nurseries, plus Christmas-tree and even wreath farms. At 25.4 miles, turn right on Hosner Road, then left onto Oxbow Drive at 25.9 miles. At 26.7 miles, begin a lovely forested descent on Oxbow before rising up to an intersection with NE Division Drive at 28.2 miles. Turn left and ride some tame rollers to a pie-shaped intersection at 29.6 miles; veer right on SE Troutdale Road. From here, reenter civilization in the form of suburban Troutdale.

MILEAGE LOG

0.0	From Troutdale, head east on Historic Columbia River Hwy.
0.7	Cross Sandy River at Glenn Otto Park (restrooms).
0.8	Bear right after bridge to stay on Historic Columbia River Hwy. (Crown Point Rd.).
4.8	Enter Springdale.
4.9	Bear right to stay on Historic Columbia River Hwy.
5.0	Bear right onto SE Hurlburt Rd.
7.1	Right onto Gordon Creek Rd.
10.9	Bear right to stay on Gordon Creek Rd.
14.0	Road becomes SE Bull Run Rd.
15.2	Right to stay on SE Bull Run Rd.
17.7	Cross Bull Run River.
18.2	Bear right to join SE Ten Eyck Rd.
19.1	Right onto SE Lusted Rd.
20.9	Cross Sandy River at Dodge Park (restrooms).
25.4	Right onto Hosner Rd.
25.9	Left onto Oxbow Dr.
28.2	Bear left to join NE Division Dr.
29.6	Bear right onto SE Troutdale Rd.
32.3	Jog left as road becomes Buxton Ave.
32.8	Finish at Historic Columbia River Hwy. in Troutdale.

40 LARCH MOUNTAIN

THE PORTLAND AREA'S "BIG CLIMB"

Difficulty:	Epic
Time:	3 to 5 hours
Distance:	46.2 miles round-trip
Elevation Gain:	3921 feet
Best Seasons:	Summer to early fall only; check whether road is open before going

ROAD CONDITIONS: Shoulder nonexistent in places, especially in 0.5 mile before Springdale. Rough patches on E. Larch Mountain Rd., particularly between mileposts 6 and 7.

GETTING THERE: On I-84 east of Portland, take exit 18 for Lewis and Clark State Park; turn left off ramp onto Crown Point Rd., drive to bridge, and take a right onto bridge. After crossing bridge, turn left into Glenn Otto Park. Free parking; restrooms and water. A small snack shop is adjacent. By bike, you can access this route from Portland several ways—most likely via Marine Dr. or NE Halsey St.

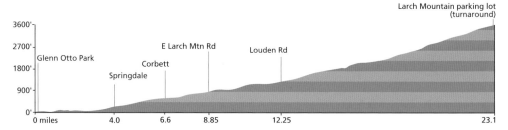

Every place you go, there's the local Big Climb. Sure, in Florida it might be an overpass, but there's always *some* place riders go to test themselves (and then later just casually slip it into conversation: "Yeah, got in a ride up Larch this morning. What'd *you* do today?").

In the Portland area that's Larch Mountain. Yes, there are plenty of steeper climbs in the West Hills. And Mount Hood is a tough, long climb, but it's on a major highway. You can't get that long, steady effort in an isolated setting without heading out toward the Columbia Gorge and taking on Larch. It's no mistake that hill-climb time-trials are held here.

Part of the reason is that you can get in an extended climb (look at the elevation profile). Part of it is that Larch is the highest point around. And part of it is that the road to the top is open only in the summer, once the snow clears from higher elevations; that lends a certain cachet to the enterprise.

So, to reiterate: For Portland, this is the Big Climb.

Start at Glenn Otto Park along the Sandy River; on any summer day you're likely to find many cyclists unloading here or pedaling by—this is the way to get to Crown Point, Multnomah Falls, and Larch Mountain.

Biking buddy Mike cranks up Larch Mountain through the deep forest. It rained on this day, just like every time I've ridden it.

But first, a note: It may just be my bad luck, but I've never enjoyed a sunny ride up Larch. My point? Unless it's a total bluebird day, consider your clothing carefully. I recommend taking at least a second jersey and a light jacket; if you're sweaty after the climb and it's not toasty-warm at 4000 feet, you're going to want to change for the downhill. If it's misty or raining at the start, take every extra piece of clothing you can carry, and try to keep them all dry going up.

You start at a whopping 58 feet of elevation here, ending up at nearly 4000. But the first 3.5 miles are relatively flat as you spin along the Sandy. The overall ascent begins with about 3 miles of reasonable climbing, through Springdale and up to Corbett, where it flattens out for 0.5 mile or so. The shoulder alternates from generous to nonexistent, as well as states in between; be careful as you climb the narrow, winding section from 3.5 miles to Springdale. There's a store here, and one in Corbett.

From Corbett, the climb is steadier but not punishing up to the Portland Women's Forum viewpoint at 8.5 miles—an excellent place to stop for the view, a snack, and possibly a clothing adjustment. Just past the

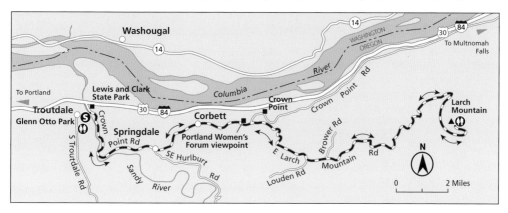

lookout, veer right up E. Larch Mountain Road. Right away you'll see a sign saying 14 miles to the top—in case you're an odometer-watcher (and who among us is *not* on a long climb?), it's actually about 14.5 miles.

The first couple miles are kind of rolling, and then it's just . . . up. It's never a punishing grade; it's just long. You ride through the kind of dark-deep-green forest that seems to soak up sound, so it's quite peaceful. Pace yourself, find a gear you can spin in, and spend some time in your happy place. Count mileposts if you must (warning: Last time I rode this, 11 and 12 were missing). When you hit the parking lot at the top, you can hike the Larch Mountain Trail a little way for a splendid view (or so I've been told).

On the descent there are a few rough patches in the road, particularly between mileposts 7 and 6. But you're looking at basically a 20-mile downhill, so I hope you get to enjoy it . . . dry and warm.

MILEAGE LOG

0.0	From Glenn Otto Park in Troutdale, head northeast (right) out of parking lot on E. Columbia River Hwy.
0.15	Across bridge, right onto Historic Columbia River Hwy. (Crown Point Rd.).
4.0	Enter Springdale.
4.35	Bear right at intersection with E. Bell Rd. to stay on Historic Columbia River Hwy.
4.5	Bear left at intersection with SE Hurlburt Rd. to stay on Historic Columbia River Hwy.
5.25	Bear left at intersection with SE Smith Rd. to stay on Historic Columbia River Hwy.
6.6	Enter Corbett.
8.5	Pass Portland Women's Forum viewpoint on left.
8.85	Bear right onto E. Larch Mountain Rd.
12.25	Stay straight at Louden Rd. on right.
13.05	Stay straight at Brower Rd. on left.
23.1	Reach Larch Mountain parking lot (restrooms)—turnaround point; retrace route back to start.
46.2	Finish at Glenn Otto Park.

41 MULTNOMAH FALLS OUT-AND-BACK

GORGE-OUS VIEWS AND OREGON'S SIGNATURE WATERFALL

Difficulty:	Challenging
Time:	2½ to 4 hours, with stops
Distance:	36.6 miles round-trip
Elevation Gain:	2339 feet
Best Seasons:	Year-round

ROAD CONDITIONS: Shoulder disappears on some sections, and you can be tight to traffic. A rear-view mirror of some kind recommended here. On weekends and in general, riding in morning is best, before tourist traffic heats up.

GETTING THERE: From I-84 east of Portland, take exit 18 for Lewis and Clark State Park; turn left off ramp onto Crown Point Rd. and then left into state park parking area. Plenty of free parking; restrooms. By bike, you can access this route from Portland several ways—most likely via Marine Dr. or NE Halsey St.

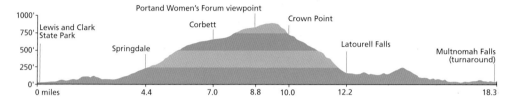

Here's the most basic endorsement for this route: On the occasions when I get the chance to host a visiting cyclist who wants to take a ride in the Portland area, this is where we go.

To me, it's the quintessential northwest Oregon ride: Not far from the city, you get to ride along a river, climb through rolling fields, enjoy expansive views at picturesque points, swoop through mossy curves under an impossibly green canopy, glide past tumbling waterfalls, and arrive at a destination sure to make your neck crane and your jaw drop. There's not too much more you could ask for.

The ride starts at Lewis and Clark State Park, tucked next to the Columbia River

where the Sandy River joins it. As you park your car and get ready to ride, take a minute to imagine this spot as those intrepid explorers saw it, before anything was really *built*.

Roll out from the park along Crown Point Road (Historic Columbia River Highway), paralleling the Sandy. Immediately you pass a bridge that leads up to Troutdale, a nice spot to have a bite after the ride. The road here is generally smooth, with just a gentle incline. You get about 3 miles of warm-up before any real climbing begins.

At 4.4 miles you reach Springdale, where there's a small general store. At this point you've turned up and away from the river,

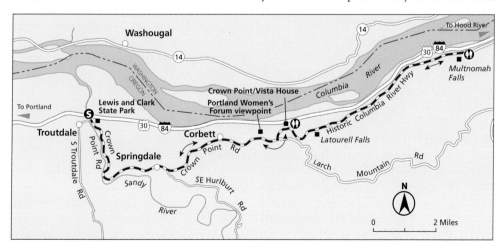

The view out the Columbia River Gorge from the Portland Women's Forum viewpoint is the first real view of the Gorge on the way out from Portland, and a must-stop. In the middle distance is Crown Point.

and you're climbing through pastureland and wheat and berry fields. Pace yourself; the uphill that started slightly at the river stretches on for roughly 6 miles. At 7 miles you pass through Corbett, another spot with a store and a few businesses. Follow signs for Crown Point, Multnomah Falls, and the Historic Columbia River Highway, which is what you're still on.

At 8.8 miles, take the time to stop at the Portland Women's Forum viewpoint, with a parking lot on the left. It's the first glimpse on this route of the grandeur and scale of the Columbia River Gorge.

As you drop down toward Crown Point, get your first taste of what kind of impressive achievement this road was in 1913, when construction began. Beyond the priceless views, nostalgic white fence lines, and gracefully arched stone support walls, this visionary road is one of the first instances in America where cliff-face road building used "modern" highway construction technologies. It resulted in one of the most beautiful stretches of road anywhere.

Crown Point and Vista House together make up an iconic spot in Oregon. Built in 1916 as part of the highway construction, Vista House was designed to be "a place of refreshment and enjoyment of the Columbia Gorge." It underwent a major restoration that was completed in 2006 (with restrooms). It's worth a stop to poke around and enjoy more views.

From Crown Point (10 miles) you get an exhilarating, winding 2.1-mile descent; the pavement here is occasionally rough, so be cautious. Another hint: If you enjoy speedy descending, wait for a gap in motor traffic; otherwise you'll get stuck behind a tourist.

Bottom out at Latourell Falls, the first of a series of spectacular falls. From here to Multnomah Falls the road includes several stretches of shady curves that are nearly tropical in their feel.

The first thing you'll see at Multnomah Falls is the small, rustic lodge (with restrooms)—and a lot of people milling around, most likely. This is the most-visited natural attraction in Oregon. But keep going, past the lodge . . . then look up. Multnomah Falls is like a framed photo: the sheer drop, the delicate white spray, the perfect little bridge near the bottom, the second drop of the falls.

After a break here, turn around and head back. It's the same road, but you get the other-side view of everything—and, of course, you get the 2.1-mile climb up to Crown Point. But once you top out at the Portland Women's Forum, you can enjoy miles and miles of flat or downhill, back down to the Sandy River and the start.

MILEAGE LOG

0.0	From Lewis and Clark State Park, head south on Historic Columbia River Hwy.
4.4	Enter Springdale.
4.6	Bear right to stay on Historic Columbia River Hwy.
4.8	Bear left at intersection with SE Hurlburt Rd. to stay on Historic Columbia River Hwy.
5.5	Bear left to stay on Historic Columbia River Hwy.
7.0	Enter Corbett.
8.8	Reach Portland Women's Forum viewpoint.
9.2	Bear left at intersection with E. Larch Mountain Rd. to stay on Historic Columbia River Hwy.
10.0	Reach Crown Point and Vista House viewpoint (restrooms).
12.2	Pass Latourell Falls.
18.3	Reach Multnomah Falls (restrooms)—turnaround point; retrace route back to the start.
26.6	Reach Crown Point and Vista House viewpoint.
30.4	Bear left to stay on Historic Columbia River Hwy.
36.6	Finish at Lewis and Clark State Park.

42 THE WATERFALL RIDE

SEVEN MAGICAL WATERFALLS IN LESS THAN 10 MILES

Difficulty:	Moderate
Time:	1½ to 2 hours, with stops
Distance:	9.75 miles one way
Elevation Gain:	545 feet
Best Seasons:	Year-round

ROAD CONDITIONS: Historic Columbia River Hwy., first road through Columbia Gorge, opened in 1915. It's a narrow, winding road that you have to share with tourists in motor vehicles of varying sizes. But most of them drive slowly, gawking at the same natural beauty you are. A good tip is to pedal this route in morning—even on summer weekends, traffic doesn't get hopping on this road until late morning.

GETTING THERE: From I-84 east of Portland, take exit 28 for Bridal Veil; turn right off ramp on E. Bridal Veil Rd. First stop sign is at Historic Columbia River Hwy., the road you're going to ride. To do this route, turn right and drive approximately 2 miles to Latourell Falls parking area. By bike, you can access this route as part of the Multnomah Falls Out-and-Back route (Ride 41)—but starting at Latourell Falls eliminates a very strenuous climb back up to Crown Point and makes this section much more friendly for average riders.

If the good folks at Disney decided to build an Oregon road-bike ride, this might be what they'd come up with: something that's fun for the whole family, is a bit of a thrill ride, feels a little magical, and might be too beautiful to be real. But this is the real deal, folks—Mother Nature's chance to show what "water feature" really means.

In a gently rolling ride along a narrow, picturesque road, you'll pass no fewer than seven major waterfalls, in fewer than 10 miles. There may not be another collection of falls like this anywhere, much less all along one easily accessible road. This ride will beckon you to stop, look, photograph, and maybe hike. I suggest you bring a good bike lock along so you can take as much time as you want and wander as far as you like.

Some variation of the term "leafy green canopy" gets used a lot when describing Oregon rides.
This is a good example of what it means.

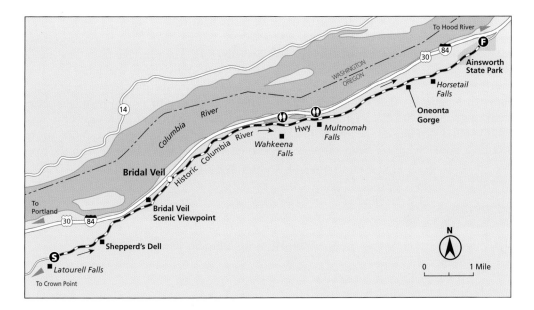

This geological wonder is available for your pedaling pleasure thanks to the fury of volcanoes. The Columbia River, which is what these waterfalls plunge into, once flowed much farther south, through roughly the middle of Oregon. But 25 million years of lava flows gradually pushed it farther north. As the lava piled up—there are six different layers of basalt lava visible in these cliffs—the drop-off got higher and higher. And that's how you get 542 feet of Multnomah Falls.

The ride, done west to east, starts at Latourell Falls, a straight-plunge falls with brilliant green streaks of algae on the rock face next to it. Short trails go both up and down from the parking area for different views.

As you start riding down the road, enjoy the sinuous white fences bordering many corners—and note occasional portions of the original stone walls, with their arched-support design.

At 1.1 miles come upon Shepperd's Dell, a sideways-twisting falls featuring a path down to a creekside overlook at water's edge. At 2 miles, reach Bridal Veil Scenic Viewpoint for a look at your third falls. After a slightly less interesting stretch of road, reach

Wahkeena Falls at 5.3 miles. There's a nice park across the road, with a picnic area and restrooms. Wahkeena is a multi-tier falls, with a path up to a lovely stone-arch bridge. This is also a jumping-off point for several good hiking trails.

At 5.8 miles is the showpiece of the ride: majestic Multnomah. This is the second-most-visited attraction in Oregon (behind a casino . . . sigh). There's a beautifully rustic lodge with a restaurant, gift shops, restrooms, and visitors' information area. Check out the outdoor food vendors if you feel you've already earned some ice cream.

This is a good time to lock up your bike at one of the racks and hoof it a little. The trail up to the stone bridge just above the second drop of the falls is absolutely worth it; this trail extends up to the top of the falls if you're feeling adventurous.

Back on the road, next up is Oneonta Gorge, at 8.2 miles. The first thing you're sure to notice is the cool tunnel just past the gorge—part of the original road that was only recently restored and now beckons riders and walkers with a geometric perfection of wooden support beams.

But the true allure of Oneonta awaits only the hardy. A scramble up the creek, over the log-debris pile, and onto the sandbar reveals what lies on the other side of the canyon: a nearly perfectly round bowl, formed by rock, into which pours . . . Punchbowl Falls. You'll want to go there—it's like a porch light to a moth—but depending on the season it might require a wade or full-on swim through the narrow canyon. You've been warned. Or maybe just enticed.

Your final falls is Horsetail, at 8.4 miles. This is a shorter, wider spray that nicely evokes its namesake. You can hike from here into a network of trails above, including one that takes you above the punchbowl in Oneonta Gorge. You can turn around right here, head up the road a short stretch to Ainsworth State Park, or—as mapped here—continue on to where this road meets back up with the freeway at 9.75 miles.

MILEAGE LOG

0.0   From Latourell Falls, head east on Historic Columbia River Hwy.
1.1   Shepperd's Dell.
2.0   Bridal Veil Scenic Viewpoint.
5.3   Wahkeena Falls (restrooms).
5.8   Multnomah Falls (restrooms).
8.2   Oneonta Gorge and Punchbowl Falls.
8.4   Horsetail Falls.
8.7   Ainsworth State Park.
9.75   Finish at interchange with I-84.

43   HISTORIC COLUMBIA RIVER HIGHWAY (PART 2)

SLICES OF A SLICE OF HISTORY

Difficulty: Moderate
Time: 45 minutes to 1½ hours
Distance: 11.2 miles one way
Elevation Gain: 724 feet
Best Seasons: Year-round

ROAD CONDITIONS: Uneven pavement after Tooth Rock trailhead and again before tunnel under I-84; mossy trail edges after tunnel. Long, steep staircase at 1.2 miles; walk your bike.

GETTING THERE: From I-84 east of Portland, take exit 40 for Bonneville Dam. Stay right off ramp; trail crosses immediately, but parking lot is farther down the road. You can also access this section via bike (see explanation below).

The restoration of the Historic Columbia River Highway is an ongoing project, with visions of one day having an uninterrupted stretch of bike-pedestrian trail generally following the original route of this historic byway, from Portland to The Dalles. And make no mistake: The HCRH has some of the most breathtaking vistas and scenery you'd ever want to pedal past.

The problem is that it's not a complete route. As it stands now and for the foreseeable future, to connect the entire route you have to spend some time riding on the shoulder of Interstate 84. And, after riding and/or reviewing the entire route, I can't recommend that you ride it all unless you are (a) a totally fearless rider and (b) slightly obsessive.

So here's the deal: What I consider the rideable portions of the overall HCRH, from Troutdale to The Dalles, are all covered in this book, but in pieces. For Troutdale to Warrendale, follow the Multnomah Falls Out-and-Back (Ride 41) and keep going a bit past the end, on the frontage road to Dodson and Warrendale. The second and shortest section is covered in this ride. And Hood River to The Dalles is covered by the route of the same name (Ride 45).

This section features some bike trail, some road through town, and some back roads with one strong hill.

Start at exit 40 off the freeway; the bike trail intersects the small access road just to the south of the freeway. It starts with a steady 1-mile climb paralleling the freeway; at 0.4 mile pass Tooth Rock trailhead. Just after cresting, watch out for uneven pavement caused by tree roots. At 1.2 miles you have to do a little cyclo-cross, taking your bike down a long and steep staircase; grooves are provided

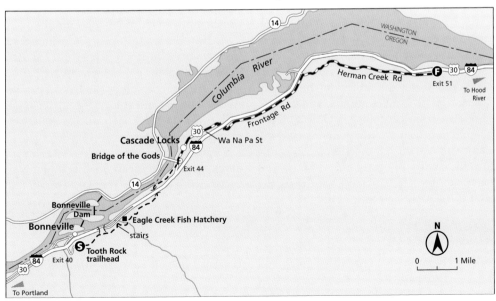

As you ride any part of the Historic Columbia River Highway, imagine what it must have been like for people to drive this in the 1920s. The stunning views haven't changed much. Carl Kloos

to guide your bike wheels alongside you.

At 1.5 miles, jog left-right through the entry to the fish hatchery and the Eagle Creek trailhead (a great hiking trail), and soon after turn away from the freeway. Another short climb precedes a downhill with more root damage; at 2.7 miles tunnel under I-84. From here it's gently rolling, and the trail can be quite mossy at the edges; don't make any sudden moves. At 3.8 miles cross under the grandly named Bridge of the Gods as you enter the town of Cascade Locks; cross the road to the right and pick up the bike lane,

which takes you through town past stores, restaurants, and restroom opportunities.

At the other end of town, cross under the freeway and pick up the access road. At 7.55 miles, take a right onto Herman Creek Road and start a formidable little climb of 1.75 miles. After a short rise and a dip, it goes up for a mile at 5–6 percent, with short pitches of 10 percent-plus, followed by a satisfying descent.

The off-freeway section peters out at an on-ramp; this section is best done as an out-and-back or with a shuttle car to take you on into Hood River.

MILEAGE LOG

0.0   From intersection of bike path and access road just off I-84 exit 40, head east on bike path.

0.4   Reach Tooth Rock trailhead parking lot.

1.1	Caution: Bumps in trail surface.
1.2	Staircase—carry bike down.
1.5	At Eagle Creek fish hatchery and trailhead parking, bike trail jogs left and then right, paralleling freeway.
2.7	Enter tunnel under I-84.
3.8	Jog right to enter Cascade Locks—trail ends under Bridge of the Gods; cross Wa Na Pa St. (US 30) to access bike lane.
5.15	Bear right to cross under I-84.
5.3	Go past freeway on-ramp; left onto Frontage Rd.
5.6	Stay right on Frontage Rd.
7.55	Right onto Herman Creek Rd.
11.2	Finish at I-84 on-ramp.

44 TWIN TUNNELS

THE BEST BIKE PATH EVER?

Difficulty:	Moderate
Time:	1 to 1½ hours, with stops
Distance:	9 miles round-trip
Elevation Gain:	1115 feet
Best Seasons:	Year-round

GETTING THERE: From I-84 east of Portland, take exit 64 for Hood River–SR 35. Follow signs for SR 35 and Mount Hood. Go up SR 35 a couple hundred yards to stop sign at top of hill and turn left onto Old Columbia River Dr. (US 30). Follow winding road up to plateau; auto-accessible portion of this road ends at the west Mark O. Hatfield trailhead parking lot. Free parking; nice restrooms as well as water fountains.

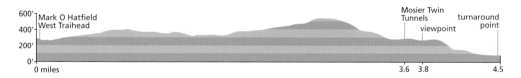

Riders doing the route from Hood River to The Dalles (Ride 45) cover this ground, but the Twin Tunnels section of the Historic Columbia River Highway merits its own route as one of the most visually stunning family-oriented rides in the country. Scenic vistas of the Columbia Gorge, rocky cliffs, fields of wildflowers, gracefully curving sections of old-style white roadside fencing . . . and tunnels! Oh, and no cars allowed. This is simply one of the very best places in the state to go for a pleasant, fairly easy ride with friends or family. Note: This route is rated Moderate only because it has a somewhat significant elevation gain; it's closer to Easy if you take your time.

From the east end of Hood River, drive the switchbacking Old US 30 for 1.2 miles up to the west trailhead, which provides ample parking and really clean facilities. If you want more of a physical challenge, you can pedal up from town, but that is not the start for young kids or those not in top shape.

At the trailhead, swing out into the broad, nicely paved path among riders, walkers, and joggers; be courteous in your speed—this is not a racetrack. The initial section is slightly downhill, after which it turns upward, rising 250 feet in about 1 mile—certainly noticeable, but not overly strenuous if you're not pushing it. After a 0.5-mile descent, there's a second similar climb. But along the way you'll enjoy huge trees, water trickling down rocky hillsides, craggy outcroppings, and million-dollar views out over the gorge.

After the second crest, it's a nice glide down for another 0.5 mile, turning uphill just as you get to the Mosier Tunnels—doubly cool in that they're tunnels *and* they provide views. It's uphill through the tunnels, but out the other side it's just a short way to a magnificent viewpoint down a short side trail to the left.

If you keep going you'll come to a set of posts in the trail at about 4.5 miles; the trail joins up with a public road just after, so this is a good turnaround point. On the way back, see all the same great things from another point of view.

This viewpoint just past the Mosier Twin Tunnels provides a chance to stop and soak in the vast scale of the Columbia River Gorge.

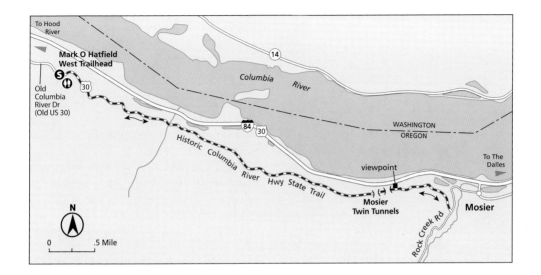

MILEAGE LOG

0.0   From west Mark O. Hatfield trailhead, head east on bike-pedestrian trail.
3.6   Reach Mosier Twin Tunnels.
3.8   Bear left onto side trail to viewpoint.
4.5   Reach gateposts, followed by end of trail—turnaround point; retrace route back to start.
9.0   Finish at west trailhead.

45 HOOD RIVER TO THE DALLES

TAKING THE BACK WAY THROUGH THE COLUMBIA GORGE

Difficulty: Moderate (**Variation:** Challenging for hilly return)
Time: 1½ to 2 hours (**Variation:** 3 to 4½ hours round-trip)
Distance: 20.2 miles (**Variation:** 40.9 miles round-trip on hilly return)
Elevation Gain: 1407 feet (**Variation:** 3753 feet round-trip on hilly return)
Best Seasons: Year-round

GETTING THERE: From I-84 east of Portland, take exit 64 for Hood River–SR 35. Follow signs for SR 35 and Mount Hood. Go up SR 35 a couple hundred yards to stop sign at top of hill and turn left onto Old Columbia River Dr. (US 30). Small public lot with free parking immediately on right.

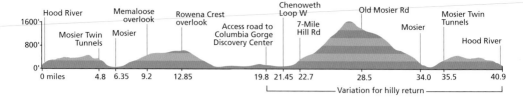

This is the classic cycling route in the Columbia Gorge: a nearly perfect combination of low traffic, spectacular scenery, and enough climbing to be a challenge—especially if you make it a round-trip. It works well as a quick one-way, a straight out-and-back (the scenery doesn't get any worse the second time around), or a hillier round-trip lollipop loop via the fairly fearsome 7-Mile Hill.

The beginning of the route is the same as for the Twin Tunnels ride (Ride 44), but while casual riders and families will want to start at the west Mark O. Hatfield trailhead parking lot, I'm guessing a more ambitious cyclist would rather ride switchbacks than drive them any day, so start at the intersection of SR 35 and Old US 30 at the convenient parking lot. This allows you to warm up your legs with a brisk 1-mile climb out of the gate, twisting up above Hood River with the first of many top-notch views. It's only a few hundred feet of gain, and the grade isn't punishing.

When you plateau, make a short jaunt to the trailhead, after which you'll bask in the freedom of carless riding on the wide and smooth trail. Do be considerate of slower riders and modes, and don't miss the chance to take in views.

After the trail joins Rock Creek Road at its eastern terminus, slither downhill to Mosier, following signs for US Highway 30. In Mosier there's a quirky little business combining ice cream and vintage Porsches(!) on the right.

Climb your way out of Mosier to a short section of flat road, then begin a long, steady ascent through the fertile land of the renowned Hood River Valley. The orchards here are so plentiful and bountiful that a local tourist trail is called the Fruit Loop. All in all, it's about 10 miles of up, but again the grades are humane, and the surroundings are captivating.

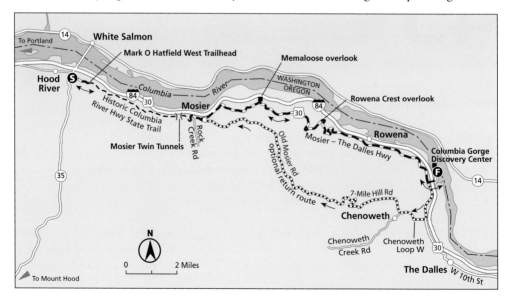

The simple white fence lines hark back to the original choice for guardrails on the Historic Columbia River Highway, far above the mighty river. Phil Bard

At 12.85 miles, take the short loop out onto the Rowena Crest overlook for a quick break and some long views. It's always fun to look down at the switchbacks you're about to savor. Speed down to the tiny town of Rowena, losing 600 feet in just over 2 miles, and then spin pretty easily on smooth roads lined by picturesque white wood fences and rocky canyon walls as you approach The Dalles.

For this one-way ride, a convenient pickup point is the Columbia Gorge Discovery Center, a well-appointed natural museum; to end the ride there, turn left at the sign at 19.8 miles and follow the "driveway" to the museum.

Route Variations: If you want to head into

The Dalles, go another couple miles past the Discovery Center turnoff to reach the strip-mall end of town.

If you'd like a round-trip out-and-back, turn around anywhere and retrace your route.

If you'd like a hillier round-trip, at 21.45 miles turn right onto Chenoweth Loop West (go past the Discovery Center turnoff) and follow the mileage log instructions below for **Variation: Hilly Return.** The route skirts Chenoweth to access 7-Mile Hill Road, which starts off with a 5-mile climb (you expected it to be 7, didn't you?) at a 5 to 8 percent grade before dropping you down on Old Mosier Road into Mosier, where you can enjoy the Twin Tunnels trail on your way back to the start.

0.0	From small parking lot on southeast corner of SR 35 and US 30 in Hood River, head uphill (east) on Old US 30.
1.2	Reach west Mark O. Hatfield trailhead and enter no-cars trail.
4.8	Reach Mosier Twin Tunnels.
5.7	Left onto Rock Creek Rd.
6.15	Bear right, then left, toward US 30 intersection.
6.35	Right onto US 30 into Mosier.
9.2	Pass Memaloose overlook on left.
12.85	Right to Rowena Crest overlook.
15.9	Reach Rowena.
19.8	Left onto access road to Columbia Gorge Discovery Center.
20.2	Finish at Columbia Gorge Discovery Center (**Variation:** Turnaround point for out-and-back; retrace your route back to start).
19.8	**Variation—Hilly Return:** Continue straight on US 30.
21.45	Right onto Chenoweth Loop W.
22.05	Right onto Chenoweth Creek Rd. (W. 10th St.).
22.7	Right onto 7-Mile Hill Rd.
28.5	Bear right onto Old Mosier Rd. (State Rd.).
34.0	Enter Mosier; road becomes Third Ave.
34.25	Right onto Washington St.
34.3	Left onto US 30; retrace route back to Hood River.
40.9	Finish at parking lot in Hood River.

46 CHERRY HEIGHTS

AN ASCENT THROUGH THE ORCHARDS

Difficulty:	Challenging
Time:	1 to 1½ hours
Distance:	15.65-mile loop
Elevation Gain:	1050 feet
Best Seasons:	Year-round

GETTING THERE: From I-84 east of Portland, take exit 84 for The Dalles; ramp drops you right onto US 30. Follow US 30 a block or two to Thompson Park, on the right; entrance is at near end of park. Plenty of free parking; well-appointed public restroom.

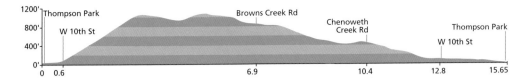

Let's start with a lame little cycling riddle: When is a bike route like a mullet? When it's business up front, party in the back (end). Ouch. But that does describes this ride: Virtually all the work is in the first 3 miles, and the reward spreads out over the rest of it.

Both Hood River and The Dalles feature almost magically fertile valleys, where the local fruit in particular is renowned far and wide. This route takes you up through the cherry orchards, delivering views that showcase the fact that the Columbia River Gorge is good for something besides water sports. It's not a long ride, but it's a great way to spend an hour on the bike and get a good workout for your legs, lungs, and eyes.

Start in Thompson Park, a classic small-city affair with picnic areas, a swimming pool, and bored teenagers hanging out. Turn left out of the parking lot and go about one block before turning left onto Cherry Heights Road (you can probably get away with riding up the bike lane on the left side of the road to avoid crossing it twice, but officially you didn't hear that from me).

Wind your way through a generic stretch of commercial development, crossing a couple intersections, and then see the climb starting in front of you—all of this still on Cherry Heights Road. Grind up a 6 to 7 percent grade for 3 miles, quickly gaining nearly 1000 feet. Don't hesitate to pull over and enjoy the expansive views over the orchards and across the valley—tell yourself you're merely stopping to smell the cherry blossoms; aerobic recovery is just a pleasant side effect.

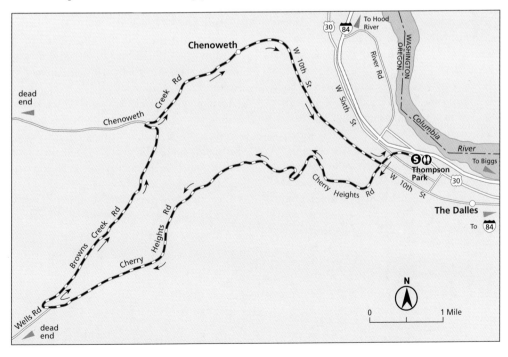

After you climb up through the cherry orchards, the drop down into the small valleys beyond can reveal plentiful wildflowers... and wildlife.

At 3.5 miles, top out and ride a plateau for a bit before dropping down through treed meadows that teem with wildflowers in the spring. At 6.5 miles it's a steep drop through a series of dipping S curves; after the intersection with Wells Road on your left, the road takes a right hairpin and becomes Browns Creek Road.

Here's where you start to party. You're descending the creek drainage in one of those wonderful stretches where you can pedal a slight downhill at up to 25 or 30 miles per hour, including a couple faster swoops. At the T intersection at 10.4 miles, turn right onto Chenoweth Creek Road and knock off a quick little climb before a more gradual descent as signs of town settlement return when you glide through Chenoweth.

At about 12.3 miles, suddenly a broad bike lane appears, just in time for a downhill that can take you to 35 miles per hour if you like, followed by a right curve that becomes W. 10th Street. Enjoy the bike lane all the way back into town; if the wind is coming from the west (a high likelihood here), it can blow you back into town at quite a nice clip over the flat ground.

A quick note about the wind: Gusty winds are a pretty constant fact of life in this part of the gorge, so be mentally prepared. And keep your hands on the bars—this is not the place to sit up and eat an energy bar as if you're a Tour pro.

Turn left when you reencounter Cherry Heights Road, and retrace your route back to the park.

MILEAGE LOG

0.0	From Thompson Park, turn left (northwest) on US 30.
0.05	Left onto Cherry Heights Rd.
0.4	Cross W. Sixth St.
0.6	Cross W. 10th St.

6.9	Bear right at intersection with Wells Road; Cherry Heights Rd. becomes Browns Creek Rd. at hairpin turn.
10.4	Right at T intersection onto Chenoweth Creek Rd.
12.8	Road becomes W. 10th St.
15.05	Left onto Cherry Heights Rd.
15.25	Cross W. Sixth St.
15.6	Right onto US 30.
15.65	Finish at Thompson Park.

47 SUMMIT TO SURF

FROM SNOWBOARDING TO BOARD SAILING, IN ONE RIDE

Difficulty:	Epic
Time:	4½ to 7 hours
Distance:	64.9 miles one way
Elevation Gain:	5676 feet
Best Seasons:	Summer and early fall

ROAD CONDITIONS: Heavy traffic on US 26, Timberline Rd., and SR 35. Uneven road surface on West Leg Rd.

GETTING THERE: From Portland, take US 26 east to E. Welches Rd.; from Sandy, it's approximately 16 miles to stoplight at E. Welches Rd. Either use parking lot at shopping center at southeast corner of intersection or, about 1 mile before intersection, turn right to Wildwood Recreation Area (road to parking goes quite a way into woods, but it's not a free parking lot; you'll need a Northwest Forest Pass).

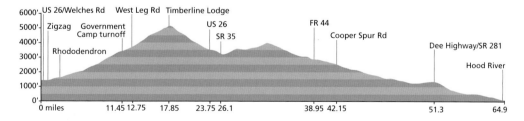

For some years, a charity ride called "Summit to Surf" climbed up and around Mount Hood and then plunged down into the town of Hood River. It was one of my very favorite event rides; if you chose to add the tough Timberline Climb to the route, at the top

they took your picture and gave you a medal. Cheesy? Yeah, well, I still have those medals somewhere.

So, in honor of the event and the route, here's the chance to re-create it. First, a caveat: Most of this route follows major highways, so it's not the serene backwoods experience many cyclists crave. But when you can ride to the top of the highest paved road on the state's highest mountain, that appeals to a certain type of rider. You know if that's you.

This ride can start anywhere along US Highway 26; the event actually started at a school. I picked an arbitrary spot at a stoplight-intersection that constitutes the "town" of Wemme. Make your transport plan: This would be an extreme round-trip ride, so a shuttle for a one-way is a good idea, or you can just do an out-and-back to Timberline Lodge.

The long slog all the way up to Timberline Lodge doesn't officially start until after Zigzag at 1.5 miles, so enjoy the warm-up. Actually, the first few miles of climbing are pretty gradual, passing through the village of Rhododendron; it's not until around 7 miles that gravity truly becomes your adversary. But as you creep up the curvy parts, the view makes up for it: The world falls away to your right, down a steep ravine carpeted with old-growth timber.

After a left curve at a popular hiking trailhead, the road levels off heading into Government Camp. You can veer off into "Guvy," as the local board-heads call it, for plenty of services. At the top end of town there's a rest area off to the left with restrooms, next to the ski hill.

Just past that intersection, look for the left turn to West Leg Road. This quiet road roughly parallels the main Timberline Road. It's not officially open to driving up; if you can't access it, use the main road. If you can get on it, do—it's a big difference.

Assuming you're on West Leg, the climb to Timberline is 6 miles of steady grind, 6 percent and up, through the forest. There aren't too many breaks, but you can find a groove here. At the top you pop out onto the main road for the loop up to the lodge area, at 6000 feet. If you haven't been inside the lodge, check it out (but that might mean carrying the extra weight of a lock up here). It's a massive, classic log-style lodge.

If you're afraid of traffic, you wouldn't be on this route, so go ahead and take the main road down—it has a better surface by far, and you can get some real speed going if you like. At the bottom, turn left onto US 26 and keep going down for a while. Split off onto SR 35 toward Hood River—be careful with merging traffic through this interchange—and then discover that you're not done scaling the heights. You have to negotiate two more passes, each a couple miles long, before you get your just deserts.

After topping the second one, get ready for fun: 20 straight miles of descent, some of it alongside the gorgeous Dog River. And it's not grip-and-tuck; it's a gradual 3 to 5 percent. A pace line can cruise steadily at 30 miles per hour for miles and miles. Of course, you should say a small prayer beforehand to not have a strong headwind, which most certainly can happen through here.

There's a small bump or two on the way down into the Hood River Valley, but mostly it's just rivers and orchards and grand views out to the north. When you hit the town of Hood River, head into downtown for some good food and beverage.

Route Variation: When you enter Hood River, instead of turning left as the mileage log indicates, you can cross under Interstate 84 and end up at a nice waterfront park to watch the wind-sports show on the Columbia River.

< *The long slog up Highway 26 is mitigated by two things: a very wide shoulder and an unparalleled view of your target ahead.*

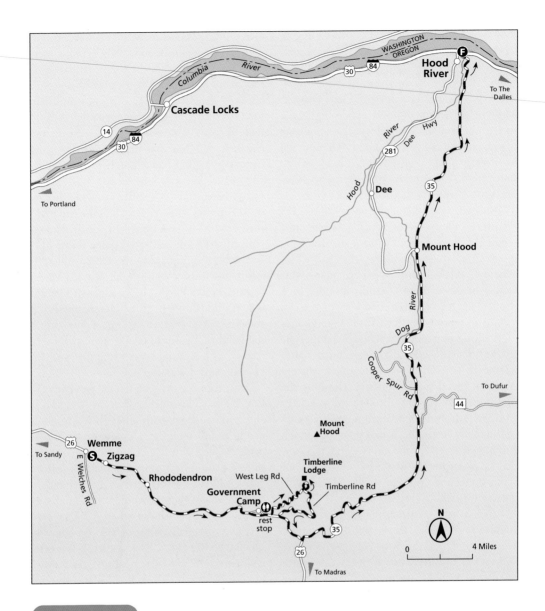

MILEAGE LOG

0.0   From intersection of US 26 and E. Welches Rd., head east on US 26.

1.0   Enter Zigzag; climb begins afterward.

2.8   Enter Rhododendron.

11.45   Pass west turnoff to Government Camp on left.

12.6   Pass east turnoff to Government Camp on left; rest area (restrooms) on northeast corner of intersection.

12.75   Left onto West Leg Rd.

17.85   Left onto Timberline Rd.

17.9	Bear right on one-way loop to Timberline Lodge.
18.9	Bear left at intersection with West Leg Rd. to stay on Timberline Rd.
23.75	Left onto US 26.
25.6	Bear right at junction; follow signs for SR 35 and Hood River.
26.1	Join SR 35 merging lane—caution.
38.95	Pass FR 44 on right.
42.15	Pass Cooper Spur Rd. on left.
51.3	Continue straight at intersection with Dee Hwy. (SR 281) in town of Mount Hood.
64.4	Left onto US 30 (State St.).
64.75	Jog right, then left onto Oak St.
64.9	Finish at Oak St. and N. Second St. in Hood River.

48 LOLO PASS

A CLIMB WITH A VIEW

Difficulty:	Challenging
Time:	2 to 3½ hours
Distance:	32.05 miles round-trip
Elevation Gain:	2779 feet
Best Seasons:	Summer and early fall; check whether road is open

ROAD CONDITIONS: E. Lolo Pass Rd. changes to chip seal for 0.25 mile before Muddy Fork Rd.; a ways beyond, washout where road narrows to one lane, then short stretch of gravel. Surface at beginning of FR 1828 pretty uneven; stay sharp watching out for nasty potholes and portions of road beginning to slide away. These conditions prevalent mainly on lower portion of road; it's not at all unrideable going up.

GETTING THERE: From Portland, take US 26 east; after passing through the town of Sandy continue just less than 12 miles to traffic sign for Brightwood and a left turn lane to Brightwood Loop Rd. Turn left onto Brightwood Loop Rd. and go about 0.5 mile to "town." If you ask permission, it's likely you can park off to the side of small commercial intersection with a store.

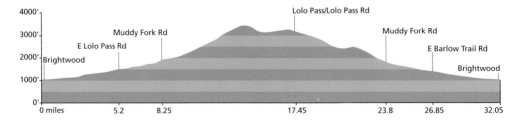

A lot of people know about Lolo Pass (Forest Road 18), which runs over the west shoulder of Mount Hood and down into Hood River on the Columbia Gorge—but because it has a substantial unpaved section, it's unfriendly as a point-to-point for road bikes. And, frankly, the climb up Lolo Pass Road is good but not great.

But then there's FR 1828 . . . and that makes all the difference.

Whereas the main Lolo Pass Road follows a major powerline up a clear-cut alley, FR 1828 dives deep into the forest, producing an entirely different—and much more soul-satisfying—experience. I wouldn't ride here if FR 1828 didn't exist. But it does, so enjoy it.

Picking up at E. Barlow Trail Road, the first 5 miles meander tranquilly, paralleling the Sandy River past mountain cottages tucked in the forest shadows, and heading slightly uphill at a 1 to 2 percent grade. Because this road parallels US Highway 26, it has only local traffic.

Turning onto E. Lolo Pass Road, you're still along the bank of the Sandy, with evidence of the washout that obliterated sections of this road in 2010. The road is still in good condition here, and the grade inches up more toward 3 and 4 percent.

At about 8 miles, the county road maintenance ends, and so does the good road

Three interpid riders scale Lolo Pass in the shadow of Mount Hood, the state's tallest mountain. This rewarding view appears suddenly, after quite a bit of work.

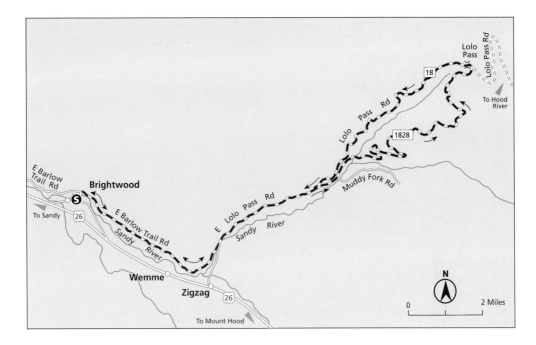

surface—hello, rough chip seal. Just after this, take a right onto Muddy Fork Road. Follow this new road 0.7 mile to a bridge that goes off to the right, with what looks like a driveway going to the left. The one to the left is FR 1828.

Immediately the feel of the ride changes; it's like entering a fun house at the circus—you plunge (well, uphill) into a tunnel through the forest, with a vivid green ceiling and light splattered on the road like a Jackson Pollock painting. On a hot day, the shade is invigorating.

When you reach a sharp left curve, get ready, because it's going to get steep. It's a mix of 8, 10, 11 percent for about 2 miles, but if you can, settle in and focus on the surroundings—all you'll hear are wind, water, and wildlife. After the first couple miles, the pitch eases to 6 percent, which feels easy at this point.

At about 12.9 miles come around a right corner and Mount Hood is right up in your face. It's a startling sight; maybe it's the mixture of adrenaline and exertion, but the view always feels particularly exhilarating at this moment.

You're not quite done climbing, but from this point it feels relatively easy; it's more of a ridge with rise than an ascent. Then it's a dip of just over 1.5 miles; be careful of the road surface and shadows—a couple nasty spots here. But don't worry, you'll get your jollies soon enough.

One more moderate climb, and you join back up with Lolo Pass Road at its peak. Turn left and start down the road, and you'll understand why you're riding this configuration. You can see the road, the surface is generally fine, it's wider . . . perfect for a descent. Pedal or tuck in—you won't spin out of your top gear much here. At about 20.5 miles the road flattens out for a bit, and there's a short stretch of gravel; after the descent resumes, be ready for a stop sign where a washout has reduced the road to one lane.

Keep flying past the junction with Muddy Fork Road to complete the lollipop, as the slope gradually lessens. When you turn back onto E. Barlow Trail Road, the route back to the finish is perfect for a fast pace line—silky smooth, slightly downhill—and you can get in a nice bit of work between the descent and the end.

Route Variations: You can start at any different number of points if you want to add length to this ride; start in the town of Sandy, going out Ten Eyck Road to Marmot Road to E. Barlow Trail Road, to add 30 miles (round-trip) of big-roller back roads. I've also just parked the car along Marmot Road at a distance to match the amount of time I have.

MILEAGE LOG

0.0	From Brightwood Loop Rd. at Brightwood Country Store, head northeast on Brightwood Loop Rd. (becomes Brightwood Bridge Rd.).
0.3	Right onto E. Barlow Trail Rd.
5.2	Left onto E. Lolo Pass Rd. (FR 18).
8.25	Bear right onto Muddy Fork Rd.
8.95	Bear left onto FR 1828.
17.45	Left onto Lolo Pass Road (FR 18).
23.8	Pass Muddy Fork Rd. to left.
26.85	Right onto E. Barlow Trail Rd.
31.75	Left onto Brightwood Bridge Rd. (becomes Brightwood Loop Rd.).
32.05	Finish at Brightwood Country Store.

49 TIMOTHY LAKE THE BACK WAY

TAKE A RIDE ON THE WILD SIDE

Difficulty:	Epic
Time:	4½ to 7 hours
Distance:	68-mile loop
Elevation Gain:	4964 feet
Best Seasons:	Summer and early fall

ROAD CONDITIONS: Traffic, especially motorcyclists, on Skyline Rd. (FR 42).

GETTING THERE: From Portland, take I-205 south, then SR 224 east to Estacada. From Estacada, continue on SR 224 toward Detroit Lake; from junction where SR 211 splits off to right, it's 24.6 miles to Ripplebrook Ranger Station. Free parking at ranger station; please park off to side from main building, and ask permission inside if it's open—they're very nice about it. Restrooms at lower end of parking lot. You can get snacks in ranger station and tap into water spigot outside.

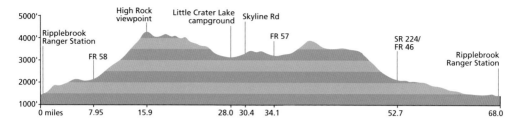

Some years ago I heard about a road up through Mount Hood National Forest that had had a washout—which meant no cars, but bikes could make it if you didn't mind carrying them a little. It turned out to be a wild, epic haul through pristine forests—with one of the best descents in Oregon—but we did have to truck our bikes through a small canyon. So we found a different way to do roughly the same ride, and this is it. Ironically, though, the first route actually went to Timothy Lake, and this one just loops

around it. But if you must see the lake, you can take a short side trip to it.

It takes some doing just to get to this ride; find your way to Estacada and then keep going, another half hour (at least) up to Ripplebrook Ranger Station. The folks who work here have always been very nice about our presence and parking, probably because we've always been very polite (hint).

Start by continuing down State Route 224 (Forest Road 46) for 0.5 mile and then turn left onto FR 57, clearly marked on a sweeping

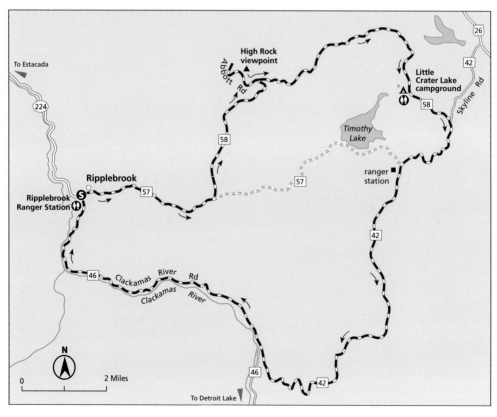

A quiet road, a worthy climb, good friends, and very tall trees . . . this is the essence of forest riding in Oregon. Phil Bard

left-hand curve. After an initial fairly steep bit, the climbing is gradual as you drink in the smells, sights, and sounds—mostly silence—of a verdant forest setting.

Just before 8 miles, turn left at the junction with FR 58—FR 57 continues but turns to gravel. By now the true climbing has commenced. It's an unrelenting stretch of about 8 miles overall and several thousand feet of gain, at pitches from 5 to 10 percent. The last 2 miles before you reach a four-way intersection at 14.9 miles is the toughest stretch.

When you reach this intersection, I urge you to put in the extra mile of climbing to your left up to High Rock. If you do, when you come around the corner to a gravel parking area on the right, the view will stun you. It's a cliché, yes, but it's as if you could reach out and touch the peak of Mount Hood. And there's nothing but wilderness between you and it.

Rocket back down to the intersection and go straight through it. Other than a few rolling sections, it's essentially a long downward glide through the forest. At 28 miles, consider taking the time to stop at Little Crater Lake campground—if you turn right into the campground road, 100 yards or so in there's a path on the right to a good old-fashioned water pump with fresh, cold water. And if you explore the campground you can find out why it has its name.

A couple miles later, turn right onto Skyline Road (FR 42), a more-traveled road with traffic but a terrific downhill stretch toward the main intersection at 34.1 miles. Just past this is a small ranger station with water available, and if you don't have some, get some—because there's one more sturdy climb, and it's exposed to the sun. It's almost 3 miles long, and it never fails to feels longer.

But the payoff awaits. As you push through some rolling terrain, the road morphs into one of those smooth, one-wide-lane forest roads that unwinds like a magic carpet before you. Starting at about mile 45, the 7-mile downhill is just about perfect—if you want to fly, you can pedal without spinning out, or you can just tuck in and enjoy. A word of warning, though: Motorcyclists love this road, too, so don't cut blind corners.

When you stop at the bottom, adrenalized from the descent rush, turn right onto SR 224 (FR 46) and follow the Clackamas River downstream. It's a great stretch to pace-line—a steady downhill until the last little stretch before the finish.

Route Variation: If you want to see Timothy Lake, at the intersection at 34.1 miles, turn right onto FR 57 for a short mile.

MILEAGE LOG

0.0	From Ripplebrook Ranger Station on SR 224 (FR 46), approximately 25 miles southeast of Estacada, head southeast on SR 224.
0.55	Left onto FR 57.
7.95	Left onto FR 58.
14.9	Left at four-way intersection—not sharpest left, but other one.
15.9	Reach High Rock viewpoint; turn around and backtrack to four-way intersection.
16.9	Go straight through four-way intersection to return to FR 58.
28.0	Reach Little Crater Lake campground (water stop, restrooms).
30.4	Right onto Skyline Rd. (FR 42).
34.1	Bear left at intersection with FR 57 to stay on Skyline Rd. (FR 42); ranger station just beyond (water stop).
52.7	Right onto SR 224 (FR 46).
68.0	Finish at Ripplebrook Ranger Station.

THE CASCADES

The Cascade Range serves as a natural dividing line within Oregon. With the rich valleys and the coast to the west, and the vast and more arid environs to the east, the lofty Cascades rise above the entire state. And this chain of volcanic peaks offers a wealth of both beauty and adventure, with summits to climb, lakes to fish, rivers to paddle, trails to hike— and epic roads to ride.

50 CAMP SHERMAN

OVER THE RIVER AND THROUGH THE WOODS

Difficulty: Moderate
Time: 1½ to 3 hours, with stops
Distance: 21.4 miles round-trip; shorter variations possible
Elevation Gain: 479 feet
Best Seasons: Spring through fall

GETTING THERE: From US 20 just east of Santiam Pass, turn north onto FR 14, clearly marked for Metolius River–Camp Sherman. Follow it 2.4 miles and bear left onto FR 1419. At 4.8 miles turn right to stay on FR 1419. In 0.5 mile reach Camp Sherman store, just across bridge over Metolius River. Small parking lot to right, marked "Metolius overlook," has six spaces; if that lot is full, please don't park in store lot—it's OK to park alongside roads in the vicinity if you pick a reasonable spot. Restrooms just across road from Metolius overlook lot.

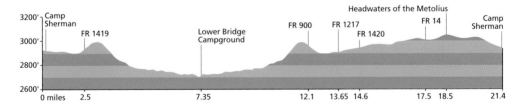

The Central Oregon Cascades have a plethora of resort developments; between the numerous fair-weather activities and the proximity to superb skiing at Mount Bachelor, this is prime vacation territory. And most resorts here are built around golf courses, condos, and chalets or trophy homes. But just west of the hubbub, Camp Sherman is a hidden wonderland of rustic authenticity tucked into the eastern base of the Cascades. Five miles off the highway, it's a bit inconspicuous; I think the locals prefer that. And it's built

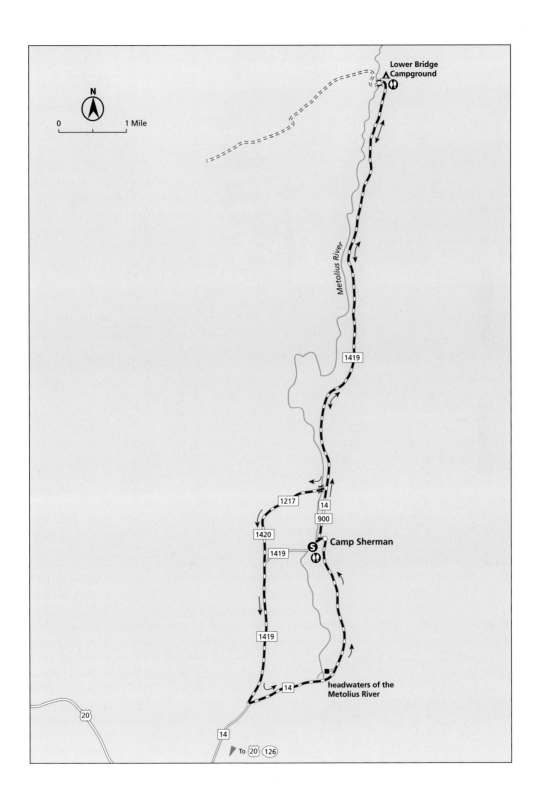

After you've ridden your fill alongside the peaceful Metolius River, you might want to try your hand at fishing it.

around a river, not a golf course. So although there are cabins and a couple resort lodges, the whole place has a different feel that's nicely low key.

And this ride reflects that feel. It's not physically overwhelming, and it can be approached as a pleasant meander through the woods, suitable for just about any rider who's comfortable on the road. It's probably best experienced at a conversational pace, in a group, with as many stops as everyone wants.

As you approach the Camp Sherman store and cross the Metolius River, odds are you're going to see some folks fly-fishing down on the banks or in the water. The Metolius is one of the premier spots in the West for this artistic form of angling.

Just after you start out from the store, as

you turn onto Forest Road 900, you follow the river's wanderings, sometimes right along its edge. It's a combination of small riffles and flat, smooth water, thick with vegetation on the banks and in its channels. Maybe it's the effect of the altitude (the ride starts at nearly 3000 feet), but riding through ponderosa pines next to a body of water, inhaling the foresty smell of the high desert, always makes me feel a bit juiced.

Follow FR 900 and then continue on FR 1419 all the way north to Lower Bridge Campground (restrooms). Hint: For more aerobic work, take FR 1419 from the start; it has some nice up-and-down sections. From the campground, the road crosses the river at a picturesque juncture; this is the turnaround point (the road turns to gravel just past here). Plenty of campgrounds along the way in both directions have restroom facilities.

It may have felt as though you were going downhill all the way out—you were following a river downstream, after all—but the return route doesn't feel too hard. It's not so much rollers here as just that the road tilts—a bit up, a bit down. At about 11.5 miles, there's a bit bigger tilt up, right before you turn back onto FR 900.

Add to your adventure by turning right at the Allingham Junction at 13.65 miles, crossing the river on FR 1217, then turning left onto FR 1420 at 14.6 miles. An extra loop down FR 1419 to FR 14 takes you to a turnoff for the headwaters of the Metolius—a remarkable sight: The river basically emerges, full-blown, from the side of a hill. It's worth seeing whether you bike there or drive there. Continue north on FR 14 to return back to the junction at the store.

Route Variations: You can skip the Allingham Junction turn at 13.65 miles and return straight to the finish for the shortest ride. Or you can skip the FR 14 loop to the headwaters of the Metolius and take a left onto FR 1419 to return to the finish for the next-shortest option.

MILEAGE LOG

0.0   From Camp Sherman store, turn right onto Camp Sherman Connector Rd., following signs toward FR 1419.
0.25   Left onto FR 900.
2.5   Continue on FR 1419.
7.1   Bear left downhill toward river and campground, staying on FR 1419.
7.35   Cross Metolius River at Lower Bridge Campground—turnaround point; retrace your route back on FR 1419.
12.1   Bear right onto FR 900.
13.65   Right onto FR 1217 (Streibel Rd.). (**Shortest variation:** Continue straight on FR 900 back to Camp Sherman store.)
13.75   Cross Allingham Bridge.
14.6   Left onto FR 1420 (Rankin Rd.).
15.3   Continue straight across intersection as FR 1420 becomes FR 1419. (**Next-shortest variation:** Left onto FR 1419 to return to Camp Sherman store.)
17.5   Left onto FR 14.
18.5   Reach turnoff for headwaters of the Metolius (0.5-mile loop on left).
19.2   Bear right to stay on FR 14.
21.05   Left onto Camp Sherman Connector Rd.
21.4   Finish at Camp Sherman store.

51 McKENZIE PASS

YOU'RE GONNA LAVA THIS

Difficulty: Challenging
Time: 2½ to 3½ hours
Distance: 37 miles one way
Elevation Gain: 2152 feet
Best Seasons: Summer and fall; check road accessibility before going (see Road
                   Conditions)

ROAD CONDITIONS: Don't judge accessibility on this seasonal route by whether the road is open to cars: One of my favorite things to do on a bike is to ride McKenzie Pass in spring or early summer, before cars are allowed—the road is often plowed to bare pavement, one lane wide, with walls of snow up to 10 feet tall on either side at the top. It's like a bobsled run on a bike, and it's also hauntingly quiet and beautiful. Check with bike shop in Sisters for current info; they always know the score.

GETTING THERE: Take US 20 or SR 126 to Sisters, northeast of Bend. Go three blocks south of main highway to Village Green City Park, at S. Fir St. and E. Washington St. Free street parking; restrooms and water.

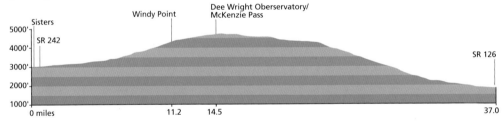

One of the great things about taking people on this ride is seeing their jaws drop when they get their first glimpse of the volcanic-lava moonscape at the top—usually at Windy Point, coming from the Sisters side. It's like absolutely nothing else you'll see from your bike, ever. But that's not the only reason to do this ride; it's also a quintessential Cascades forest ride, offering both a climbing challenge and some delightful descending.

You can approach this route in several ways (see Route Variations). I start in Sisters because that's where most tourists and locals congregate to ride. There's not much to say in the way of directions—head out of town westbound on State Route 242 (McKenzie Highway) and keep going. The first 8 miles have a very gradual rise; when you hit the 90-degree right-hand corner, it's time to work. But from the Sisters side it's not really bad; the first 1.5 miles is the steepest, at 6 to 7 percent, but generally it's just a good hard spin up the hill. Notice the change from the

When I say "lunar landscape," it's not hyperbole. The lava fields of McKenzie Pass are a unique signature of this ride. Greg Lee/Cycle Oregon

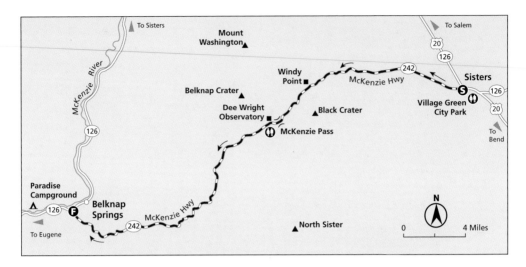

sparse juniper and lodgepole pine forest of the high desert surrounding Sisters to the fir mix of the east slopes of the Cascades; even the smell changes.

When you reach Windy Point, the road gets more level and the view gets better. Millions of years of volcanic activity created this bleak but impressive landscape; there are more volcanoes and glaciers right here than anywhere in the contiguous United States. Stop and soak it in—although the spot is aptly named, and you may want to get back on the bike before the wind chills you.

Continue through some fast and fun rollers and then climb a bit more, up to the unique Dee Wright Observatory (restrooms), a cool, roundish building constructed entirely of lava rock. Scramble up the rock stairs to peer through windows positioned to frame peaks in all directions, or get on the roof for a 360-degree panorama.

From this acme, the ride down the other side of McKenzie Pass is first otherworldly and then thrill-ride-worthy. Slalom between bizarre lava walls, pass through some high meadows, and then wiggle your way down a series of steep switchbacks that pose a challenge to even the best bike-handlers. Watch out for gravel in the corners, as well as recreational vehicles and trucks that occasionally disregard the clearly posted vehicle-length limits at the bottom of the road.

When you reach the intersection with SR 126, two convenient places to meet up with someone are Paradise Campground (to the left) or Belknap Hot Springs Resort (to the right). Both are just a short way down the road.

Route Variations: You can ride this one-way in either direction, or out-and-back for a round-trip—both directions are spectacular, although starting in Sisters means less climbing if you're going one way. You can also make a pretty epic loop out of this by continuing north on SR 126 and then east on US 20–SR 126 back to Sisters—again, you can do this loop in either direction.

MILEAGE LOG

0.0 From Village Green City Park in Sisters, head north on S. Fir St.
0.1 Left onto E. Hood Ave.
0.65 Left onto SR 242 (McKenzie Hwy.).
7.8 Make 90-degree right—begin climb.

11.2   Reach Windy Point viewpoint.
14.5   Reach Dee Wright Observatory (restrooms) at McKenzie Pass.
37.0   Finish at junction with SR 126.

52   AUFDERHEIDE MEMORIAL DRIVE

ONE RIVER UP, ANOTHER RIVER DOWN

Difficulty:	Epic
Time:	4 to 6 hours
Distance:	63.6 miles one way
Elevation Gain:	4308 feet
Best Seasons:	Road cleared year-round, but likely safe only spring through fall

GETTING THERE: From I-5, take exit 188 for SR 58 east to Willamette Pass and follow the very scenic highway 35 miles to Oakridge. Go through town and then turn right into Greenwaters Park. At fork in park entry road, go right into rest area section; free parking, restrooms.

The first time I heard of Aufderheide (OFF-der-HY-dee) Memorial Drive was from friends who liked to take their motorcycles on it. Some funny-named road off in the forest . . . whatever. Then I got to ride it on a bike, and it immediately hit my Top 10 list of Oregon rides, with a bullet.

What makes it so special? It's a combination of factors. For one, the scenery is unbeatable. In the direction this route is mapped, you follow one gorgeous river up the hill, pick up another one on the way down, and then skirt the shoreline of a sizeable jewel-like lake. It's a tough climb followed by a truly exhila-

rating descent. The traffic tends to be quite light, and the road surface is mostly glassy-smooth. What's not to like?

Start at Greenwaters Park in Oakridge, a town that has become a nationally recognized mountain-biking destination. With the fat-tire crowd has come a bit of a revival of this logging town—you can get a fine microbrew here and not get sneered at for wearing bike clothes. From the park, take a quick jaunt west down State Route 58 to the turnoff north toward Westfir. At 4 miles, when you turn right onto North Fork Road, check out the superb covered bridge—the Office

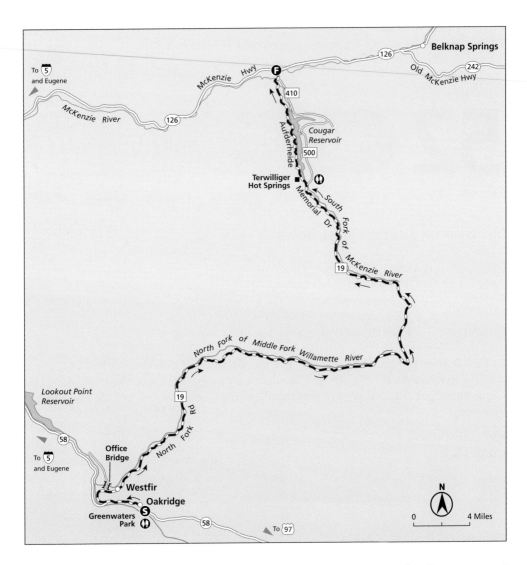

Bridge, at 180 feet the longest covered bridge in Oregon.

Once you're on North Fork Road, the real climbing doesn't start for about 10 miles, so enjoy the peaceful surroundings. The road is thusly named because it follows the (stay with me now) North Fork of the Middle Fork of the Willamette River. Don't worry about the name; just listen to its burbling and watch its flowing action.

Once the road tips upward, I'm not going to lie to you: It's 20-plus miles of ascent. But the incline hangs at a grade of between 1 and 4 percent for a very long time; it's actually like nine separate climbs, and only the last one will truly hurt. Just after mile 35, it steepens to 7 and 8 percent for a couple miles. Push on through and crest like a champion, because you're about to be richly compensated for your efforts.

From the top, the next 16 miles are deliciously downhill—steeply at first, then gradually. This section feels like an exhibition of the smooth efficiency of a bike—agile cornering,

Descending the last of the long drop from the summit of the Aufderheide, ready to flatten out on the shores of Cougar Reservoir. Greg Lee/Cycle Oregon

maximum speed for a minimum effort—as you glide down through the forest, now following the South Fork of the McKenzie River as it glints in the sunshine. I've been in a pace line through the last half of this descent that was rolling at 25 to 30 miles per hour for miles on end; it's a magical ride.

The long dive ends at Cougar Reservoir, where you bear left to hug the west shoreline (restroom at the junction with Forest Road 500 to the right). The road rolls up and down, with some fairly strenuous short pitches. At about 54.7 miles you pass the trailhead for

the short hike to Terwilliger Hot Springs, a mildly notorious hangout that has been cleaned up considerably since the Forest Service started charging a small fee and monitoring it. Clothes are still optional, though; if there's a chill in the air, it's quite nice to soak a bit, clad or unclad.

When you pass the dam that forms the reservoir, there's another fun, swervy descent before the road bottoms out in a valley of the McKenzie River. When you reach the intersection with FR 410, go left and reach SR 126, the main road through these parts.

MILEAGE LOG

0.0	From entrance to Greenwaters Park in Oakridge, head west on SR 58.
2.75	Right onto Westfir–Oakridge Rd. (Old Willamette Hwy.).
4.05	Bear right onto North Fork Rd. (Westfir Rd.).
5.8	Reach Westfir; stay straight on North Fork Rd. (FR 19).

54.7	Bear left at intersection with FR 500 to stay on Aufderheide Dr. (FR 19) (restrooms 500 ft. to right).
60.25	Bear left at intersection with dam road to stay on Aufderheide Dr. (FR 19).
63.15	Left onto Cougar Dam Rd. (FR 410) (restrooms).
63.6	Finish at intersection with SR 126.

53 COTTAGE GROVE TO OAKRIDGE

A PAVED PATH THROUGH (FOREST) PARADISE

Difficulty:	Epic
Time:	4 to 6 hours
Distance:	59.6 miles round-trip
Elevation Gain:	5003 feet
Best Seasons:	Summer and early fall

GETTING THERE: From I-5, take exit 174 at Cottage Grove and head west on overpass, dropping down onto SR 99, which curves around and becomes Ninth St. At intersection with Main St., turn left; Row River trailhead is on left at 10th St. downtown. Free street parking; several restrooms along initial trail section.

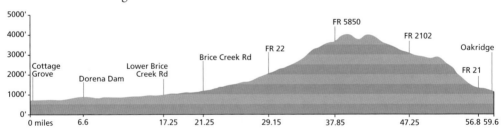

There are so many rides like this in Oregon—start from a small town, go up a big climb through an old forest, come over a pass with views for miles, and rip down the road to another small town—that it can be difficult to describe them all differently. But I know this: I never get tired of them. It's not that any one thing makes the whole thing perfect; it's what movie types call *mise-en-scene*: the way everything in the surroundings comes

together to create the desired effect.

Starting in Cottage Grove, connect with the Row River Trail (Ride 30) heading southeast out of town, following it around the northeast shore of Dorena Lake. Just before the Culp Creek trailhead at the end of the trail, connect to Row River Road.

The turn onto Lower Brice Creek Road is a worthwhile sidetrack—a narrow country lane that rolls up and down through vaulted tree

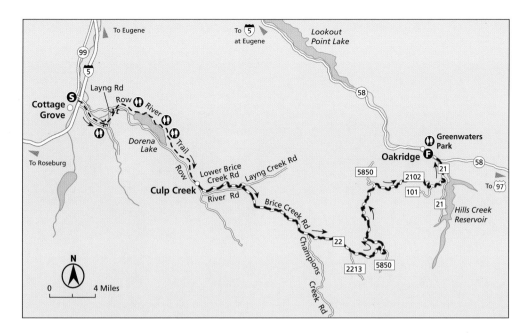

tunnels and beside pastures. A superb, rocky swimming hole on Brice Creek to the right draws local crowds on hot days.

Once you take a quick jog on Layng Creek Road to get to the main Brice Creek Road, the terrain is wide open for a couple miles, and then it starts to get a little wild. The road narrows perceptibly around 23 miles in, and you're riding through green-filtered sunlight past moss-draped trees and thick under-growth. Multiple campgrounds with toilets are along this stretch.

As you can see from the elevation profile, the grade increases in pitch ever so slightly for a long time. About the time the road becomes Forest Road 22, where Champions Creek Road veers off to the right, the grade is much more than slight now. FR 22 alternates between being one lane and having a feeble center stripe in sections.

At 33.85 miles, where FR 2213 goes off to the right, is a section of road that was first paved only a few years ago, and it shows. Velvety smooth, one lane with frequent pull-outs, it's a joyous surface—but joy may not be foremost on your mind as you slog up

the steepest part of the day, nearly 8 miles of extreme challenge. The best way I can describe it is, it just keeps coming. Don't be fooled by the cruel false summit at about 36.5 miles; there's more suffering left—including after the turn onto FR 5850.

Once you're on FR 5850 it's a combo of straight-up climbing and some ridge-running, with views off to forever—miles and miles of trees. At 40 miles you get an extended respite, with a mile of steep downhill, before another equally staunch final ascent. Watch for a short section of gravel in between. After the climb, stay to the right on the paved road at the T intersection.

Once you're actually at the top of this world, there's a series of curious "summit meadows"—not what you'd expect up here, but a nice break before you start on the downside.

This descent is the kind that makes you feel like a slalom skier—lean right, lean left, scrub some speed, bomb the short straightaway. The first section is about 6 miles of steady 6 percent and steeper; about halfway through, be careful when you hit three short patches of

This route passes through some very remote forestland; it's the kind of ride where you're truly immersed in your environment. Greg Lee/Cycle Oregon

gravel on a steep stretch right before the junction with FR 2102.

After a few miles of relative flatness, drop out of the mountains through more slalom turns—4 miles of sheer plunging at 8 and 9 percent. If you have time to notice your lush and leafy surroundings, ponder this: How many shades of green are there in a forest like this?

From the left turn onto FR 21, the remainder of the ride is just a bit downhill. When you hit State Route 58, traffic may seem like the Indy 500 after where you've been, but there's a good shoulder on the way into Oakridge. The turn into Greenwaters Park is at the bottom of a hill using the left-turn lane. Once you're in the park area, the road splits; take the right into the rest stop section.

MILEAGE LOG

0.0	From Row River trailhead, E. 10th St. and E. Main St. in Cottage Grove, head east on Row River Trail.
0.3	Cross 16th St.
0.5	Cross Gateway Blvd.
0.95	Cross Thornton Lane.
1.6	Cross Row River Rd. (by weigh station).
3.1	Reach Mosby Creek trailhead (restrooms); view south to covered bridge.
3.8	Cross Layng Rd.
4.7	Cross Oak Rd. and Row River.
4.8	Cross Row River Rd.
6.0	Cross Row River Rd.

6.6	Dorena Dam (restrooms).
8.5	Harms Park (restrooms).
11.5	Bake Stewart Park (restrooms).
15.95	Join Row River Rd.
17.25	Left onto Lower Brice Creek Rd.
20.9	Right onto Layng Creek Rd.
21.25	Left onto Brice Creek Rd.
29.15	Bear left at intersection with Champions Creek Rd. as Brice Creek Rd. becomes FR 22.
33.85	Left at intersection with FR 2213 to stay on FR 22.
37.85	Left onto FR 5850.
47.25	Right onto FR 2102.
54.8	Stay left on FR 2102 when FR 101 comes in on right.
56.8	Left onto FR 21.
57.55	Bear right at La Duke Rd. to stay on FR 21.
57.85	Left at T intersection onto FR 23.
58.35	Left onto SR 58.
59.45	Left into Greenwaters Park.
59.6	Finish at Greenwaters Park rest stop (to right on park entrance road).

54 DIAMOND LAKE TO COTTAGE GROVE

LONG DOWNHILL, SHORTER UPHILL

Difficulty:	Epic
Time:	6 to 8 hours
Distance:	89.4 miles one way
Elevation Gain:	3563 feet
Best Seasons:	Summer and early fall

ROAD CONDITIONS: Highway traffic for first 40 miles, sometimes with narrow shoulder. Watch for rock debris on road after intersection with Rock Creek Rd.

GETTING THERE: From I-5 near Roseburg, take SR 138 east and follow signs on SR 138 for Diamond Lake North End. From I-5 near Medford, take SR 62 and SR 230 northeast to SR 138 and Diamond Lake. From US 97 just north of Crater Lake, take SR 138 west to Diamond Lake. Turn off SR 138 into Diamond Lake Resort, which has a store, restaurant, and lodging. Route starts at intersection of SR 138 and Diamond Lake Loop Rd., just north of the resort; parking and restrooms at resort.

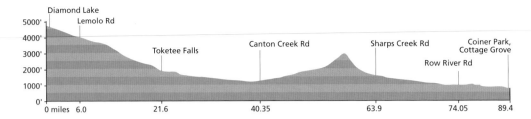

Four words you don't hear very often: 40 miles of downhill. This route gives you the chance to cruise down the road for a couple hours along the idyllic North Umpqua River, then take a quiet forest road up into the sky, grip the handlebars for a scintillating and steep descent, and finish with a pleasant pedal past a lake and on into a historic town. Really, what more could you want out of an Oregon ride?

From Diamond Lake, the highway is

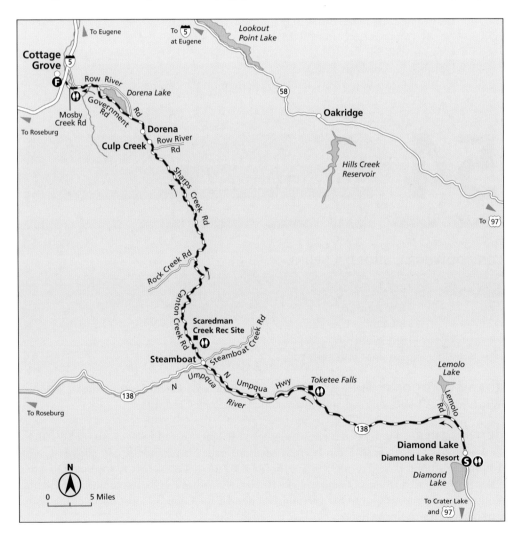

The thing about bike touring is, you've got all day. Take some time to relax, enjoy the view, check out the inside of your eyelids. There's no more picturesque spot to do it than here. Greg Lee/Cycle Oregon

confined to Oregon, it would cover the entire state with a layer 8 inches deep. It was a big blowout.

Now go ride. Start at historic Crater Lake Lodge, refurbished in the mid-1990s. (A comfy chair on the sidewalk "deck" is a prime spot to contemplate your ride afterward.) Turn right out of the lot, past the café–gift shop onto Rim Drive W., and coast down for a bit, looking out at the barren Pumice Desert before taking on the first major climb, heading up toward the Watchman, a rock tower that rises above the lake's Wizard Island. Stop at a viewpoint to check out the island; it was formed by a second, smaller eruption; the only

boats allowed on the lake ride out to the island and drop people off to explore it on foot.

Just after 6 miles, stay to the right at the junction with the North Entrance Road and attack a smaller climb on Rim Drive E. before reveling in a long, satisfying drop for several miles. Cleetwood Cove, where the only trail to the lake takes people down to the boat dock, comes at 11 miles. After you pass Round Top at 13 miles, gird yourself for the burliest climb of the day, a 3.5-mile push at up to 8 percent that takes you to the Cloudcap overlook turnoff at 17.3 miles; if you have the legs, ride up to the parking lot there for a splendid view.

Over the rest of the ride, the route swings away from the lake several times, reminding you that the views are good on the left side of the road, too. One last twisting climb, which levels out mercifully for the last mile or so, brings you back to the lodge parking lot.

You've conquered the rim. Now go and mingle with the tourists, knowing that you didn't need a car to ride the rim.

MILEAGE LOG

0.0	From Crater Lake Lodge parking lot, at far southeast end of parking loop road, head out of parking lot.
0.4	Bear right onto Rim Dr. W.
6.25	Turn right at intersection with North Entrance Rd. to stay on rim road—now Rim Dr. E.
11.0	Pass Cleetwood Cove hiking trail to lake.
17.3	Pass Cloudcap Overlook to right.
21.15	Bear right at intersection with Pinnacles Rd. to stay on Rim Dr. E.
29.4	Bear right at intersection with Munson Valley Rd. to stay on rim road—now Rim Dr. W.
32.2	Right into Crater Lake Lodge parking loop road.
32.6	Finish at Crater Lake Lodge.

56 CRATER LAKE UP-AND-OVER

YOU VERSUS THE VOLCANO

Difficulty:	Challenging
Time:	4 to 6 hours
Distance:	58.65 miles one way
Elevation Gain:	3100 feet
Best Seasons:	Summer and early fall; road to park cleared year-round, but probably not safe for riding except in warmest months

ROAD CONDITIONS: Tourist traffic on park roads. Uneven road surface on SR 62 west of park boundary.

GETTING THERE: From I-5 at Medford, take exit 30 and follow SR 62 northeast to Fort Klamath. From US 97 at junction just north of Klamath Falls, take SR 62 northwest to Fort Klamath. In Fort Klamath, a very small town, follow SR 62 to post office on Third St., with a store across the street. Park anywhere out of the way.

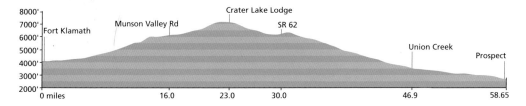

If just riding around the rim of Crater Lake isn't your favored strategy—if you want to ride *to* the lake—this is the prettiest approach. Plus you can ride up to it, decide if you want to ride around it, and then swoop down for miles and miles and end up in the remote and beautiful town of Prospect. The route as mapped here doesn't include circling the lake's rim, but it's configured for a seamless connection; see Crater Lake Rim Road (Ride 55).

Begin at the tiny outpost of Fort Klamath (yes, there's still a fort; just south of town they have a kind of living museum there). You start at a pretty healthy altitude—right about 4000 feet. The first 5-mile stretch is roughly level, giving you a chance to

acclimate. Ride past pastureland so fertile that the cows are in it up to their knees in the summer. The rise begins almost imperceptibly, and soon you're spinning easily through the forest.

As you ride up State Route 62, Crater Lake Highway, take note of the amazing canyon that frames Annie Creek—you'll get frequent glimpses off to your right, but you should pick a spot to get off the bike and look around. The canyon walls look as though they were chipped away by some giant Norse god with a very large chisel. It's quite an unusual effect.

There are a couple spots to stop for a rest on the way up; at around 12.5 miles the incline increases for a mile or so, and the flat plateau that follows is bliss before you

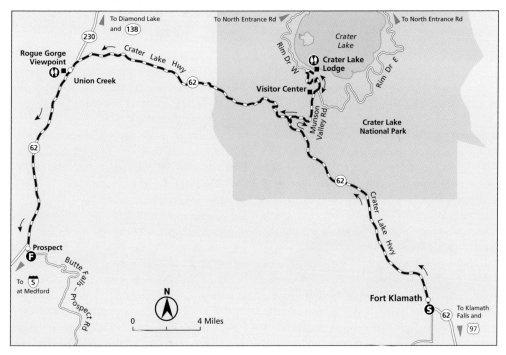

Beckie's, in Union, tends to draw a crowd for its wide varieties of delicious pies...
especially if there are bikers in the vicinity. On this ride, you've already
burned it off before you eat it. Phil Bard/Cycle Oregon

resume a gentler climb. A note: I rated this ride Challenging rather than Epic, because some of my riding partners didn't think this was a particularly difficult climbing day; they eventually clued me in to the fact that if you don't seek pain on a hill, sometimes you don't find it. You can take your time up the climbs on this route; it's not a long day unless you're riding the rim road too.

At 16 miles, turn onto the road for Crater Lake National Park (Munson Valley Road). Even on a bike you'll have to pay at the ranger station. The first couple miles after the gateway are flat and smooth, giving way

to a moderate grade up to the visitor center (restrooms) on the left. At 19.9 miles join Rim Drive W.; at this point the road begins switchbacking its way up at a steady 5 and 6 percent. It's not brutal, and it's kind of fun. Do be careful with slick spots on the road due to snowmelt runoff, and of course there are tourists in vehicles to deal with. But you're riding up a *volcano*.

When the climb eases up, the contrast feels like it's downhill; another 1.5 miles takes you to the parking lot loop road for Crater Lake Lodge, 3000 feet above where you started the day. If you're not riding around the rim, this

58 LOWER BRIDGE ROAD

HIDDEN VALLEYS AMONG THE RIMROCK

Difficulty:	Moderate
Time:	2½ to 3½ hours
Distance:	38-mile loop; longer options possible
Elevation Gain:	925 feet
Best Seasons:	Spring through fall

ROAD CONDITIONS: Highway traffic on SR 126.

GETTING THERE: From SR 126 between Sisters and Redmond, turn south into Cline Falls State Park, clearly marked with state park signs. A narrow road takes you down to expansive parking area right on Deschutes River; restrooms, picnic tables . . . fish-cleaning stations.

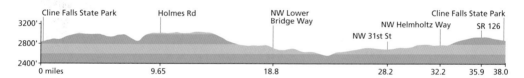

If you drive through the open space of Oregon's high desert, you might get the impression that everything around you is either trees or rocks as it blurs by at highway speeds. One of the reasons I like this ride is because it takes you back into some lusher and more fertile pieces of land you'd never see—or maybe even suspect were there—passing through here in a car. The back roads are low-traffic, sections of the pavement are terrific, and the scenery is somehow calming. As a local rider described this ride: "There's not a bad mile in it."

The only drawback to the overall vibe is that you have to start and end on State Route 126; it's a matter of river and road geography. But there are many worse places to ride a highway—the shoulder is nearly always ample and the surface is good.

Start out going west on the highway; at about 8 miles drop down into a canyon and climb up out the other side; this is the only noteworthy climb of the ride. Just at the top of the rise, the pavement squeezes between rock walls, getting tight for a short stretch. Otherwise it's not a bad bit of highway.

Still, you'll probably breathe a little easier once you turn north onto Holmes Road. The pavement stretches ahead through the pines, and the drop-off in traffic is wonderful. Wind through some flats to around mile 15, where you drop down past a horse farm and turn right into a long, narrow valley. At around 17 miles, watch the fence line to your right for some interesting rock art, leading up to an ostentatious gate.

After a right turn onto NW Lower Bridge Way, pass through more fertile land, irrigated

The rugged landscape of Central Oregon matches the foreboding weather on this day. But Central Oregon enjoys 300+ days of sun per year.

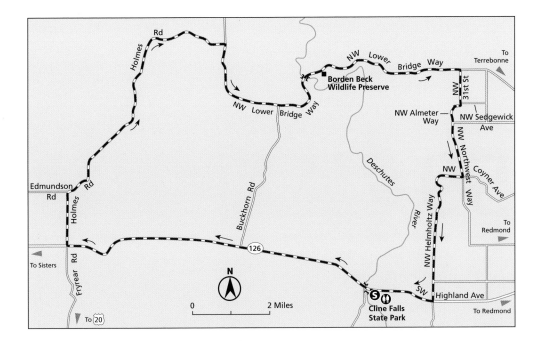

in circle patterns. Between 21 and 22 miles, check out the alpacas on both sides of the road.

At mile 23, begin a dip down to a crossing of the Deschutes, worth a stop to look. Just around the corner is a small parking lot for Borden Beck Wildlife Preserve; this river marshland is a haven teeming with wildlife species.

Continuing on Lower Bridge Way, climb sharply above the river and emerge into flatland. After a few curves the road straightens out, with views to the east of tall and craggy Smith Rock, a magnet for rock climbers from all over. A few zigs and zags on the western

outskirts of Terrebonne eventually put you on NW Helmholtz Way, where velvety asphalt extends out ahead of you for a smooth ride back to the highway.

Just before turning right onto SR 126, on the right is a reindeer farm; since most of us haven't seen one of these outside an animated TV Christmas special, it's worth a gander. There are some impressive racks.

Back on the highway, it's a short jaunt back to Cline Falls State Park; a convenient pullout on the right shoulder just across from the entrance allows you to safely assess traffic before making your crossing.

MILEAGE LOG

0.0	From Cline Falls State Park, where parking-loop road comes together, head out to highway.
0.25	Left onto SR 126.
9.65	Right onto Holmes Rd.
11.1	Right at intersection with Edmundson Rd. to remain on Holmes Rd.
18.8	Right onto NW Lower Bridge Way.
28.2	Right onto NW 31st St.
29.15	Right onto NW Sedgewick Ave.

29.4	Bear left to stay on NW Almeter Way as it becomes NW Northwest Way.
31.45	Right onto NW Coyner Ave.
32.2	Left onto NW Helmholtz Way.
35.9	Right onto SR 126.
37.7	Left into Cline Falls State Park.
38.0	Finish at parking area in Cline Falls State Park.

59 TWIN BRIDGES LOOP

DANCE WITH THE DESCHUTES

Difficulty:	Moderate
Time:	2½ to 3½ hours
Distance:	32.9-mile loop
Elevation Gain:	850 feet
Best Seasons:	Spring through fall

ROAD CONDITIONS: Short stretches of riding on busy highways.

GETTING THERE: From US 20 in Sisters or US 97 in Redmond, head south to Bend and follow signs for downtown off US 97. This puts you on NW Division St.; turn right on NE Revere Ave., followed by a quick left onto NW Wall St. Follow Wall St. into downtown, through three blocks of congestion, taking a right at stoplight at NW Franklin, which becomes NW Riverside Dr. as you drop down to Harmon Park in downtown Bend. Two small free parking lots to right on NW Riverside Dr.; also free parking along street. Restrooms in park.

There's a reason Bend has been one of the West's fastest-growing cities, attracting businesses and people like a magnet for several decades: There's a bounty of outdoor activities available, year-round. Of course, that kind of rapid growth can overwhelm city planning, and that certainly happened here; traffic can be a nightmare. But on a bike you can get out of town fast.

One of the showpieces of Bend is its collection of downtown parks where the Deschutes River pools wide at the heart of the city, forming the equivalent of a pond. The ride starts here, where you'll find walkers and runners

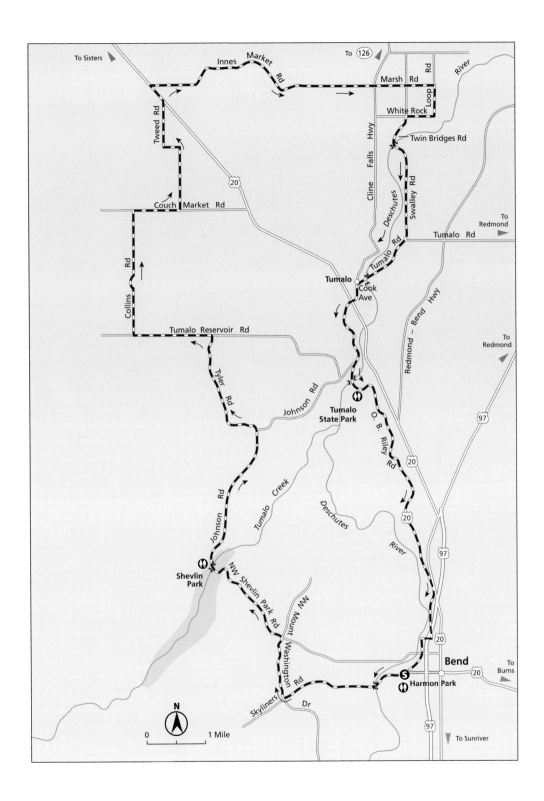

This route winds up, down, and all around the Bend-Redmond area, including this fun plunge down Tyler Road.

on the paths, kayakers on the water, and a general activity level befitting the hardy local population.

After crossing the river, head uphill on Galveston Avenue through a section of small commerce, climbing for 1 mile as you leave the town's core and head for its "suburbs." You have good bike lanes for the first 9 miles. Experience a taste of Europe with four traffic roundabouts in the first 3 miles, as well as the local signature architecture: cute little Northwest Craftsman lodges.

There's some more climbing interspersed, and then at 4.2 miles swoop down for 0.5 mile to Shevlin Park (restrooms) and your second crossing of the river. It's the same 0.5 mile up and out, but the result is some of that tasty gradual downhill that lets you build up speed like the truly efficient machine you are.

Be careful not to miss the left onto Tyler Road at 7.4 miles; the road you're on sweeps right, but you want the left. Say goodbye to bike lanes for a while—but the traffic is low; you're likely to see almost as many deer and other cyclists as vehicles. When you turn left onto Tumalo Reservoir Road, you're heading straight toward the Three Sisters mountains, and when you turn north onto Collins Road, they loom over your left shoulder. Ride the rollers past horse farms and irrigated fields, along with some fairly ridiculous trophy homes.

After the right turn onto Couch Market Road, don't miss the left onto Tweed Road; it can sneak up on you. After a couple bends, Tweed spills out onto US Highway 20, which you have to follow for only a short stretch before spinning off onto Innes Market Road.

slight uphill, but you do get glimpses of the Three Sisters, Broken Top, and Mount Bachelor to your right.

When you reach SW Reservoir Road and turn left, there's a staging site for off-roaders that has a bathroom. This road is more of the same, with a bit of roller coaster to it, for another 7 miles.

But then, when you turn onto SR 27, immediately scream down a twisty, delicious descent with views of the reservoir below and to your right. This is just plain fun, if you happen to enjoy leaning into corners with the occasional judicious application of the brakes. After skirting the reservoir shore for a good bit, cross the dam and dip down into the canyon. Again, the road snakes out ahead of you like an invitation, and the views are astounding. Think back to your 23 miles of sagebrush straightaways—you'd never imagine that something like this cuts through the vast flat desert.

You pass multiple campgrounds, official and unofficial, scattered along the Crooked River as you slide between sheer rock cliffs above or next to the water. After a while the land widens a bit, then narrows again, then opens up into a broad, fertile valley as you return toward town. But it's the canyon you'll remember.

Route Variation: To ride this as an out-and-back, connect to SR 27 in Prineville and follow it out until you decide to turn back; to the dam it's just under 20 miles.

MILEAGE LOG

0.0	From Stryker Park, at NE Dunham Ave. and NE Fourth St., head west on Fourth St.
0.65	Left onto NW Locust Ave.
0.7	Right onto US 26.
0.75	Bear left to take fork onto SR 126.
3.4	Left onto Millican Rd.
19.1	Left onto SW Reservoir Rd.; ATV site (restrooms) across intersection.
26.0	Follow as now SE Reservoir Rd. turns 90 degrees right.
26.7	Left onto SR 27.
30.0	Cross dam.
49.65	Cross US 26 in Prineville.
49.7	Right onto NW Fourth St.
49.9	Finish at Stryker Park.

EASTERN OREGON

The population of Oregon is mostly squeezed into Portland and the Willamette Valley—and that's why the eastern reaches of the state are so appealing. From the remote alpine wilderness of the Wallowas to the craggy history of the John Day Fossil Beds to the stark contrasting beauty of Steens Mountain and the Alvord Desert below it, the variety of landscape in eastern Oregon is nearly limitless. The variety of riding follows suit, as this collection of disparate routes shows.

61 THE WINDMILL RIDE

A SUBLIME AND SURREAL ROLLER RIDE

Difficulty:	Challenging
Time:	4 to 5 hours
Distance:	49.7-mile loop
Elevation Gain:	2762 feet
Best Seasons:	Year-round, unless snow levels get very low

ROAD CONDITIONS: Some highway riding; watch traffic on the SR 206 descent to Columbia River.

GETTING THERE: From I-84 east of Portland, take exit 109 for Rufus; turn right off ramp and quickly right again onto Biggs–Rufus Hwy. (frontage road into Rufus proper) for about 0.25 mile. Look for empty parking lot on right just past a restaurant-tavern; park there for free.

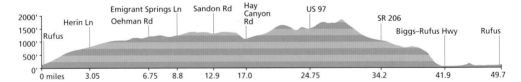

Yes, Oregon can boast of offering riding scenery to match almost anything you'll find in the rest of the country—forest, desert, mountains, rivers, beaches—but here's a ride that you might not find anywhere else. It features a roller-coaster route past, around, and between hundreds of giant white wind machines. Besides the gentle beauty of new green wheat fields rippling in the wind, there's the sublimely surreal, *Gulliver's Travels* experience of riding in the literal shadows of these graceful behemoths.

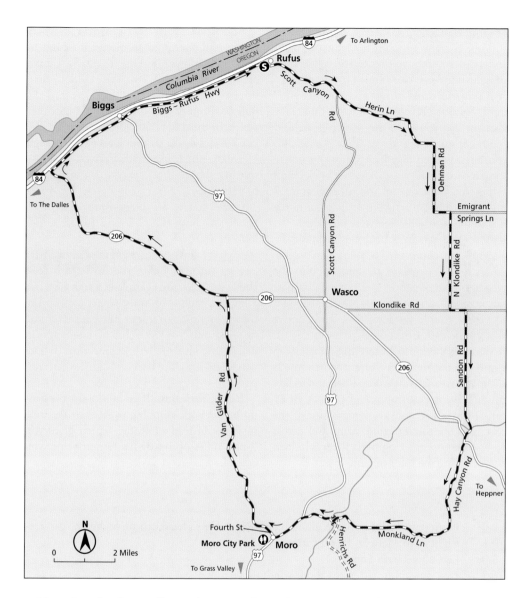

Note that there's a really good reason all these windmills are here: It's quite often very, very windy in this area. The locals will tell you that the wind is neither seasonal nor better in the morning; if it's a windy day, it's windy. You might check the weather report.

Starting from Rufus, immediately climb Scott Canyon, a 3-mile rise that winds upward at around 6 percent for 1.5 miles and then levels off to more like 3 percent. At 2.5 miles you get your first glimpse of windmill blades on the horizon. After turning left on Herin Lane, continue climbing gradually until you've risen 1000 feet in a little over 4 miles. At this point you're not likely to see any cars, and the only sounds may be crickets and the windmills, which sound like far-off jet engines when they turn.

The climb basically peaks at 6.2 miles, where a roadside viewpoint has information on windmill energy. After a bit of down-and-up, a right turn onto Oehman Road, and a quick climb, you hit classic rollers on a straight-line road, surrounded by windmills.

A series of turns brings more of the same, until Sandon Road dips down into Hay Canyon and you leave the windmills behind (sigh). A quick jog across State Route 206 continues you up Hay Canyon, where you're less exposed to the wind. Another brisk climb brings you back out on top of it all at 21.3 miles; you'll be surprised to see how far north it is to the windmills you were just amid.

A drop down to a bridge is followed by a significant climb of 0.6 mile, then a glide down to US Highway 97 and on into the pleasant town of Moro. You can go a bit past the mapped turn at Fourth Street into town to visit a couple restaurants, a store, and a shady little park (restrooms).

Back on the route, hump up a short, steep climb past the Sherman County courthouse as the road becomes Van Gilder Road and snakes through the undulating fields of wheat. At 29 miles, top a rise and get a view out all the way past the distant wind farms and across to Washington; the Columbia River is hidden down among the folds of land.

And don't forget that the river is where you're ending up; that means it's time to savor some downhill. First it's nearly 5 miles of smooth descent on Van Gilder, then more of the same on SR 206. Don't miss the hollowed-out church on the left, 2 miles after you turn onto SR 206. And be careful: The last 2 miles down to river level twist through a canyon much like Scott Canyon earlier—ride like the wind, and maybe cars won't have to pass you.

Once you're on Biggs–Rufus Highway, paralleling both the river and Interstate 84, look to your left across the river to see austere Maryhill Museum, high on a bluff. After passing through Biggs, rise up onto a shelf above the river and again look left to pick out a life-size replica of Stonehenge, also on the hills across the water and just beneath a line of windmills—a lovely bit of juxtaposition of ancient and modern engineering. Before you know it, you're back in Rufus, where you parked.

Route Variation: If you like a little warm-up before your climbing work, start this ride in Biggs instead of Rufus, which gives you 7-plus miles of mostly flat terrain before you ascend.

MILEAGE LOG

0.0	From parking lot in Rufus along Biggs–Rufus Hwy., head east on highway.
0.1	Right onto Main St. (Scott Canyon Rd.).
3.05	Left onto Herin Lane.
6.2	Pass viewpoint with signs about windmill energy.
6.75	Right onto Oehman Rd.
8.8	Left onto Emigrant Springs Lane.
9.4	Right onto N. Klondike Rd.
12.4	Left to stay on N. Klondike Rd.
12.9	Right onto Sandon Rd.
16.85	Left onto SR 206.
17.0	Right onto Hay Canyon Rd.
19.7	Bear right as road becomes Monkland Lane.
23.5	Bear right at intersection with Henrichs Rd. (dirt) to stay on Monkland Rd.
24.75	Left onto US 97.

There's something both graceful and imposing about a group of wind machines on the horizon.
But it's much more impressive in person.

26.0   Right onto Fourth St. in Moro (restrooms at city park).
26.65   Bear right as road becomes Van Gilder Rd.
34.2   Left onto SR 206.
41.9   Right onto Biggs–Rufus Hwy.
44.7   Cross US 97 in Biggs.
49.7   Finish at parking lot in Rufus.

62

FOSSIL LOLLIPOP

A GEOLOGIC ADVENTURE ON TWO WHEELS

Difficulty:	Challenging
Time:	4 to 6 hours (**Variation:** less for loop)
Distance:	66.35 miles round-trip (**Variation:** 46.2-mile loop)
Elevation Gain:	5748 feet (**Variation:** 4550 feet)
Best Seasons:	Spring through fall

ROAD CONDITIONS: Girds Creek is a minor road, and upkeep is commensurate. Can be good bit of scattered gravel in stretches, so be cautious on downhills; may also be some free-ranging livestock or a dude-ranch group on horseback on roadway.

GETTING THERE: From I-84 at Biggs, take US 97 south. In Wasco, follow signs to SR 206 southeast to Condon. In Condon, follow signs to SR 19 south to Fossil. When approaching Fossil, take the "City Center/W. First St." turnoff. Follow First St. to intersection with Main St. where just to left is a small public area (restrooms); park anywhere on street for free.

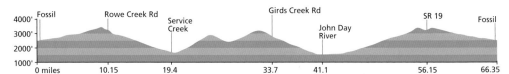

You've gotta love a town called Fossil. I mean, the local petroleum-products supplier here is called Fossil Fuels. And you can actually dig up fossils on a hillside behind the local high school, with help from a trained geological interpreter—and take away all you can hold in your hands, for five dollars. Besides, the people in town are friendly, and it's set in the middle of some of the most scientifically significant surroundings in Oregon.

So why not come out to this intriguing place and take a nice, challenging ride through prehistoric canyons, past colorful exposed rock beds, and up and over some serious geography?

Leaving from Fossil, head south on Main Street to State Route 19 and turn left, noting

the impressive outdoor antler collection dead ahead of you across the intersection. Begin a steady 9-mile climb through pine forest that takes you to Butte Creek Pass (elevation 3788 feet). Just after the pass is the intersection with Rowe Creek Road—this is where you're coming out later; stay left on SR 19 for now.

It's a steady, mesmerizing drop into Service Creek, a 4 to 6 percent grade you can spin down at up to 30 miles per hour if you pedal steadily. Service Creek itself is a marvel of compact self-sufficiency; there's a lodge, a store, a restaurant, raft rentals, and a guide service—all in two buildings. (I know a couple who used to own the town—it's a package deal—and it was zoned "Frontier Commercial.")

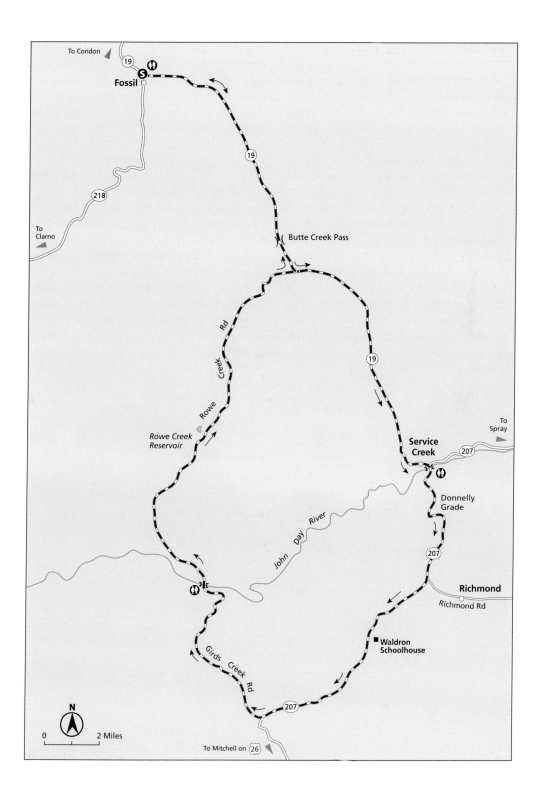

To Condon

19

Fossil

To Clarno

218

19

Butte Creek Pass

19

Rowe Creek Rd

Rowe Creek Reservoir

John Day River

To Spray

Service Creek

207

Donnelly Grade

207

Richmond

Richmond Rd

Waldron Schoolhouse

Girds Creek Rd

207

To Mitchell on 26

N

0   2 Miles

Just after Service Creek, turn right onto SR 207 toward Mitchell, crossing the John Day River; on the left there's a river-access spot with restrooms.

The next 2 miles are deceptively uphill; it doesn't look like much, but your legs will tell you. Then after a sweeping left turn, the Donnelly Grade (named for a pioneering local family) begins for real. For 3 miles, hug the hillsides at 7 percent, topping out at 24.6 miles. Don't forget to look back at the views on the way up. After the turnoff for Richmond (where there's a cool old pioneer church) to the left, descend into a patchwork valley, ride flats for a while, and then start climbing again at 28.3 miles.

Half a mile into the climb, note the 1874 Waldron Schoolhouse in a field on your left. Continue climbing; it gets steeper, but the views off to the right out to stunning green layers of exposed rock should distract you. You're up and over at 31.3 miles; just at the bottom of the next descent, turn right onto Girds Creek Road.

This is my favorite part of the ride: Follow the creek down through rimrock canyons like something out of a John Ford western, sweeping through downhill turns and narrow spots. About 6 miles later it flattens out into a long valley tucked next to the John Day River. Just before you cross the river there's a wayside launch spot with restrooms.

From here follow the Rowe Creek drainage inexorably upward, first through valley

The gradual slide down Girds Creek Road takes you through some impressive, craggy rock formations.

bottomland and then forest, passing Rowe Creek Reservoir at 47.6 miles. At 52.6 miles it transitions from incline to climb—first 1 mile of "here we go" and then 0.5 mile of "ouch," followed by 1 mile of blessed downhill.

Emerging back onto SR 19, turn left for Fossil. Go up for 0.75 mile to Butte Creek Pass before the long descent into Fossil.

Route Variation: I confess I actually prefer to do this ride as a loop starting and ending in Service Creek, a tiny outpost 20 miles into the route, skipping the ride out of and back into Fossil, which isn't the scintillating part of the route anyway.

MILEAGE LOG

0.0	From downtown Fossil at First St. and Main St., head south on Main St.
0.25	Left onto SR 19.
10.15	Bear left at intersection with Rowe Creek Rd. to stay on SR 19.
19.4	Enter Service Creek.
19.6	Right onto SR 207; cross John Day River (restrooms at river-access site).
25.1	Continue straight at intersection with Richmond Rd. to stay on SR 207.
28.8	Pass Waldron Schoolhouse to left.
33.7	Right onto Girds Creek Rd.
41.0	Bear right, toward river.
41.1	Cross John Day River (restrooms at boat launch); road becomes Rowe Creek Rd.
56.15	Left onto SR 19 to close loop.
66.1	Right onto Main St.
66.35	Finish at First St. and Main St. in Fossil.

63 HEPPNER TO UKIAH

FROM FARMS TO THE FOREST

Difficulty:	Challenging
Time:	3½ to 5½ hours
Distance:	46.9 miles one way (**Variation:** 110.55-mile loop)
Elevation Gain:	3675 feet
Best Seasons:	Summer and fall

ROAD CONDITIONS: Chip seal on Willow Creek Rd. (Blue Mountain Scenic Byway).

GETTING THERE: From I-84 east of The Dalles, take exit 147 at Heppner Junction for SR 74 south. In Heppner, city park is on left at Church St. just before downtown proper. Free parking all over.

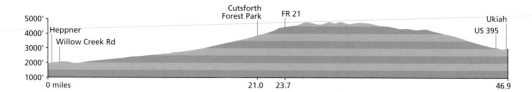

One of the problems with choosing 75 road routes in Oregon is that there are *way* more than 75 good routes in Oregon. And this book spreads them throughout the state, to give some two-wheeled love to all our regions. So as I looked around the nooks and crannies of the state, I arrived at decision points where I just had to . . . pick one. My point? There's a lot of good riding around the north-central part of the state, but this is the route I picked for this book.

Why? Partly because I love Heppner. From the first time I biked through this Irish-heritage town (there's a shamrock in the middle of the main intersection downtown), I've enjoyed its setting and its people, so that's where this route starts. And partly because I love the drop into Ukiah. You're going up and over, through two distinct vegetation zones.

After rolling through Heppner, the left onto Willow Creek Road 1 mile south of town puts you on the Blue Mountain Scenic Byway—always a good sign to have official scenic designation. The road, which is not the best sort of chip seal at this point, takes you up a steep little climb with a view back to town and then down to Willow Creek

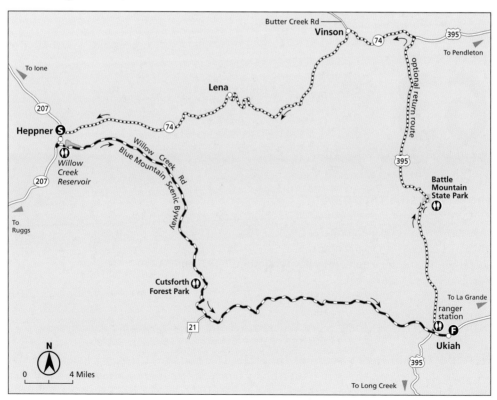

It's worth the short side trip to walk up a steep, rocky road to check out this broad view of how water flow dictates plant life.

option with restrooms and more secure parking at the start. At the end, you can continue on Court Avenue past the not-so-great part of town if the traffic doesn't bother you.

MILEAGE LOG

0.0	From off-ramp parking at exit 248 off I-84, head north on frontage road.
0.3	Cross bridge and curve left under freeway.
7.1	Enter Kamela.
11.45	Left at stop sign on freeway ramp.
11.55	Right to cross under freeway (signs to Meacham).
11.7	Left at stop sign, to Meacham.
11.8	Bear right toward Meacham, not freeway on-ramp.
12.7	Enter Meacham.
15.6	Cross over I-84.
15.85	Pass Emigrant Springs State Park (restrooms) on left.
16.85	Cross over I-84.
17.0	Bear right to follow sign to scenic viewpoint, not freeway on-ramp; road becomes Old Emigrant Hill Rd.
18.85	Stay straight at intersection with gravel road to scenic viewpoint to right.

22.05	Right at stop sign; rest area on right. At second stop sign, go straight.
26.75	Pass Poverty Flat Rd. on left.
33.65	Cross St. Andrews Rd.
37.35	Go straight at flashing stoplight at SR 331; road becomes Mission Rd.
40.55	Continue straight as US 30 merges from left.
41.3	Stay straight as SR 11 merges from right—caution; road becomes SE Court Ave.
41.6	Right onto SE 17th St.
41.8	Right at T intersection onto SE Byers Ave.
42.0	End at Kiwanis Park, SE Byers Ave. and SE 19th St.

65 TOLLGATE PASS

UP, UP, AND AWAY

Difficulty:	Epic
Time:	5 to 7½ hours
Distance:	73.9 miles one way
Elevation Gain:	5299 feet
Best Seasons:	Late spring through fall

GETTING THERE: From I-84 at Pendleton, take exit 207 (US 30). Follow US 30 into town 2.4 miles, where it splits into a one-way couplet. Follow it another 1.1 miles and turn right on SE Seventh St.; it's one block to SE Emigrant Ave., next to Till Taylor Park. Free street parking.

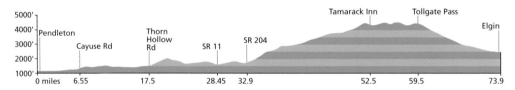

Something about the word "pass" makes some riders just want to take on the challenge. If you relish the fact that any road with the name "hill" in it is likely to dish out a little punishment, then a route that goes over a real-life pass is going to be a good time. It doesn't hurt that pass roads also tend to be visually attractive.

And so you're going to want to ride up and over Tollgate Pass when you get the chance. The thing is, it doesn't seem all that hard—it's more of a long pass than a steep pass. But you still get to climb a mile up.

One thing about this pass route: It's pretty much upward and onward from the start, for nearly 60 miles. But it starts out lightly, letting you find your climbing legs before they're really tested. Find your way out of town on

It's perfectly justifiable to feel triumphant when you've conquered a long, steady climb like Tollgate Pass. Greg Lee/Cycle Oregon

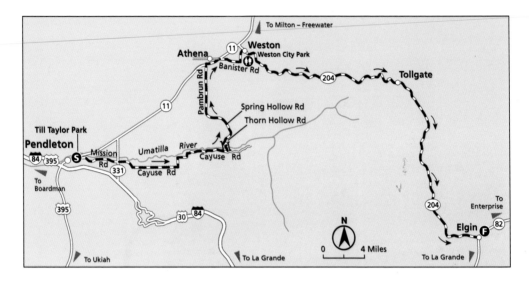

Mission Road, then turn onto Cayuse Road. After a couple jogs, connect to the Umatilla River, paralleling the water for a nice 4 miles before crossing it.

And here comes a surprise: A gorgeous little climb twists up a canyon for a bit more than 2 miles. It's one of those climbs where the setting—switchbacks and rugged country—enhances the effort. It's as if you've disappeared in your own little world, until you emerge at the top. And when you do, you get to coast for a while—bonus.

The next 12 miles or so are occupied with getting you over to State Route 204, the pass road, out of Weston. A fair number of steep rollers go through here, in wide-open country. Once you blow through Weston—there's a nice little park (restrooms) in town for lunch if you brought it—and connect to SR 204, it's "game on" between you and the pass.

Tollgate throws a big punch right away—the first 4 miles are actually the steepest, at a steady 6 percent. But, as always, you can fight it or you can spin it. It's more than 23 miles to the top, so I recommend spending your energy wisely.

As you ascend, the terrain and the views gradually change, as a more alpine feel creeps in. Absorb some nice ridgeline vistas as you work, and don't forget to savor the fresh pine scent in the air. And hey, after just a few hours, you're at the top!

Or so you think. The first real peak, at the Tamarack Inn (about 52.5 miles) is not the last one. There are actually four high points over the next 8 miles as you roll through winter-vacation-home territory; the last one tops out over 5000 feet and precedes an extensive and well-deserved slide down to the finish.

And quite a slide it is. When I rode this, I actually got kind of tired of going downhill; you may not be similarly afflicted. It's a grade of 3, 4, 5 percent for about 10 miles; if you want to pedal you can really fly, or you can just coast it on home. There's not really a flattening-out at the end; you just sort of drop into town in Elgin.

Route Variations: This route starts from Pendleton, partly because it's the most happening town in the area. You could just as easily start from Athena or Weston, but you'd miss some nice stretches of road. Also, this route avoids taking the straight shot on SR 11 from Pendleton up to Weston, to stay away from busy highway traffic and to take in sections like the very cool Thorn Hollow Road canyon—but adapt as you like.

0.0	From SE Emigrant Ave. and SE Seventh St. in Pendleton, next to Till Taylor Park, head north on SE Seventh Ave.
0.1	Right onto US 30.
1.0	Bear right at intersection with SR 11 to stay on US 30.
1.5	Bear right onto ramp for Mission Rd.
4.95	Cross SR 331.
6.55	Left onto Cayuse Rd.
11.2	Bear left at intersection with Burke Rd. to stay on Cayuse Rd.
12.2	Bear right at 90-degree turn to stay on Cayuse Rd.
14.0	Bear left at intersection with Jackson Rd. to stay on Cayuse Rd.
17.5	Bear left onto Thorn Hollow Rd.
17.8	Cross Umatilla River; Thorn Hollow Rd. becomes Spring Hollow Rd.
23.75	Right onto Pambrun Rd.
28.45	Right onto SR 11.
29.85	Right onto Banister Rd.
32.2	Bear left at 90-degree turn as Banister Rd. becomes S. Water St. in Weston (city park with restrooms).
32.9	Bear right at fork to access Weston–Elgin Hwy. (SR 204).
52.5	Pass Tamarack Inn.
59.5	Reach Tollgate Pass high point, 5000-plus feet.
73.5	Enter Elgin; road becomes Division St.
73.8	Left onto N. 12th Ave.
73.9	End at Tom McDowell Park, on Baltimore St. and N. 12th St. in Elgin.

66 JOSEPH–ENTERPRISE LOOP

WALLOWA-ING IN THE BEAUTY OF IT ALL

Difficulty:	Moderate
Time:	1 to 2½ hours
Distance:	20.05-mile loop
Elevation Gain:	577 feet
Best Seasons:	Spring through fall

GETTING THERE: From I-84 in La Grande, take exit 261 and follow signs for SR 82–Wallowa Lake. Turn right off exit (coming from either direction) and follow SR 82 approximately 70 miles to Joseph. Ride starts at SR 82 (S. Main St.) and First St. Ample free parking along Main St.

Hurricane Creek Road, just outside Joseph, with hay in the foreground and the Wallowa Mountains looming in the distance. Greg Lee/Cycle Oregon

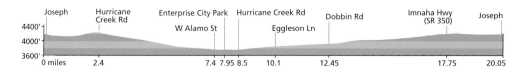

If you've never been to the northeast corner of Oregon, start planning the trip now. The rugged Wallowa Mountains, known rightfully as the Oregon Alps, are here, complete with a dizzying tram ride up Mount Howard. There's also unique Wallowa Lake, tucked in the shadows of the peaks and flanked on both sides by glacial moraines. And the Wallowa Valley is as peaceful and eye-pleasing a spread as you could ask for.

Take all that scenery and add the impressively cosmopolitan small towns of Enterprise and Joseph, and you have a reason to head up what amounts to a very long dead-end road to Joseph to spend some time. Not that you'd be the first. Joseph has wholeheartedly embraced the tourist economy, evidenced by plenty of restaurants, bed-and-breakfasts, and artsy shops. It's a destination.

So while you're there, do some riding.

For this ride, start in the heart of Joseph, on a very broad Main Street lined on both sides with merchants. Head down to the main highway junction and take a left to scoot out of town past the fairgrounds. Following Airport Lane, feel the immense presence of Chief Joseph Mountain over your left shoulder. Pedal past old barns, hay fields, and pastures as Airport Lane becomes Hurricane Creek Road.

This road is a blast to ride, because it's just a little bit downhill all the way; you're blithely breezing along, taking in the sights and going as fast as you want to. Soon enough (about 7 miles in) you reach the outskirts of Enterprise, which has historically been the governmental and financial center of Wallowa County.

The route as mapped takes you to a convenient little park with restrooms, but it's worth it to cruise around town for a bit, checking out some of the graceful old homes and the stately courthouse. There's also a quite popular local brewpub in town, if you enjoy adult beverages.

When you've had your fill of Enterprise, find your way back onto the route and retrace your path to the intersection with Eggleson Lane. Turn left here and make your way across the valley floor, crossing State Route 82 in 2 miles. There's a little right-left-right jogging to be done on Dobbin Road, so pay attention to the mileage log.

After Dobbin swivels its way to the south, turn onto Imnaha Highway (SR 350) to head back into Joseph. From here Wallowa Lake is hidden behind the east moraine; once you reach town, if you haven't seen the lake yet, continue up Main Street and follow the road up a hill to get a perfect view of the deep-blue lake framed by jagged peaks.

Route Variations: This ride is just one sample of the fairly easy routes you can piece together through the valley; grab a map and talk to a local to find more roads to explore.

MILEAGE LOG

0.0	From intersection of Wallowa Lake Hwy. (SR 82), aka S. Main St., and First St. in Joseph, head north on Main St.
0.2	Left onto W. Wallowa Ave., which becomes Airport Lane.
2.4	Bear right to join Hurricane Creek Rd.
5.8	Cross Eggleson Lane.

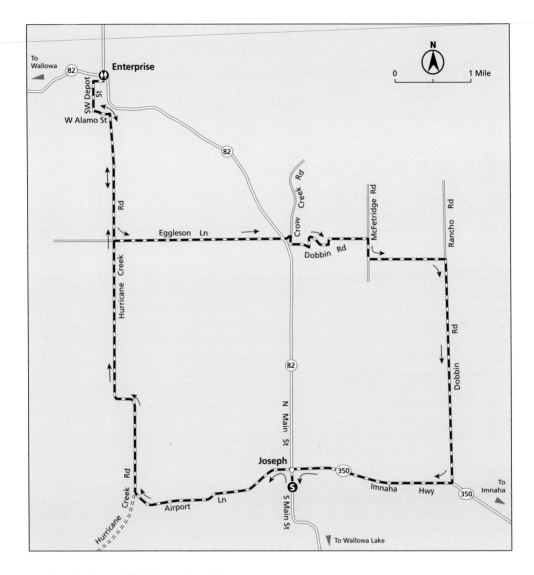

7.4	Left onto W. Alamo St. in Enterprise.
7.6	Right onto SW Depot St.
7.95	Enterprise City Park (restrooms)—turnaround point; head south on SW Depot St.
8.3	Left onto W. Alamo St.
8.5	Right onto River St. (Hurricane Creek Rd.).
10.1	Left onto Eggleson Lane.
12.25	Cross Wallowa Lake Hwy. (SR 82).
12.35	Right onto Crow Creek Rd.
12.45	Left onto Dobbin Rd.
13.65	Jog right at McFetridge Rd. to follow Dobbin Rd.
13.9	Jog left to stay on Dobbin Rd.

14.9   Right at 90-degree turn at Rancho Rd. to stay on Dobbin Rd.
17.75   Right onto Imnaha Hwy. (SR 350), which becomes E. Wallowa Ave. into Joseph.
19.85   Left onto Wallowa Lake Hwy. (SR 82), aka Main St.
20.05   Finish at intersection with First St.

67   UNION LOOP

UP THE CREEK WITHOUT A CARE

Difficulty:	Challenging
Time:	5 to 7½ hours
Distance:	75.9-mile loop
Elevation Gain:	2710 feet
Best Seasons:	Spring through fall

ROAD CONDITIONS: Short stretch on busy highway.

GETTING THERE: From I-84 south of La Grande, take exit 265, turn right onto SR 203 (coming from either direction), and follow it about 8 miles into Union. Ride starts at intersection of SR 203 and SR 237—N. Main St. and Beakman St.—at a nice city park on right side of N. Main St. Free parking along street; clean restrooms in park.

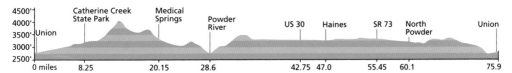

Certain towns, for whatever reason, just keep drawing you back. For me, Union is one of those towns. I've been there to ride at least four times, and it's always been memorable, in a good way. The town sits in a picturesque spot beneath golden foothills, with the Elkhorn Ridge of the Blue Mountains on the western horizon, and it has that friendly Western-small-town vibe. Plus, both the roads heading southerly out of town are sublime to ride—and this loop lets you cover both. It showcases both the rolling parts of the foothills and the

flat parts of the Powder River Valley, and it's not a particularly taxing 75-mile ride.

Start in downtown Union; the city park with the gazebo and veterans' memorials along Catherine Creek is a good spot to set up. Then head out of town to the southeast on State Route 203, Medicine Springs Highway. The first 10 miles deliver a positively bucolic start to the day, as you make your way up Catherine Creek. This is one of my favorite stretches in the state; the road rises, but in a cooperative way, as you follow the creek upstream. There are little dips and bumps, and the road curves along the water. When you reach Catherine Creek State Park (restrooms), you should be properly blissed out.

Take that bliss and put it to the test with the major challenge of the day, an ascent of 1000 feet over 5 miles. The pitch never really goes over 6 percent, but it's a tester as you work up through the piney forest. Once you get over the top, a roller-coaster drop takes you down through Pondosa and Medical Springs to the Powder River—long downhill stretches punctuated by a couple short, stout climbs.

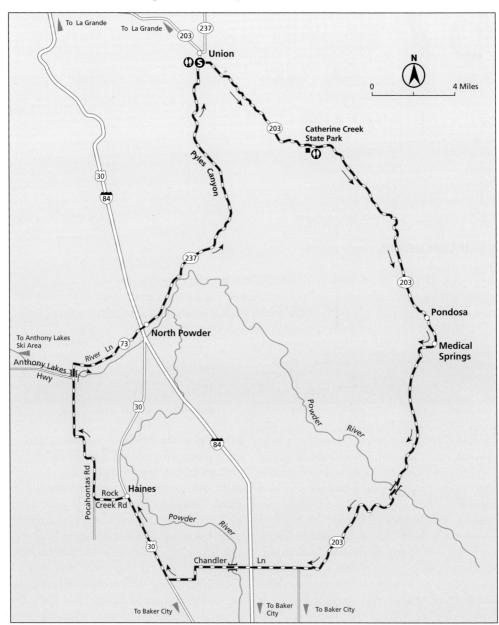

Sometimes the most indelible moments come after a ride. The low hills outside Union glow as the sun sets on another great day of riding. Greg Lee/Cycle Oregon

Once you cross the Powder at about 28.6 miles, head back uphill again—a smaller version of what you just came down, with bigger rises and smaller dips. Five miles later, you're blasting downhill toward Baker City and Interstate 84.

Once you cross the freeway, you're in the heart of the valley. It's cattle and pastureland and an even closer sense of the Blues, first in front of you and then to your left. A short stretch on US Highway 30 (yes, it's busier, but the shoulder is better—the usual trade-off) takes you into the small town of Haines at 47 miles, where you cut to the west to get back on some smaller roads. After a series of 90-degree curves, the Anthony Lakes Highway (SR 73) joins up and you head back east, across the freeway and into North Powder.

From North Powder back to Union is another spectacular piece of road. After a short initial decline, the road twists languidly upward through broad fields, carves through rocky Pyles Canyon, and then plunges down and back into Union. It's a fitting ending for a ride that started so well.

Route Variations: If you want to make a longer day of this, as you approach Baker City take the road that parallels I-84 on the east side, just before you cross over, and then catch SR 86 into town. Baker City has a great downtown with good places for lunch. Find your way through Baker City to US 30 north to rejoin the route south of Haines. This variation adds roughly 10 miles overall to the ride.

0.0	From city park at N. Main St. and Beakman St. in Union, head east on Beakman St. (SR 203).
8.25	Pass Catherine Creek State Park (restrooms) to right.
20.15	Enter Medical Springs.
28.6	Cross Powder River.
38.25	Continue straight at T with W. Airport Rd. (**Variation:** Left for side trip to Baker City.)
38.35	Cross I-84; road becomes Chandler Lane.
42.75	Right onto US 30.
47.0	Enter Haines.
47.25	Left onto Fourth St. (Rock Creek Rd.).
48.95	Right onto Pocahontas Rd. (Anthony Lakes Hwy.).
50.85	Jog left, then right, to stay on Anthony Lakes Hwy.
52.2	Jog left, then right, to stay on Anthony Lakes Hwy.
55.45	Bear right onto Ellis Lane (SR 73).
56.15	Cross North Powder River; bear right onto River Lane (SR 73).
60.1	Cross I-84 and enter North Powder; road becomes SR 237.
74.9	Enter Union; road becomes S. Main St.
75.9	Finish at N. Main St. and Beakman St.

68 BAKER CITY TO SUMPTER AND BACK

FOLLOW THE GOLD-RUSH ROUTE

Difficulty:	Challenging
Time:	4 to 6 hours
Distance:	59.2 miles round-trip
Elevation Gain:	1345 feet
Best Seasons:	Late spring through fall

ROAD CONDITIONS: Narrow road where railroad bisects SR 7 south of Baker City; use sidewalk.

GETTING THERE: From I-84 in Baker City, take exit 304 for SR 7. Turn west off exit onto Campbell St. (SR 7) and go 0.4 mile before turning left onto Grove St. A city park is on left, several blocks long. Free street parking; restrooms in park.

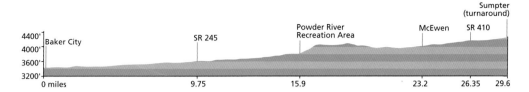

If you have any interest in Oregon's history, here's a route that starts on the Oregon Trail and goes to a site of Oregon's version of the gold rush—with tasty scenery in between.

Start in downtown Baker City, which hosts the nearby Oregon Trail Interpretive Center. From the city park, jog west on Washington Avenue to connect to State Route 7 through town. You'll get a good feel for this quiet city in the couple miles it takes to get to the other side of it. Where the railroad overpass bisects SR 7 at the 1-mile mark, take the sidewalk rather than the street; it's a tight squeeze otherwise.

Leaving town, ride a straight road through broad grasslands and arid hills before entering a short, narrow, rocky canyon of the Powder River. Coming out the other side, the road still hugs the river. After meandering pleasantly beside the water, just before 16 miles, take a few minutes to stop at the Powder River

Recreation Area, a long and narrow parking area that accesses a path along the bank of the river. The water is downright soothing, and you can sit on benches along the trail to watch people fly-fishing or just contemplate the beauty of nature.

Back on the road, quickly encounter a 0.75-mile climb that rises up above Phillips Lake, created by a dam in the river. This is the sole true climb of the ride, the only time the grade rises above about 3 percent. Fingers of the lake extend into several coves, and several excellent viewing opportunities are along the left side of the road (of course, they'll be on the right side coming back). The road rolls up and adjacent to the lake for 5 miles before beginning a steady and gradual rise toward Sumpter. Just after Phillips Lake, pass through McEwen, a one-store town.

At 26.35 miles take the turnoff to Sumpter, a town that may have seen its heyday quite

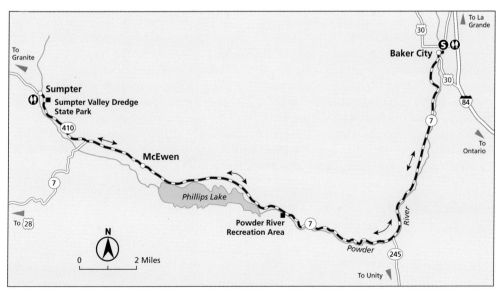

The comparison to a warehouse is fitting; this historic relic in the Sumpter Valley Dredge State Park gives you an idea of the kind—and scale—of mining work it performed.

soon after its founding in 1862. This was dredge-mining country, and the piles of tailings that greet you alongside the road into town attest to the scale of the mining efforts. Stop at Sumpter Valley Dredge State Park (restrooms) to look at, and even walk into, a preserved dredge, which is the size of a large warehouse. These machines chewed up massive bites of land and digested it while extracting any gold and then excreting the tailings. It was horrible environmentally, but that wasn't a consideration at the time. There's also the Sumpter Valley Railroad here, a working concern that gets fired up on special occasions.

Sumpter has several resources for food, beverages, and interaction; this is the normal turnaround point for the ride.

Route Variation: If you'd like to test yourself, keep going up the road toward Granite, a town that makes Sumpter look like Metropolis. It's an up-and-over that adds 33 miles and completely changes the ride into a climbing challenge, with 1200 feet of gain in each direction at grades of 6 to 8 percent.

MILEAGE LOG

0.0   From city park on Grove St. just south of Campbell St. (SR 7) in Baker City, head south on Grove St.

0.25   Right onto Washington Ave.

0.45   Left onto Main St. (SR 7).

0.65	Bear right to stay on SR 7 as road to left becomes Dewey Ave. (US 30), then Elm St.
1.0	Take sidewalk at underpass below I-84.
9.75	Bear right at intersection with SR 245 to stay on SR 7.
15.9	Pass Powder River Recreation Area on left.
23.2	Enter McEwen.
26.35	Right onto SR 410–SR 220 to Sumpter; pass Sumpter Valley Dredge State Park (restrooms) near town.
29.6	Enter Sumpter; continue to intersection of Mill St. and Granite St.—turnaround point; retrace route back to Baker City.
32.85	Bear left to join SR 7 heading east.
49.45	Bear left at intersection with SR 245 to stay on SR 7.
58.7	Right onto Washington Ave.
58.9	Left onto Grove St.
59.2	Finish at Baker city park.

69   SUMMIT PRAIRIE

ONE BIG SUMMIT, TWO REMOTE PRAIRIES

Difficulty:	Epic
Time:	4½ to 6½ hours
Distance:	65.2 miles round-trip
Elevation Gain:	3816 feet
Best Seasons:	Late spring through fall

GETTING THERE: Take US 26 to Prairie City, just east of US 395 at John Day; US 26 serves as the main street in Prairie City. When you hit town, turn south on Bridge St. to a small but nicely appointed city park. Parking along street; restrooms in park.

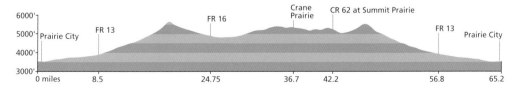

Some routes just name themselves. This one has a hellacious summit, followed by a prairie—OK, two prairies, but you get the point.

Start in Prairie City, a truly pleasant little town that's a big step above your average dot on the highway map that you blow through (or stop at for gas if you're desperate). The

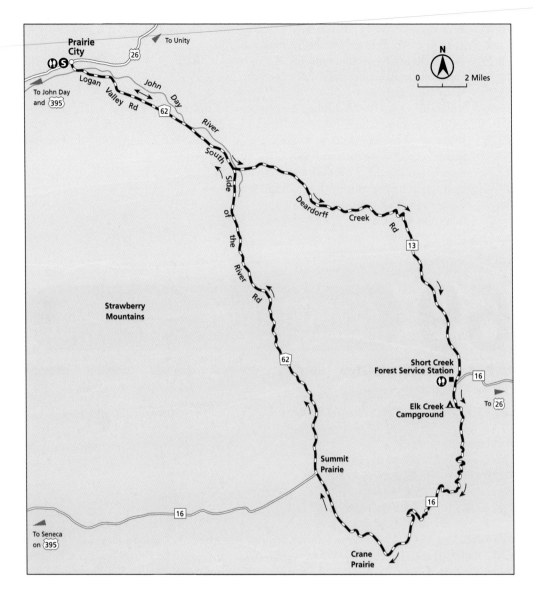

downtown is festive and quaint in an authentic way, not a contrived one. Stop in and drop some money on the local economy.

The ride heads out of town on County Road 62, which starts by paralleling US Highway 26 for a while. The road surface is not bad, and traffic is nearly nonexistent. The jagged peaks of the Strawberry Mountains rise over your right shoulder, typically with snow still hanging on until midsummer or later. If the

I don't know who put this rock here (near Elk Creek campground), but I'm pretty sure it wasn't Mother Nature. >

town's moniker wasn't enough of a hint, this is rolling prairie country, with grassy swells in all directions.

About 8.5 miles in, turn left onto Forest Road 13 (Deardorff Creek Road), which has a coarser surface here. Quickly you're swallowed up into a canyon—suddenly the prairie land is a memory and it's close-in, rocky forest. You're following Deardorff Creek, but it's not challenging . . . yet. At around 11 miles, pass the Malheur National Forest sign and the pitch increases almost imperceptibly; your legs will notify you. And soon thereafter you'll have to acknowledge that, yes, this is an extended climb. But hopefully this is the kind of ascending environment where you can find a smooth gear, spin, and tune in to the surroundings. Butterflies are flitting, the creek is murmuring; look at all the variations of deep green.

And then you hit the right-hand hairpin at 16.1 miles and it's no more fooling around. The next 2 miles to the top (actually, it's a little less—but program your brain for 2 miles and you'll be done early) is capital-H *hard*. It's a steady grind of roughly 10 percent, sometimes more. But when you summit and hit that downslope on the other side, the joy will be palpable. It won't take very many pedal strokes to get to the junction at 24.75 miles—you can just glide for long stretches.

At the junction with FR 16, on the right is Short Creek Forest Service station, with a pit toilet here and (usually) water from a hose attached to the building. There's a picnic table, but I'd recommend going a mile farther on to the shady little Elk Creek campground if you want a stop.

The first part of FR 16 is still down, but at 27 miles it's climb-time again. But you've already conquered the worst this route can dish out, so this feels like nothing . . . relatively. After 4 miles of low-grade incline there's a false summit, where the road surface inexplicably narrows and deteriorates markedly for 7 miles. Not all of that is uphill; there are some drops and some ridge-running.

And then, about the time you're thinking, "This seems like more down than up, lately," right around 36.7 miles, boom! Off to your left is Crane Prairie, an isolated pocket of mountain bounty. As you slip down beside the prairie, the road widens and gets a center line.

Several miles later you emerge at the namesake Summit Prairie, equally pastoral. Here, take the right fork back onto CR 62. Since you're leaving a prairie, you may not be surprised by a 1-mile climb, but then you remember it was a *summit* prairie—and so you get to ride downhill all the way home. You'll enjoy the glide, too, and about 9 miles into it you dramatically emerge from the forest back into the broad prairie land. Two miles later it flattens out, but it's still down to town, retracing your route out.

MILEAGE LOG

0.0	From city park on Bridge St. just south of Front St. (US 26) in Prairie City, head south on Bridge St.
0.5	SW Bridge St. becomes CR 62.
8.5	Left onto FR 13 (Deardorff Creek Rd.).
24.75	Bear right where FR 13 ends at FR 16 to follow FR 16 (pit toilets).
36.7	Pass through Crane Prairie.
42.2	Bear right at fork at Summit Prairie to take CR 62.
56.8	Continue straight at intersection with FR 13 to stay on CR 62.
65.2	Finish at city park on Bridge St.

70

BURNS TO FRENCHGLEN VIA THE NARROWS

THE ROAD TO . . . SOMEWHERE

Difficulty:	Moderate
Time:	4 to 6 hours (**Variation:** 6 to 9 hours)
Distance:	60.1 miles one-way (**Variation:** 90.2 miles one-way)
Elevation Gain:	961 feet
Best Seasons:	Spring through fall

GETTING THERE: To get to Burns, a bit right of the center of Oregon, take US 20 east or west or US 395 south or north. From junction of US 395–US 20 with SR 78 in Burns, go three blocks north and three blocks east to Washington Park at E. Adams St. and N. Cedar Ave. Free parking in gravel on park's perimeter; restrooms. If you're leaving a vehicle overnight, talk to a local merchant about a safe place to leave it.

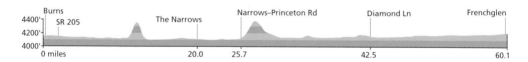

I was going to call this route (combined with Frenchglen to Burns, Ride 71) The Road to Nowhere, but some folks in Diamond let me know that they don't appreciate the term "the middle of nowhere" for their location (population 7). So, while this route travels a very remote road, it's not nowhere—in fact, there are some amazing things along the way.

When planning this book, I needed to spread the routes around the state. No problem—until you come to southeastern Oregon, which is a bit like Saudi Arabia's Empty Quarter. It's a wonderful place to visit by car—more on that later—but it's awfully stretched-out for bicycling. So I included two routes you can combine for a loop tour.

Here's my recommendation: Choose to either ride to Frenchglen in one day and stay overnight there, or ride on to Diamond and

stay there (see Route Variations, below). But here's another suggestion: If you can, have someone come along with a car, in the fall, and take a day off the bike in Frenchglen to drive the loop road up Steens Mountain. Once you're out here, you really should see it. Really. (More on that below.)

A few extra notes on this route, as well as the next ride's route back to Burns: It's a long way between resources out here; be especially conscious of your fluid intake and supply, make sure someone knows where you're going and when, bring a lot of sunscreen . . . and, from mid-June to whenever all the hay gets mowed, plaster yourself with the strongest bug spray money can buy. The mosquitoes are voracious and relentless, but once the hay is cut, they're gone.

OK, the bike route. First of all, note that

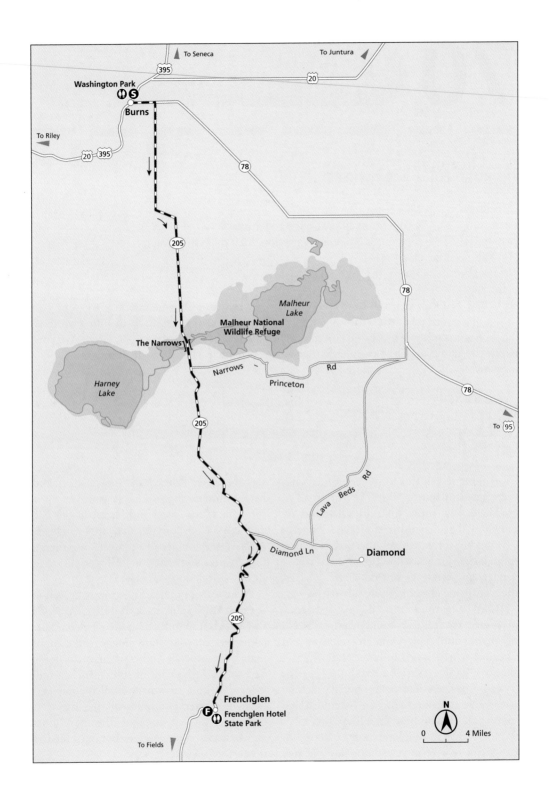

To Seneca

To Juntura

395

20

Washington Park

Burns

To Riley

20 395

78

205

Malheur
Lake

Malheur National
Wildlife Refuge

The Narrows

78

Harney
Lake

Narrows ~ Rd

Princeton

205

78

To 95

Lava Beds Rd

Diamond Ln

Diamond

205

Frenchglen

Frenchglen Hotel
State Park

To Fields

N

0   4 Miles

The Frenchglen Hotel, an oasis in the vast expanse of southeastern Oregon, is also an official Oregon State Park. It's a great jumping-off point for a side trip up Steens Mountain.

(Ride 70) route description in more detail: Things are spread out here, so plan your fluid supplies accordingly, leave an itinerary with someone, and don't forget the sunscreen . . . and bug spray.

Starting from Frenchglen, go north up SR 205 to the Diamond Lane turnoff. It's hard to believe, but initially Diamond Lane seems even more desolate than what you've been riding through (the surface isn't as nice, either). But after a few miles you break out into the surprisingly fertile Diamond Valley, home to a large number of family ranches that go back as many as five generations. At the junction with Lava Beds Road, choose whether to make the 5.6-mile side trip to Diamond and back.

On Lava Beds Road, pass through the Diamond Craters, a remarkable series of formations that look a lot like what an alien spaceship would cause if it landed on Earth in a Hollywood movie: charred, buckled impact zones. At 45.5 miles (34.4 miles if you skipped the side trip to Diamond) is the turn-off for the famous Pete French Round Barn; it's a pretty cool building, but it's also 1 mile of rutted dirt road off the highway. Whether you go or not, here's the quick skinny on this Pete French character from back in the day: land and cattle baron; influential but greedy, and a bully—not well liked; shot in the back by a rival rancher, who was acquitted of the murder although there were witnesses. Ah, the Old West.

The next section feels more uphill over-all, although not egregiously so, and you're back in the great wide open. When the route rejoins SR 78, it's likely you'll appreciate the pavement more than resent the increased traf-fic. Just before the turnoff to go into the town of Crane, there's a store on the left. And at 72.3 miles (61.2 miles if you skipped the visit to Diamond) you can't miss Crystal Crane Hot Springs. Here you can get a cold drink and a hot soak—either in a communal pond requiring clothing (bike clothes OK) or in a do-what-you-like private soaking cabin. There's also camping available.

As you approach Burns, the final 10 miles is on a great surface—which, after the miles that preceded it, will feel like zipping along one of those people-movers at the airport.

MILEAGE LOG

0.0	From Frenchglen Hotel, head north on SR 205.
17.6	Right onto Diamond Lane.
24.4	Continue straight at intersection with Lava Beds Rd. to stay on Diamond Lane. (**Variation:** Left onto Lava Beds Rd. to skip side trip to Diamond.)
30.0	Diamond—turnaround point; retrace Diamond Lane back to intersection.
35.5	Right onto Lava Beds Rd. (**Variation:** Resume mileage log here.)
45.5	Pass dirt road to Pete French Round Barn on right.
55.8	Bear right at Narrows–Princeton Rd. to stay on Lava Beds Rd.
58.9	Bear left at cutoff to join Steens Hwy. (SR 78).
68.5	Bear left at turnoff for Crane to stay on SR 78.
72.3	Pass Crystal Crane Hot Springs on right.
95.0	Cross intersection with SR 205.
96.6	Right onto N. Cedar Ave.
96.7	Finish at Washington Park at E. Adams St. in Burns.

MULTIDAY ROUTES

If you have the time, there's no better way to get in touch with the natural wonders of Oregon than by seeing a large swath of it from a bike. Road touring in Oregon is a popular activity, and for good reason: You can string together day after day of matchless beauty, warm and welcoming towns and people, and wandering roads to take you through it all. Here are four multiday routes that offer four different viewpoints of the state.

72 THE OREGON COAST ROUTE

BORDER TO BORDER, BEACH-STYLE

Difficulty: Epic
Time: 4 to 8 days
Distance: 359.8 miles one way
Elevation Gain: 12,809 feet
Best Seasons: Year-round, but late summer through fall ideal

ROAD CONDITIONS: Highway traffic on US 101; tunnel at Arch Cape equipped with bike-warning light.

GETTING THERE: From Portland, take US 26 west to US 101 and follow it north to Astoria, where official Oregon Coast Bike Route begins. Official route, which assumes you're coming from Washington state on US 101 over Astoria–Megler Bridge, starts at foot of bridge, on W. Marine Dr. (US 101–US 30). I don't necessarily recommend parking a car there for a week or more, so you might want to make other arrangements (see Route Variations, below).

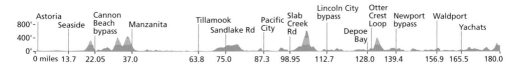

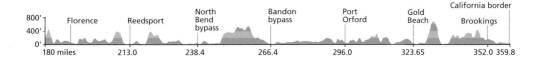

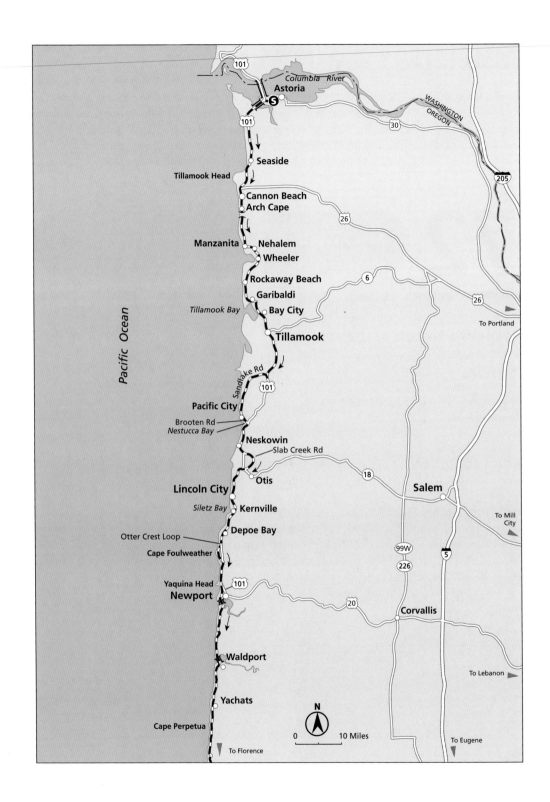

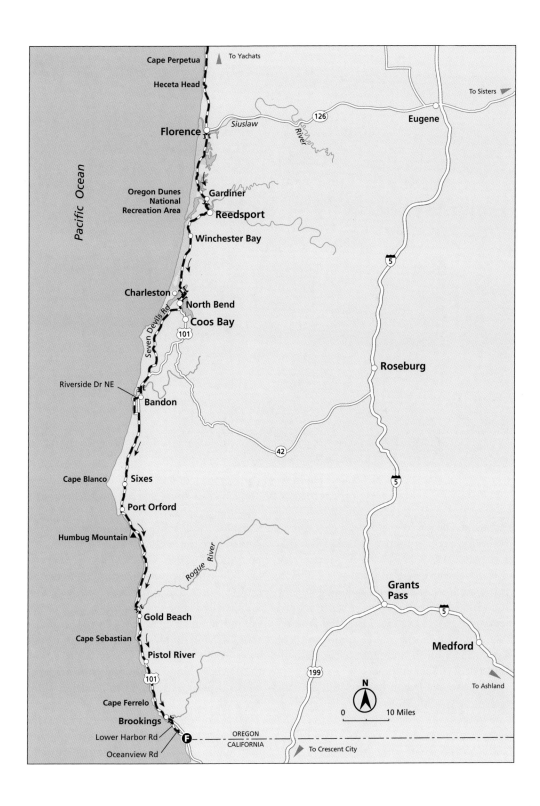

Cape Perpetua

To Yachats

Heceta Head

Siuslaw

126

To Sisters

Florence

Eugene

River

Oregon Dunes
National
Recreation Area

Gardiner

Reedsport

Winchester Bay

5

Charleston

North Bend

Coos Bay

Seven Devils Rd

101

Roseburg

Pacific Ocean

Riverside Dr NE

Bandon

42

Cape Blanco

Sixes

5

Port Orford

Humbug Mountain

Rogue River

Grants
Pass

5

Gold Beach

Cape Sebastian

Pistol River

Medford

101

199

To Ashland

N

Cape Ferrelo

Brookings

0   10 Miles

Lower Harbor Rd

F

Oceanview Rd

OREGON
CALIFORNIA

To Crescent City

The Ben Jones Bridge arches over the water at the beginning of the Otter Crest Loop, a sublime section of the Oregon Coast Route that veers off Highway 101.

Riding the Oregon coast is a major checkoff on the list for any bike tourist. Whether you ride it as part of an epic Canada-to-Mexico trek or just cycle the length of Oregon, it's a treat. This route has just about everything going for it: unparalleled scenery (massive capes, rugged headlands, pastoral valleys, iconic lighthouses, long unspoiled beaches) and a combination of beachy small towns and larger cities with all the services you might need.

The state of Oregon has made it as convenient as possible to go down the coast on two wheels, with a detailed map of the route (www.oregon.gov/ODOT/HWY/BIKEPED /docs/oregon_coast_bike_route_map.pdf) that includes a list of campgrounds, parks,

waysides, and more. This route starts in Astoria, so the mileages pretty well match up with the state's map. Oregon State Parks has bike-camping spots set up at numerous campgrounds along the way—in fact, they unofficially claim that even if a park campground is full, cyclists are allowed to find a spot, so you shouldn't find yourself turned away. And if you want to stay under a roof, there's everything from motels to cottages to bed-and-breakfasts to yurts available along the way.

If you're camping, keep an eye on the State Parks map to pick your stopping points each night. If you're employing the plastic-payment plan, here are a couple suggested itineraries. If you prefer shorter-mileage days, stopping at Wheeler, Pacific City, Depoe Bay, Yachats, Reedsport, Bandon, and Gold Beach takes eight days total and provides 40 to 50 miles a day on average—and lands you overnight in some very charming small towns. If you like more mileage, try a five-day trip that averages just over 70 miles a day: Take the Three Capes Scenic Route option out of Tillamook to stay in Oceanside, then Newport, Winchester Bay, and Port Orford. This has been my approach, and it's not that hard to get in that many miles: Sleep in and have a huge breakfast, hit the road for a couple hours (30 miles or so), stop for a leisurely lunch, ride for three hours (40 to 45 miles), and you're there. Throw in a couple hours for random photo ops and stops along the way, and you're still rolling into your overnight town in the late afternoon, ready for food, a nap, and then more food again.

OK, let's talk about a few downsides: First, you're likely to do this ride in the summer (weather-wise, mid-July to mid-September is the most reliable; you're likely to be miserable at some point at other times), exactly the same time that hordes of tourists invade the same roads. Having done this entire route, I'd say that for making me nervous on the bike, it's a tie between clueless drivers of recreational vehicles and road-hogging log-truck drivers. But honestly, over 300 miles of coast, I felt truly crowded (or buzzed) by vehicles only a half-dozen times. Not bad, really.

Second, there are some significant climbs—in this geography, capes—along the way: a dozen distinct ascents, mostly in the 500- to 700-foot range, but a couple upward of 1000 feet. If you're loaded-touring, that will take some exertion. So be sure you're fit enough and have a low enough range of gearing to take your time heading up these climbs.

Finally, weather is a joker in the deck of coastal rides; I've seen plenty of rain-sodden riders slogging down US Highway 101 in the middle of summer. Don't neglect to pack some wet-weather supplies.

Last notes: If you have a choice, ride this north-to-south. The winds tend to help rather than be in your face (and you *will* have wind), plus for my money the southern section is the best, so save it for last. If the mileage log seems confusing at all, follow the green Oregon Coast Bike Route signs—they're thoughtfully and frequently placed. I advise you to carry a copy of the state's map as well as information from this book.

OK, let's ride. Leave Astoria with a sense of the immensity of the mouth of the Columbia River, then head down through some flatlands to Seaside, a kitschy tourist town for Portlanders who want to eat their ice cream at the beach. Then, after your first up-and-over (Tillamook Head), the route takes a side trip through Cannon Beach, a higher-end attraction with a wonderful beach and Haystack Rock to explore.

Back on US 101, things get twisty and upward, ascending Arch Cape. The tunnel here can be a little nerve-wracking, but it's equipped with a bike-warning light; don't forget to stop and activate it before going through. Two distinct climbs through here have a sharp descent between them, and then you drop down and turn inland, around placid Nehalem Bay and through the small, peaceful villages of Manzanita, Nehalem, and Wheeler.

After a long, straight stretch through Rockaway Beach, turn inland again and go over a few rollers coming into the sweep around broad Tillamook Bay, passing through Garibaldi and Bay City. Just out of Bay City, enter dairy farmland, where you leave behind the salty scent of the ocean for another mix of smells. Tillamook has a nice old downtown, as well as the cheese factory if you feel like a free sample of curds. Here you can choose to veer off, just past 64 miles, for the entire Three Capes Scenic Loop (Ride 3), or continue south on an inland portion of US 101 until turning west on Sandlake Road.

Either way you'll end up dropping down off Cape Kiwanda into Pacific City, a funky hangout for surfers and families that offers a good brewpub and a collection of cafés and fish shops. After a stretch alongside Nestucca Bay, it's back on US 101 and through Neskowin. Then you've got massive Cascade Head to negotiate, and you have a choice: Take it straight on US 101, or take the recommended Coast Route, swinging out on Slab Creek Road, where the same elevation gain is spread over more miles for a gentler experience and less traffic. If you take Slab Creek, at the point where it turns onto Three Rocks Road, consider taking a quick jog to the left into Otis and its nationally famous café.

Lincoln City is a long, sprawling small city that isn't really conducive to riding through; I'm a fan of the alternate route closer to the beach, even though it involves a lot of turns and jogs. Once clear of the majority of the mayhem, head out through the Siletz Bay flats at Kernville and then past Salishan Resort and a flat, straight run through Lincoln Beach (great bike lane!). After a couple bumps alongside the crashing waves of Boiler Bay and Pirate Cove, glide into Depoe Bay, the world's smallest harbor.

South of Depoe Bay, just past Whale Cove, is one of my favorite sections of the entire route: Otter Crest Loop. A few years back this included an abandoned section of road that the forest was reclaiming inch by inch, but it's since been refurbished as a one-way corridor with a dedicated bike lane. From the graceful arching bridge at the beginning of the side loop to the tree-framed views of the Cape Foulweather headlands, to the narrow lane slicing through moss-draped coastal forest, the atmosphere here is simply special. After cresting Cape Foulweather—a great viewpoint to the right—drop down into Otter Rock, where you can take a short side jaunt to Devil's Punchbowl State Park.

Back on US 101, the road slips down to run along a couple long, sandy beaches, with the Yaquina Head lighthouse ahead in the distance. A little climbing brings you into Newport, where once again you can circumvent the main highway, winding down by the water and then through quaint Nye Beach, ending up in Yaquina Bay Recreation Site, a windswept park, before coming back to US 101 and crossing the Yaquina Bay Bridge. The mileage log looks complicated, but the roads and signs keep it easy. South of Yaquina Bay, enjoy long stretches of seaside roadway by a crossing of scenic Alsea Bay to Waldport.

Just south of Yachats (pronounced YAH-hots) is the comparatively small Cape Perpetua, as you pass through two designated wildernesses; the going is a bit more rugged through here, and about 7 miles after Yachats is Cape Creek Tunnel, another somewhat nerve-jangling passage on the steep and twisting climb up Heceta Head.

Stay on US 101 right through Florence, one of the larger cities on the coast, cross the Siuslaw River, and then ride big rollers past a series of coastal lakes before scaling a sturdy climb that's not even its own cape. The downhill side brings you into the mill town of Gardiner and then to Reedsport, where you'll cross the Umpqua River on the way into town. Reedsport is a blue-collar, fishing-and-timber town that came late to the tourism party, but the area offers tons of outdoor recreation, including hiking or dune-buggying in the vast Oregon Dunes National Recreation Area, which spans the coast from Florence to Coos Bay.

Just past Reedsport is Winchester Bay, a fishing hub and the nearest coastal access for this area; here the route takes a quick detour to check out the local estuary and lighthouse. As you approach North Bend, you'll twice cross horseshoe-shaped Coos Bay; just after the second bridge look for the signs for a major US 101 bypass.

This route departs the highway nearly all

A few years back, the Otter Crest Loop road was closed to traffic and being reclaimed by the forest. Today it's a spectacular one-way road with an excellent separated bike lane.

the way to Bandon. After negotiating North Bend, head out the Cape Arago Highway to Charleston, where you turn off onto Seven Devils Road. (Consider continuing on to Sunset Bay, Shore Acres, and Cape Arago state parks, all stellar spots for a lunch stop.) Seven Devils is aptly named, because although they're not lengthy, there are seven peak-points (they're even numbered on the pavement for your pleasure) that are somehow as taxing as any cape climb. You're out in the boonies here, with no soothing seascape to concentrate on.

Back onto US 101 for a short stint, cross the Coquille River, then veer off on Riverside

Drive just before entering Bandon. Bandon's Old Town is worth exploring, before taking Beach Loop Drive—one of the best beach roads on the West Coast—out of town. The run from Bandon down to Port Orford is a great ride, with much smooth pavement. If you feel like it, the side trip out to Cape Blanco just past Sixes takes you to a cool old lighthouse you can climb up inside, as well as more photogenic views and the knowledge that you're at the westernmost point in the contiguous United States. In Port Orford, check out the harbor, one of the few in the world that gets boats out of the water by hoisting them with a crane-and-dolly setup.

The view south from Cape Foulweather, looking over Otter Rock, is emblematic of Oregon's rugged, beautiful coastline.

I have to say that Bandon to Brookings—the South Coast—is the nicest overall part of this ride. It has all the wild beauty, pounding surf, and panoramic views of the North Coast, but with fewer towns and way fewer people and vehicles. Outside Port Orford, rise up several times, including over Humbug Mountain, before arriving at Gold Beach. Here, cross over the Rogue River, the first federally designated Wild and Scenic River in Oregon. Upstream at Galice (Rogue River Ramble, Ride 32) this is world-class rafting; at this end people ride jet boats up the river.

Just a couple miles south of town, here comes Cape Sebastian, the highest point on the coast; the climb will confirm this, but knowing it's the last major haul will help, as will the descent to the Pistol River. The section between Cape Sebastian and Cape Ferrelo is so sweet that it's designated a state scenic corridor, and the drop from Ferrelo, the last cape of the route, to the sparkling waters of Harris Beach just outside Brookings is simply exhilarating; keep your eyes on the road if you can.

When you reach Brookings–Harbor, the last town(s) in Oregon, decide if your quest is over or if you need to cross the border into California. If you're going on past town, take the Lower Harbor–Oceanview side loop, get back on US 101, and knock off the last few miles to the border.

Route Variation: If you'd like to start at a place where you can park a vehicle, try Tapiola Park in Astoria. It's on State Route 202, southeast of the traffic circle at the 0.4-mile mark of the main route. It's roughly the same distance from the traffic circle as the official start, so your mileage should be pretty close.

MILEAGE LOG

0.0	From foot of Astoria–Megler Bridge, on W. Marine Dr. (US 101–US 30), head southwest on W. Marine Dr.
0.4	Continue south on US 101 at traffic circle, crossing Youngs Bay bridge.
13.7	Enter Seaside.
19.1	Continue south at intersection with US 26 to stay on US 101.
22.05	Right onto Beach Loop road toward Cannon Beach; comes out on Fir St., which becomes Elm Ave. in Cannon Beach.
22.65	Jog right on Elm Ave., left on Spruce, right on Third, left on Hemlock; follow Hemlock south through Cannon Beach.
25.6	Right onto US 101.
37.0	Enter Manzanita.
38.9	Enter Nehalem.
41.2	Enter Wheeler.
49.0	Enter Rockaway Beach.
53.8	Enter Garibaldi.
63.8	Enter Tillamook.
75.0	Right onto Sandlake Rd.
79.45	Left at intersection with Cape Lookout Rd. to stay on Sandlake Rd.
87.3	Enter Pacific City.
88.3	Left onto Pacific Ave.; cross bridge over Nestucca Bay.
88.5	Right onto Brooten Rd.
91.2	Right onto US 101.
97.75	Enter Neskowin.
98.95	Left onto Slab Creek Rd.
108.3	Right onto NE Three Rocks Rd.
108.9	Left onto US 101.
112.7	Right onto NW 40th St. approaching Lincoln City.
112.95	Left to stay on NW 40th St. to Jetty Way and jog right-left onto NW Jetty Ave.
114.1	Jog right at end of NW Jetty Ave onto NW 21st St.; then jog left onto NW Harbor Ave.
114.6	Jog left onto NW 12th St. and then right onto NW Inlet Ave.
114.9	Left onto NW Second Dr., then right onto US 101.
115.35	Right from US 101 onto SW Ebb Ave.
115.75	Jog left at SW Ninth St., then right onto SW 11th Dr., then left onto SW Coast Ave.
116.55	Right onto SW 24th Dr., which curves to right and becomes SW Anchor Ave.
117.35	Left onto SW 35th St., then right onto US 101.
117.95	Right onto SW Beach Ave.
118.35	Jog left onto NW 48th St., then right on NW Dune Ave., then left on NW 50th St.
118.8	Right onto US 101.
128.0	Enter Depoe Bay.

130.5	Right onto Otter Crest Loop.
132.3	Bear right to stay on Otter Crest Loop.
134.0	Right to rejoin US 101.
139.4	Right onto NW Oceanview Dr. approaching Newport.
140.85	Jog right onto NW 12th St., left onto NW Spring St., right onto NW Eighth St., then left onto NW Coast St.
141.55	Jog right onto W. Olive St.; it jogs left and becomes SW Elizabeth St.
142.4	Right onto Government St., into Yaquina Bay Recreation Site.
142.8	Bear left at fork; don't go under bridge—follow signs for US 101 south, turn right, and cross bridge over Yaquina Bay.
156.9	Cross bridge over Alsea Bay; enter Waldport.
165.5	Enter Yachats.
190.0	Enter Florence; cross bridge over Siuslaw River.
213.0	Cross bridge over Winchester Bay; enter Reedsport.
217.4	Right onto Eighth St. in town of Winchester Bay.
217.55	Left onto Beach Blvd., then right onto Salmon Harbor Dr.
218.7	Left onto Lighthouse Rd.
219.95	Bear right to stay on Lighthouse Rd.
220.35	Right onto US 101.
238.4	Cross bridge over Coos Bay; right onto Florida St. in North Bend.
238.65	Left onto Monroe St.
239.0	Right onto Virginia Ave. (Cape Arago Hwy.).
239.55	Left onto Broadway St. (Cape Arago Hwy.).
240.5	Bear right at Newmark St., following signs for Cape Arago Hwy.
242.45	Left onto S. Empire Blvd., following signs for Cape Arago Hwy.
247.5	Left onto Seven Devils Rd. in Charleston.
253.85	Bear left onto W. Beaver Hill Rd.
258.3	Right onto Whiskey Run Rd.
260.75	Left onto Seven Devils Rd.
263.6	Right onto US 101.
266.4	Cross Coquille River; right onto Riverside Dr. NE in Bandon.
268.0	Right onto First St. SE; curves left and becomes Edison Ave. SW.
268.65	Right onto Fourth St. SW; curves left and becomes Ocean Dr. SW.
269.3	Road turns 90 degrees left and becomes Beach Loop Dr.
273.55	Right onto US 101.
296.0	Enter Port Orford.
319.8	Right onto Old Coast Hwy.
322.9	Road curves left and becomes Wedderburn Loop.
323.65	Right onto US 101; cross Rogue River into Gold Beach.
352.0	Enter Brookings.
354.3	Right onto Lower Harbor Rd., just across bridge over Chetco River.
355.35	Sharp right, after curve on Lower Harbor Rd., onto Oceanview Dr.
358.95	Right onto US 101.
359.8	Finish at Oregon-California border.

73 WILLAMETTE VALLEY SCENIC BIKEWAY

A TRANQUIL TOUR OF THE HEART OF OREGON

Difficulty: Moderate
Time: 2 to 4 days
Distance: 132.9 miles one way
Elevation Gain: 1758 feet
Best Seasons: Year-round

ROAD CONDITIONS: Some riding in city or highway traffic.

GETTING THERE: From I-5 south of Portland, take exit 278 and turn west onto Ehlen Rd. NE. Follow this road 5.15 miles (it becomes Yergen Rd. NE and then McKay Rd. NE) and turn right onto French Prairie Rd. Follow this road for 1.2 miles and turn right onto Champoeg Rd. NE. Entrance to Champoeg State Park is 0.2 mile on left on N. Champoeg Rd. Just inside park entrance, a loop to right offers ample free parking; nice clean restrooms. Many cyclists congregate here.

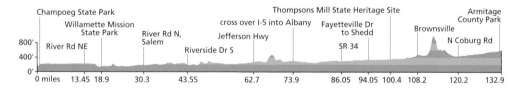

There are plenty of cycling visionaries in Oregon, and the state's groundbreaking Scenic Bikeways program is a prime example. Scenic Byways exist all over the country (Oregon alone has 17), but no one ever thought to build a Scenic Bikeway—until a group that included Cycle Oregon and Oregon's Department of Parks and Recreation started hatching plans for designated, signed, mapped, and promoted routes that highlight the very best of Oregon cycling. The idea? Attract even more cyclists out on the road, and give them great routes and helpful structure and resources.

For the first one, they chose an accessible, moderate shot right through the Willamette Valley, where something like 80 percent of the state's population lives and which produces a mind-bending array of agricultural products, from grass seed to hops, tulips to hazelnuts. This route won't excite hard-core climbers, but you can make it a one-day, long-distance challenge if you like—or poke along for days. There are a lot of places to stop for meals, lodging, or just hanging out along the way, so pick a section or do it all—just follow the green-and-white signs.

The official Scenic Bikeway map shows your camping options along the way. If you want to stay in a more solid-structure

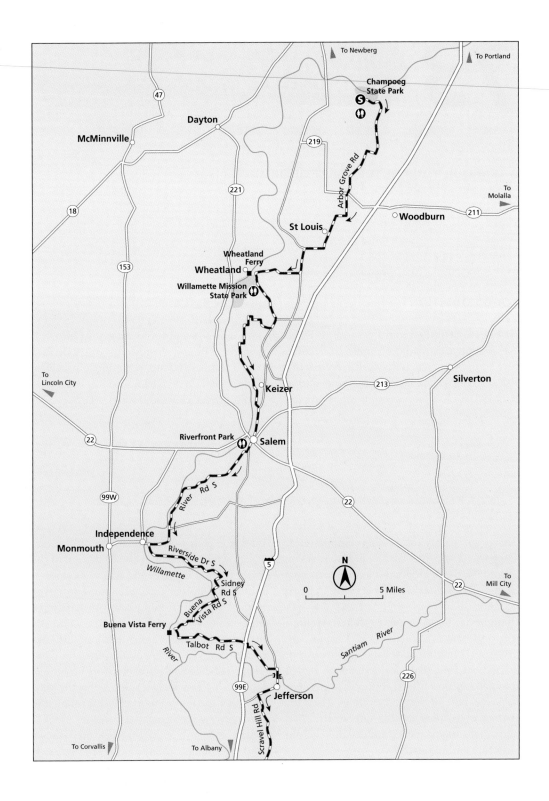

To Newberg

To Portland

⑰ 47

Champoeg
State Park

Ⓢ
Ⓧ

Dayton

McMinnville

18

221

219

Arbor Grove Rd

To
Molalla

211

Woodburn

St Louis

153

Wheatland
Ferry

Wheatland

Willamette Mission
State Park
Ⓧ

To
Lincoln City

Keizer

213

Silverton

22

Riverfront Park
Ⓧ

Salem

99W

River Rd S

22

Independence

Monmouth

Riverside Dr S

5

Willamette

Sidney
Rd S

N

0   5 Miles

To
Mill City

22

Buena Vista Ferry

Buena
Vista Rd S

Talbot   Rd S

Santiam   River

226

River

99E

Jefferson

Scravel Hill Rd

To Corvallis

To Albany

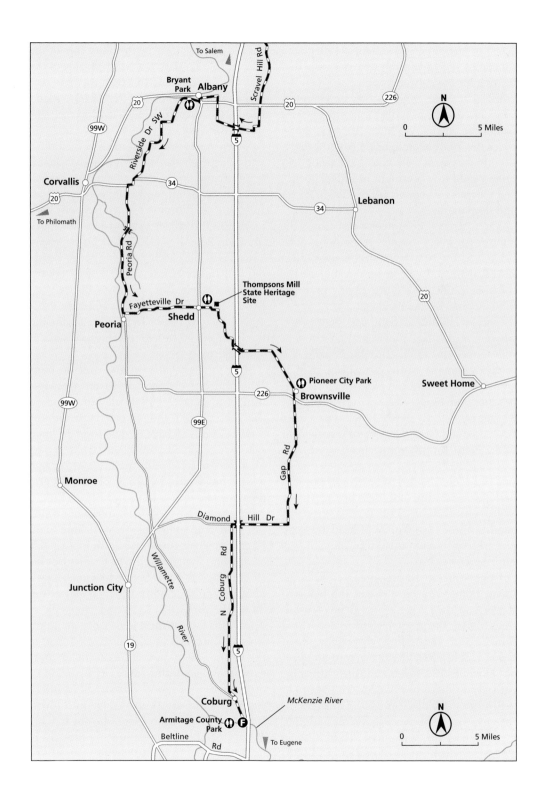

accommodation, here are a couple suggested itineraries. For a leisurely five-day trip that leaves a lot of time for stopping to smell the crops, plan your stops in Salem, Jefferson, Corvallis, and Brownsville; this will give you daily rides of 21 to 33 miles. If you'd like to cover this route more quickly, a good three-day itinerary with daily mileage of around 45 miles would stop overnight in Independence and Corvallis—both great little towns to eat and sleep in.

The state's documentation for the Willamette Valley Scenic Bikeway is quite helpful; access it at www.oregon.gov/OPRD /PARKS/BIKE/WVSB_main.shtml. Note: The mileages in this book differ slightly from the official Scenic Bikeway materials.

Start at historic Champoeg State Park, where Oregon's first provisional government was formed in 1843. This huge park is a camper's paradise and a great place to start a tour. Set out from the park in lightly rolling hills and zigzag your way down the valley, getting an early sense of the bounty these lands produce. Go through the old settlement of St. Louis with its immaculate white chapel, then decide if you want to take a quick side trip across the tiny Wheatland Ferry and back just for the fun of it, right before passing Willamette Mission State Park (restrooms), another historic site. Follow Wheatland Road past hop farms and other crops on your way into Keizer.

Once you hit Keizer, prepare for some urban riding. You have to get through first Keizer and then Salem, and there's no real way around them, so just bear down and think about the valley vistas that await beyond. When you reach the core of Salem on Commercial Street and then the bike path paralleling Front Avenue, to your right is Riverfront Park (restrooms), a true oasis in the city, with a lot of space, picnic and kids' facilities, and the Willamette River running alongside (Salem Family Fun Ride, Ride 20).

As you head south out of downtown, River Road is a bit tricky; when you first join it, the bike-pedestrian path is on the left side of the road; it's better to use this than the right side of the road. But when you reach Minto Island Road, cross over to the bike lane on the right side of the road.

When you're just about to cross the bridge into Independence, the route puts you on a right-hand loop back under the bridge. But Independence, only a mile away, has an authentic old downtown and a great city park on the river; consider a stop there. This entire stretch of River Road–Riverside Drive–Buena Vista Road pleasantly wanders along beside the Willamette before turning away toward Jefferson. When you turn from Buena Vista Road S. onto Talbot Road S., you have a second chance to take a ferry ride just for the fun of it; just go straight on Buena Vista S. if you'd like to.

Ride through Jefferson and over the concrete bridge at the Santiam River; when you turn onto Scravel Hill Road NE, there's a short, steep bump and railroad tracks. Almost 6 miles later, you have to do a little 0.1-mile right-left jog on busy US Highway 20. A couple turns later you're in the heart of Albany, where you'll pass by some of the historic downtown as well as attractive Bryant Park.

Riverside Drive SW is a pleasant, winding road that spills out on very busy State Route 34, where the route jogs right, then left to pick up White Oak Road heading south. (If crossing SR 34 to White Oak makes you nervous, continue down the right side of SR 34 to the pedestrian light and crosswalk at Peoria Road; cross there and rejoin the route where White Oak intersects Peoria.) But at this point you're only a couple miles from Corvallis, a handsome small city with a busy downtown core, good parks, and a lovely waterfront just across the bridge into town. It's worth considering a trip into (or stay in) town (Corvallis–Philomath Trails, Ride 24, is just one option from this town).

White Oak cuts across to Peoria Road, a

The Willamette Valley Scenic Bikeway isn't so much a riding challenge as it is a chance to pedal through Oregon's history as well as its agriculture. Phil Bard/Cycle Oregon

favorite among local riders for its smooth pavement, undulating curves, and relatively low traffic. Once again you end up riding along the Willamette. Just before reaching the actual town of Peoria, turn left and head east through the flyspeck community of Shedd. A little over a mile later, Thompsons Mill State Heritage Site (just past where the route turns onto Roberts Road) has restrooms.

Soon after, storm the town of Brownsville, with one of those truly authentic downtowns—something you'd see in a movie (and actually probably have; Brownsville was "Castle Rock" in the movie *Stand By Me*). It's a place to linger, and Pioneer City Park (restrooms) is a good spot. South of town, Gap Road throws the biggest hill of the bikeway at you; it's not a mountain pass, but it gains about 400 feet pretty quickly. Pick a good gear and be patient; it won't take long. Once you're "through the gap" (you'll understand when you're there), it's about as wide-open and flat as western Oregon gets. It can be a bit windy through here; let's hope it's at your back.

After crossing under Interstate 5 one last time, run parallel to it on the straight country road of N. Coburg Road for about 10 miles—here's where the wind will have a say. Pass right through Coburg—another cool old village—and continue on to Armitage County Park (restrooms), a sprawling facility along the banks of the McKenzie River right before it joins the Willamette outside Eugene.

Route Variations: If you feel like continuing on past Armitage Park, consider adding a scenic lollipop route via McKenzie View Drive (Ride 28), or follow Coburg Road toward town and turn right onto Crescent Avenue, following the end directions of the McKenzie View route into Eugene.

0.0	From intersection of Champoeg State Park entrance road and Champoeg Rd. NE, head east on Champoeg Rd. NE.
0.95	Right onto Case Rd. NE.
4.4	Right onto St. Paul Hwy. NE (SR 219).
4.95	Left onto Arbor Grove Rd. NE.
8.0	Stay straight as SR 219 temporarily joins Arbor Grove Rd. NE from right and then turns off left.
9.4	Jog right at 90-degree turn and then another 90-degree jog left, onto Manning Rd. NE.
11.5	Enter St. Louis.
12.15	Right onto Keene Rd. NE.
13.45	Left onto River Rd. NE.
15.0	Right onto Matheny Rd. NE.
18.1	Bear left at intersection for Wheatland Ferry as road becomes Wheatland Rd. NE.
18.9	Pass Willamette Mission State Park (restrooms) on right.
21.7	Right onto Ravena Dr. N.; follow paved road through series of bends and names.
23.8	Left onto Windsor Island Rd. N.
28.75	Continue straight as road becomes Shoreline Dr. N. into Keizer.
29.05	Jog left onto Wayne Dr. N. and then right onto Rivercrest Dr. N.
29.5	Continue straight on connecting bike path on Rivercrest Dr. N.; after slight jog right, it becomes Willamette Dr. N.
30.1	Left onto Delmar Dr. N.
30.3	Right onto River Rd. N. into Salem.
30.55	Bear left to Commercial St. NE (SR 99E) on one-way couplet.
31.85	Road becomes two-way again.
32.1	Bear right onto bike path just after passing under bridge, then back into roadway lane after passing merging bridge traffic near Riverfront Park (restrooms).
32.8	Bear right onto Commercial St. SE (no longer SR 99E).
33.2	Jog right onto Mission St. SE, then jog left onto Saginaw St. SE.
33.55	Right onto Miller St. SE.
33.85	Left onto River Rd. S.; use bike-pedestrian path on left side of road.
34.8	At Minto Island Rd., cross to bike lane on right side of road.
43.55	Take loop to right to cross under bridge onto Riverside Dr. S. (**Option:** Continue straight for side trip to Independence.)
49.7	Bear left at 90-degree turn; Riverside Dr. S. becomes Sidney Rd. S.
51.1	Right onto Buena Vista Rd. S.
54.7	Left onto Talbot Rd. S. (**Option:** Continue straight for side trip to Buena Vista Ferry.)
59.65	Cross over I-5.
62.7	Right onto Jefferson Hwy. (SR 99E), which becomes N. Second St. into Jefferson; cross bridge over Santiam River.
65.05	Left onto Scravel Hill Rd. NE.
70.85	Right onto US 20.
70.95	Left onto Kennel Rd. SE.
72.65	Right onto Grand Prairie Rd. SE.

73.9   Cross over I-5 into Albany.
75.05   Right onto Geary St. SE.
76.6   Left onto E. First Ave.
78.0   Bear left at 90-degree turn; road becomes Calapooia St. SW.
78.1   Right onto SW Third Ave., then bear right to Bryant Way SW at Bryant Park (restrooms).
79.4   Bear left as road becomes Bryant Dr. SW.
80.8   Right onto Riverside Dr. SW.
86.05   Right onto SR 34.
86.3   Left onto SE White Oak Rd.; cross bridge over Muddy Creek. (**Option:** Straight for side trip to Corvallis.)
88.1   Left onto SE Peoria Rd.
94.05   Left onto Fayetteville Dr.
99.15   Cross SR 99E at Shedd; road becomes Boston Mill Rd.
100.4   Right onto Roberts Rd. at Thompsons Mill State Heritage Site (restrooms).
103.4   Left onto Linn West Rd.—cross over I-5.
105.6   Join 7-Mile Lane, then bear right on 7-Mile Lane.
108.2   Right onto N. Main St. in Brownsville at Pioneer City Park (restrooms).
109.0   Jog right onto Bishop Way (SR 228), then left on Washburn St. (Gap Rd.).
116.55 Bear right at 90-degree turn on Gap Rd.
117.1   Continue straight onto Diamond Hill Dr. where Gap Rd. turns left.
119.9   Cross under I-5.
120.2   Left onto N. Coburg Rd.
129.95 Left to join Coburg Rd. at W. Van Duyn St. coming into Coburg.
132.9   Right to finish at Armitage County Park.

74 RIDE ACROSS OREGON

BORDER TO BORDER BY BIKE

Difficulty:	Epic
Time:	5 to 8 days
Distance:	452 miles one way
Elevation Gain:	16,440 feet
Best Seasons:	Summer and fall, for any reliability

ROAD CONDITIONS: A lot of highway riding (traffic). Gravel in corners on SR 242 (McKenzie Pass Hwy.). City traffic in Eugene.

GETTING THERE: From I-84 in Ontario, just before it crosses Snake River into Idaho, take exit 376. Turn west off exit and follow E. Idaho Ave. for 0.75 mile to SW Second Ave. and turn left. Go 0.25 mile and turn right on SW Fourth Ave. Follow SW Fourth (Olds Ferry–Ontario Hwy.) for 2 miles and turn left onto SR 201. Take highway south a little more than 10 miles; when you reach Nyssa, fork left onto US 20–US 26 toward Idaho. River Park is 0.7 mile ahead on right in Nyssa just before highway crosses Snake River into Idaho. Free parking; restrooms.

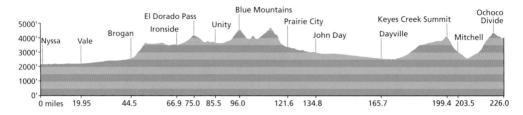

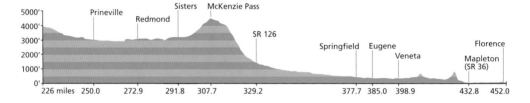

The name of this route is an homage to an event called Race Across Oregon (RAO), which officially began in 1999. The idea: Soloists, or relay teams, ride nonstop across the state—going all day, all night, and part of the next day to see who can get across the state the fastest (if this sounds like it could have started as a bar bet, it actually did). I did this several times with a team of friends, and for the first few years it actually did go across the state, by various routes. Eventually it morphed to a loop route out of the Portland area, but its soul lives on in this ride—an amalgam of RAO routes and a straighter-line approach to the coast.

Besides the twisted appeal of doing it as a race, what made a ride like RAO so great? The chance to see the whole state, in all its climatic, geographic, topographic, geologic, and other -ic variety and glory. Only when you've ridden from one side to the other do you get a real sense of the incredible natural diversity Oregon offers.

I can't give you very specific advice on how

to structure this trip—it's too long and too spread out in some regions to just provide a connect-the-dots formula for each day. This route probably lends itself to camping more than credit-card touring—or a mixture, anyway—although you might be able to find a bed each night with some good advance research.

If you don't mind small-town motels—not too many bed-and-breakfasts along the eastern stretches of this route—here are a couple possible itineraries. If you'd like to average 75 miles per day, try a six-day trip stopping in Unity, Dayville, Prineville, McKenzie Bridge (or anywhere along the McKenzie River—a lot of choices here), and Eugene. If you want more miles, average 90 miles a day and do it in five days, stopping in Prairie City (120 miles on Day 1!), Mitchell, Sisters, and Eugene.

Mostly, just get out there, take your time, and soak in all you can. Oh, and train first—there are a lot of hills in your way.

Start with a ceremonial dip of your tire in the border waters of the Snake River at

Riders wind their way up McKenzie Pass in the Cascades. The vantage point of the photographer, on the same road, shows they're not done climbing. Greg Lee/Cycle Oregon

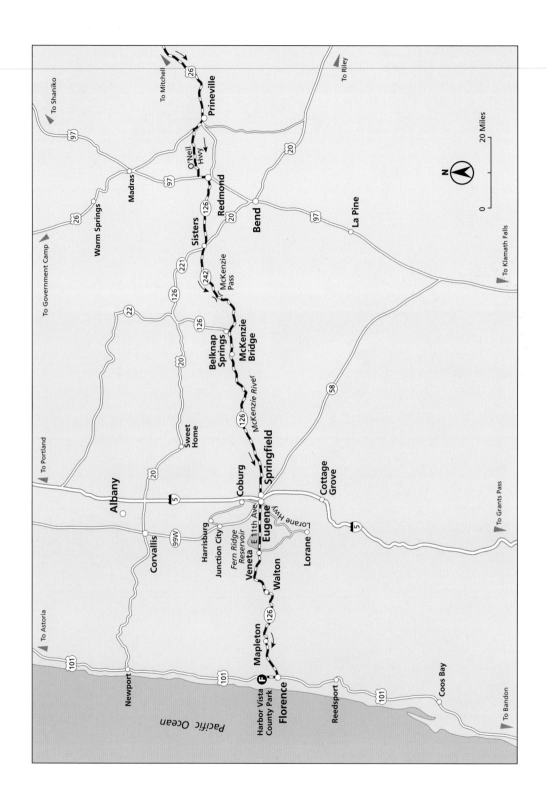

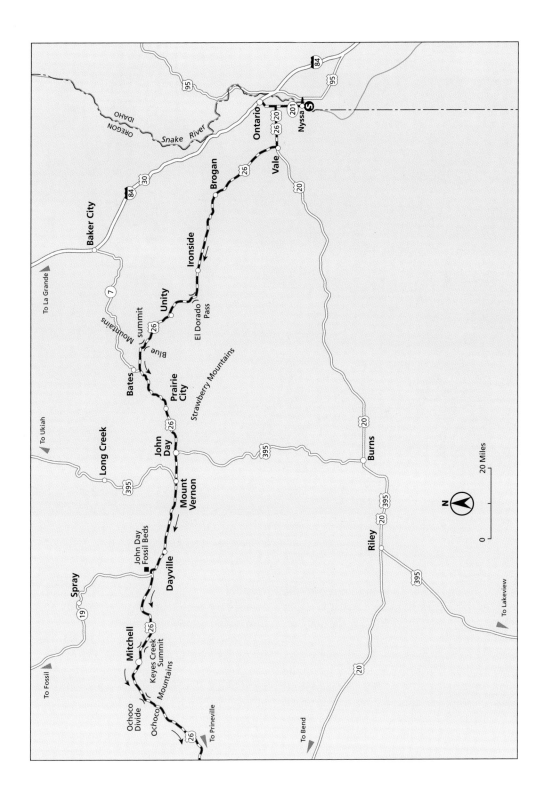

If you take on this route, try to time it so you can ride McKenzie Scenic Pass; even among the startling variety of beauty and terrain along the way, its stark lava rock is a definite visual highlight. Greg Lee/Cycle Oregon

River Park in Nyssa. Then head out into the wide-open rangelands of far eastern Oregon; many people are surprised by the agricultural bounty here, imagining everything east of Bend to be high desert. Go through Vale, crossing the Malheur River and taking on the climb up Brogan Hill, a 1700-foot gain from Vale. Now you're approaching more rugged territory; after Ironside is El Dorado Pass—a mere warm-up for the crossing of the Blue Mountains between Unity and Prairie City.

Prairie City, as its name denotes, offers vistas of tawny prairies and the white-topped Strawberry Mountains beyond, not to mention a handsome little town with a lot to offer visitors (Summit Prairie, Ride 69). Then it's on to John Day, a bustling metropolis in comparison to every town along the way so far. Follow the river of the same name out of town, through Mount Vernon and past Dayville before veering off into the imposing Ochoco Mountains. At the junction with State Route 19, where the John Day River turns north for the Columbia, you're in the

Sheep Rock Unit of the famed John Day Fossil Beds National Monument.

This junction also marks the beginning of nearly 20 miles of uphill pedaling, gaining 2000 feet by the time you hit Keyes Creek Summit before rocketing down into Mitchell with the Ochocos standing sentry to the south . . . waiting for you, beckoning you . . . because you have to get across them. The ride up to Ochoco Divide is a grinder, but of course the high-country pines and the clear, crisp air mitigate things.

I can tell you from experience that the long slide down into Prineville is a relief and a blast—nearly 30 miles of 2 to 3 percent that you can fly along. Prineville is another "major" city with all the services you might need—except maybe a bike shop. This is cowboy country.

At Prineville I choose to veer away from State Route 126 so you can enjoy the O'Neil Highway. It's a nice feeling to ride on a much-less-used road for 17 miles or so, and it basically parallels SR 126 into the Redmond area. You have to jog down US Highway 97 a little bit into Redmond, but the new bypass route actually offers probably the best pavement and shoulder–bike lane combo you're going to see on this trip.

In Redmond, head straight west on SR 126, in the red-rock, high-desert country of central Oregon, with the tangy scents of cedar and juniper in the air. Between Redmond and Sisters, a short, steep canyon is representative of the terrain in this area. Sisters is an Old West tourist town in a perfect location, serving as a gateway for three major Cascade passes and set up against the alpine backdrop of the Three Sisters. As a tourist town, it offers plenty of choices if you're feeling like pampering yourself with a good meal or a comfy bed, and there's a knowledgeable bike shop, too.

If SR 242, the McKenzie Scenic Highway, is open out of Sisters (officially or not; check with the bike shop in town to see if you can ride all the way through, because that's often

possible far before the road is opened to cars), you owe it to yourself to take it, to ride through the stark lava landscape with volcanic peaks and cones visible in all directions (McKenzie Pass, Ride 51). If it's not passable, take SR 126. The drop down SR 242 to the McKenzie River slews left and right like a giant slalom course; be careful of gravel and bad drivers in the corners.

Riding down SR 126 into Springfield is a prime example of the kind of lush forest–sparkling river riding the Cascades offer up like a gift to cyclists. Dropping elevation nearly all the way, follow the tumbling river down to the Willamette Valley, marveling at the picture-postcard scenes along the way.

The Eugene-Springfield area truly is the big-city challenge of this route, and there's no easy way around it. You can veer off toward McKenzie View Drive (Ride 28) and on into Coburg, but you'd have to go north to Harrisburg to cross the Willamette. You can head south to Lorane and over to Reedsport on the Siuslaw and Smith rivers route (Ride 6), but you have to go into Eugene to access Lorane Highway to get there. So . . . this route just plunges you right into the cities and runs you straight through. Go straight through downtown Springfield, across the river and past the University of Oregon campus, and then left on E. 11th Avenue, which eventually becomes SR 126 to the coast.

The highway is a straight, flat shot out past Fern Ridge Reservoir and Veneta before it begins to scale the Coast Range—which will seem easy compared to what you've crawled over to the east. It's just as green and mossy and leafy as a coastal pass should be. Take a left after crossing the Siuslaw River at Mapleton, and cruise on into Florence, which is not the most charming town on the Oregon coast but is convenient. The route ends at Harbor Vista County Park, or you can continue up the road a bit to Heceta Beach if you feel the need to dip your wheel in the water at the other border.

0.0	From River Park on US 20–US 26 in Nyssa, just on Oregon side of Snake River, head west on US 20–US 26.
0.75	Bear right where SR 201 joins in.
8.55	Left where SR 201 continues straight, to stay on US 20–US 26.
19.95	Bear right at split with US 20 entering Vale, to stay on US 26.
20.3	Right at 12th St. to follow US 26.
44.5	Enter Brogan.
66.9	Enter Ironside.
85.5	Enter Unity.
106.5	Continue straight where SR 7 heads to right, to stay on US 26.
121.6	Enter Prairie City.
134.8	Continue straight where US 395 joins in from left in John Day, to stay on US 26.
143.1	Continue straight where US 395 turns right in Mount Vernon, to stay on US 26.
165.7	Enter Dayville.
172.9	At junction with SR 19 to right, continue straight on US 26.
203.5	Enter Mitchell.
250.0	Enter Prineville.
251.8	Bear right to follow ramp for SR 126.
252.1	Right onto O'Neil Hwy. (SR 370).
268.85	Bear left at 90-degree turn to stay on O'Neil Hwy.
269.4	Bear right at 90-degree turn to stay on O'Neil Hwy.
269.75	Left onto US 97.
272.9	Right to follow signs to SR 126 in Redmond.
291.8	Bear right as US 20 joins in from left in Sisters, to stay on SR 126.
292.1	Left onto Hood Ave.
292.85	Left onto SR 242 (McKenzie Scenic Hwy.).
329.2	Left onto SR 126 just south of Belknap Springs.
333.8	Enter McKenzie Bridge.
377.7	Continue straight where main US 26 turns right in Springfield, onto Main St. (SR 126 alternate).
381.0	Bear right at one-way couplet in downtown Springfield.
382.5	Cross Willamette River into Eugene; road becomes Franklin Blvd.
385.0	Left onto E. 11th Ave. (becomes SR 126) from turn lane on Franklin Blvd.
398.9	Enter Veneta.
413.0	Enter Walton.
432.8	Left at junction with SR 36 at Mapleton, to stay on SR 126 across bridge.
447.1	Bear left at fork approaching US 101 in Florence; cross US 101 onto Ninth St.
448.05	Right onto N. Rhododendron Dr.
451.0	Left onto N. Jetty Rd.
452.0	Finish at Harbor Vista County Park, on N. Jetty Rd. off N. Rhododendron Dr.

75

WALLOWA MOUNTAINS AND HELLS CANYON LOOP

PEAKS AND VALLEYS AND CANYONS . . . OH MY

Difficulty:	Epic
Time:	4 to 6 days
Distance:	313.6-mile loop
Elevation Gain:	19,218 feet
Best Seasons:	Summer and early fall

GETTING THERE: From I-84 south of La Grande, take exit 265. Turn right onto SR 203 (coming from either direction) and follow it about 8 miles into Union. There's a nice city park on right side of Main St. and Beakman St. (intersection of SR 203 and SR 237) in downtown Union. Free parking along street; clean restrooms in park.

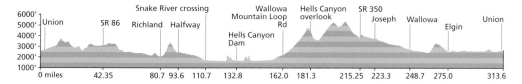

I rode this loop on Cycle Oregon, and afterward I told some friends back home about the route. They insisted I take them there . . . so the next summer I did. Eight of us retraced the route, staying in old hotels, lodges, and bed-and-breakfasts. It's about the best loop tour I can imagine in Oregon. The northeast corner of the state is a natural wonderland of amazing variety, and this route gives you the chance to ride through it all.

A few logistical thoughts about this route: Cycle Oregon rode this configuration in six days; my friends and I did it in four—which made for some long days. One of the beauties of this ride is that there are interesting towns, with good lodging and eating options, strung out along the route at good intervals. Based on that, my suggestions for

the best overnight stops are Union, Baker City, Halfway, Joseph, and Elgin. On our four-day route, we went from Union through Baker City to Halfway on Day 1; Hells Canyon (staying in Halfway again) on Day 2; Halfway to Joseph on Day 3, and Joseph to Union on Day 4. That was a lot of miles each day—but it worked for us.

Start in Union, which has a historic hotel and a few decent restaurants, with a peaceful ride up Catherine Creek (the state park has restrooms), one healthy climb, and some rollers through hilly grasslands, passing the tiny outposts of Pondosa and Medical Springs (see Ride 67). Drop down toward Baker City; if you're heading into town for lunch or an overnight, take a right instead of a left at State Route 86 and find your way into town. Baker

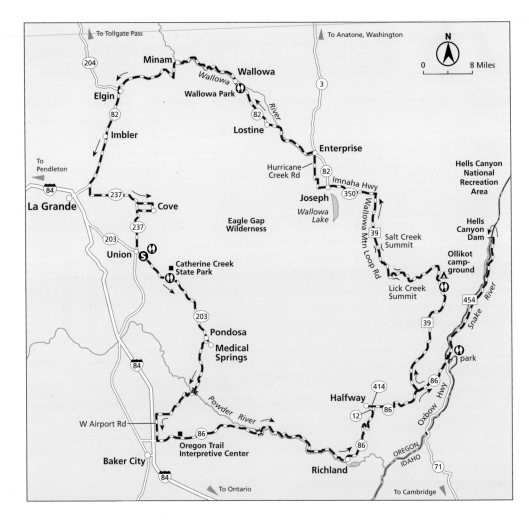

City is the metropolis of this trip, with a bustling downtown district. The Old West–style downtown is fun, with sidewalk cafés and a lot of interesting shops.

Heading east on SR 86, pass by the Oregon Trail Interpretive Center, a good spot to reflect on travelers who came before you; in spots along the road, you can walk a few feet and see ancient ruts from the Oregon Trail wagons. Roll through the Lower Powder River Valley before a breathtaking stretch inside a canyon on the bank of the Powder—miles and miles of twisting road, and a slight downhill grade to supplement the scenic pleasure. Climb a

bit coming into Richland, and think about a stop for ice cream or something stronger, because just outside town is a tough, exposed climb of more than 4 miles—with a false summit. Then rip down an equally steep back side, flattening out on the way into Halfway. Halfway is a charming if tiny town with surprisingly good choices for lodging and eating; if you do the Hells Canyon out-and-back, you'll end up here for two nights.

Leaving Halfway, after a few miles start following Pine Creek downhill, a long glide that brings you to the Snake River in Hells Canyon. Cross the bridge and ride an out-and-back on

When you ride in the country around the Wallowa Mountains and Hells Canyon, you have to adjust your concept of scale. Greg Lee/Cycle Oregon

the Idaho side of the water, marveling at what is (farther downstream) the deepest gorge in North America. You can ride all the way to Hells Canyon Dam, if you want a really full day, or just turn around whenever you feel halfway done. There's a pleasant park (restrooms) at the state-line bridge crossing that you can hit either going out or coming back. Retrace your route back to Halfway; the hill going back is one of those that really feels kind of good when you find the right gear.

On the way back up to Halfway, you pass Forest Road 39 (North Pine Road) on the right—this is the way to Joseph, which you hit the next day. This road, called the Wallowa

Mountain Loop, is one of the hardest, most remote, and awe-inspiring passes in Oregon. There are three separate climbs—18 miles, 10 miles, 5 miles—plus the option to ride up to an overlook of Hells Canyon.

Returning to the Wallowa Mountain Loop after leaving Halfway, turn onto FR 39; the first 10 miles are like riding through cycling Eden: quiet road, thick foliage, murmuring creek. The gradient is reasonable and the atmosphere superb. Then, when you notice the creek is no longer beside you, start climbing to the sky—up and around, up and around, working through the terrain. Summit at about 28 miles out of Halfway and drop back out of the sky—but don't miss the turnoff to the Hells Canyon Overlook. If you're doing this ride, it's assumed you're prepared for climbing—so add a little more. The 3.3 miles to the overlook are amply offset by the prospect of looking down into where you rode yesterday.

Back on the main road, continue down to a river crossing at the wildly beautiful Ollikot campground (restrooms), a good spot for lunch—you're not going to find a restaurant or store on this segment, so pack accordingly. The next two climbs top out at the wonderfully paired names of Lick Creek and Salt Creek; from Salt Creek Summit you can tuck into your aero position and swoop for 10 miles of mostly nontechnical descending. When you turn onto SR 350, there's a (comparatively) brief climb up to the Wallowa Valley—where the sense of space and sky contrasts sharply with the forested heights you've conquered today.

Coming into Joseph, on your left are the distinctive glacial moraines framing Wallowa Lake, a sparkling body of water worth a side trip to check out. You can take a sheer, steep tram ride up Mount Howard to get a good sense of scale in this rugged area. Joseph marks the end of the mountains for this trip. Home to many bronze artists and other metalsmiths, it's a vibrant place—a tourist haven with all the trimmings.

When you head north out of town, this route takes you over to Hurricane Creek Road, a fun back road you can speed down toward Enterprise (see Ride 66). From Enterprise, keep on trucking down the Wallowa Valley, roughly paralleling the path of the eponymous river, through Lostine and Wallowa (a good park here for a rest stop). After Wallowa, the road and the river tuck into another cool canyon before parting ways at Minam. Cross the river for one last dig up and out of the river canyon, which leads you to a series of rollers before dropping down into Elgin. Elgin is a little light on amenities but has a history of opening its heart to cyclists, so the locals will do the best with what they have.

From Elgin to Union is a flat and easy ride through the Grande Ronde Valley and the small towns of Imbler and Cove (don't miss the old chapel in Cove), skirting the base of the Eagle Cap Wilderness on the way back to Union.

MILEAGE LOG

0.0	From corner of Main St. and Beakman St. in Union, head east on Beakman St. (SR 203).
38.25	Left onto W. Airport Rd. (just before I-84).
42.35	Left onto SR 86. (**Option:** Right for side trip to Baker City.)
46.5	Pass Oregon Trail Interpretive Center on left.
80.7	Enter Richland.
92.45	Bear left onto SR 12 to Halfway.
93.6	Right onto Record St. (Pine Creek Hwy., aka SR 414) in Halfway.
94.5	Join SR 86.
103.7	Stay right at junction with FR 39 to continue on SR 86.
110.6	Stay straight at turnoff for Brownlee–Oxbow Hwy., to continue on SR 86.
110.7	Bear right to cross Snake River (rest-stop park).
111.0	Left onto Hells Canyon Rd. (FR 454).
132.8	Reach Hells Canyon Dam—turnaround point; retrace route back to SR 86.
154.65	Cross Snake River.
162.0	At junction with N. Pine Rd. (Wallowa Mountain Loop Rd., aka FR 39), either

	retrace SR 86 back to Halfway and return here next day (adding 20 miles to trip), or turn right onto N. Pine Rd. now.
181.3	Pass turnoff for Hells Canyon overlook on right.
185.1	Pass turnoff for Ollikot campground (restrooms) on right.
205.9	Reach Salt Creek Summit.
215.25	Left onto Imnaha Hwy. (SR 350).
223.3	Right to cross SR 82 in Joseph; road becomes Airport Lane.
225.5	Bear right to join Hurricane Creek Rd.
230.6	Left onto SR 82 in Enterprise.
231.0	Bear left at intersection with North St. to follow SR 82.
240.8	Enter Lostine.
248.7	Enter Wallowa (rest-stop park).
262.0	Enter Minam; cross river.
275.0	Enter Elgin.
275.3	Left to follow SR 82 in Elgin.
282.9	Enter Imbler.
291.0	Left onto Pierce Rd.
292.65	Left onto Cove Hwy. (SR 237).
303.1	Bear right at intersection with Lower Cove Rd. to follow Cove Hwy.
304.4	Bear right to follow Cove Hwy. into Cove.
312.75	Right at E. Bryan St. in Union to follow Cove Hwy.
313.05	Left to follow Cove Hwy and join SR 203 at Main St.
313.6	Finish at corner of Main St. and Beakman St. in Union.

RESOURCES

OREGON ROAD-BIKING CLUBS

Bend Bellas, www.bendbellacyclists.org. Cycling club for women, with weekly rides alternating between trail and road, May through October.

Greater Eugene Area Riders (GEARs), www.eugenegears.org. Weekly rides year-round; sponsors the Blackberry bRamble (August).

Mid-Valley Cycling Club, Corvallis; www.mvbc.com. Multiple rides each weekend; sponsors the Covered Bridge Bicycle Tour (August).

Oregon Randonneurs; www.orrandonneurs.org. Club dedicated to long-distance, noncompetitive events such as brevets, typically from 200 kilometers up to 1000 kilometers.

Pendleton on Wheels; www.pendletononwheels.org. Weekend rides starting in April each year; sponsors the Century Ride of the Centuries (CROC) Memorial Day weekend.

Portland Velo; www.portlandvelo.net. Weekday and weekend rides year-round. Saturday Signature Ride draws 100-plus riders in summer, organized in flights by riding speed.

Portland Wheelmen; www.pwtc.com. Rides nearly 365 days a year; sponsors the Pioneer Century (June) and organizes finish line of Seattle-to-Portland (July).

Salem Bicycle Club; www.salembicycleclub.org. Weekend rides year-round and weekday rides in summer; sponsors the Monster Cookie Ride (April) and Peach of a Century (September).

Santiam Spokes, Lebanon; www.santiamspokes.org. Weekday and weekend rides year-round; sponsors the Strawberry Century (June).

Siskiyou Velo, southern Oregon; www.siskiyouvelo.org. Weekday and weekend rides year-round; sponsors the Mountain Lakes Challenge (June).

Umpqua Velo, Roseburg; www.umpquavelo.org. Weekday and weekend rides year-round; sponsors Tour de Fronds (June) and Cycle Umpqua Vineyard Tour (September).

Yaquina Wheels, Newport; www.yaquinawheels.org. Saturday road rides year-round; sponsors Yaquina Lighthouse Century (August) and Trek Women Breast Cancer Awareness Ride (October).

CYCLING ADVOCACY GROUPS

Bicycle Transportation Alliance, Portland; www.bta4bikes.org. Dedicated to "creating healthy, sustainable communities by making bicycling safe, convenient, and accessible." Sponsors Bike Commute Challenge (entire month of September).

Bicycle and Ideas for Kids' Empowerment (b.i.k.e.), Portland; www.kidsofbike.org. Formed "for the purpose of providing opportunities and options for inner-city, at-risk children."

Center for Appropriate Transport, Eugene; www.catoregon.org. "Committed to community involvement in manufacturing, using, and advocating sustainable modes of transportation." Offers multiple classes and youth education programs.

City of Portland Transportation Options Division; www.gettingaroundportland.org. Offers multiple cycling-related resources, including SmartTrips and Safe Routes to School programs, plus free bike-walk maps. Also sponsors Sunday Parkways (summer and fall).

Community Cycling Center, Portland; www.communitycyclingcenter.org. Goal is to "broaden access to bicycling and its benefits through hands-on programs, volunteer projects, and a neighborhood bike shop." Sponsors both youth and adult programs, including annual Holiday Bike Drive.

Cycle Oregon, Portland; www.cycleoregon .com. Besides two annual tours (week-long and weekend rides), is heavily involved in cycling advocacy. Offers grants to cycling- and community-based projects through the Cycle Oregon Fund.

Northwest Bicycle Safety Council, Beaverton; www.nwbicyclesafetycouncil.org. Formed "to educate and promote safety and harmony between cyclists and others who share the road, as well as strengthen commu- nity and family ties through cycling-related programs and events." Offers multiple bike- safety programs for children and adults, including senior citizens.

SHIFT, Portland; www.shifttobikes.org. "Revels in expressing Portland's creative bike culture through performance events and bike fun intended to highlight the positive con- tributions of bicycling for the community at large." Sponsors Pedalpalooza (multiple events throughout June) and Breakfast on the Bridges for bike commuters, among many other events.

Washington County Bicycle Transpor- tation Coalition, Beaverton; www.washcobtc .org. Mission is "to promote bicycle transpor- tation, protect bicyclists' rights, and improve bicycling conditions throughout Washington County, Oregon, through education, advo- cacy, and community." Sponsors Harvest Century (October) as well as multiple educa- tion and safety events.

CYCLING MAPS

For a comprehensive list of bike maps avail- able in Oregon (free and otherwise), go to Ride Oregon, Travel Oregon's cycling-travel website: http://rideoregonride.com/resources /print-materials/cycling-maps/.

CYCLING EVENTS

An estimated 5000 bicycling-related events are held each year in Oregon, from one-day charity rides to guided tours, club rides, cul- tural celebrations, and some just plain weird gatherings—bike polo, anyone? Ever heard of "freak bikes"? Here are two of the best places to find cycling events:

ORbike: www.orbike.com/events.html.

Ride Oregon: http://rideoregonride.com /events/.

And here are a few of my favorite individ- ual events:

Blackberry bRamble, August; www.eugene gears.org. This ride basically follows the Wolf Creek Loop route (Ride 29) into the Coast Range on obscure roads that climb and drop in splendid seclusion. A pretty tough ride, but worth it.

Bridge Pedal, August; blog.bridgepedal .com. A unique and cool event: a chance to ride over all of Portland's bridges (actu- ally, a different number of them each year, depending on current construction or repair projects) in dedicated bike-only traffic lanes. Organizers get lanes or entire bridges closed to motor-vehicle traffic, and 15,000 or more riders take over. There's a shorter Family Ride as well as longer options. Casually pedaling your bike on the top span of an Interstate 5 bridge is surreal and not to be missed.

Cycle Oregon, September; www.cycle oregon.com. A week-long tour of Oregon's back roads and small towns, with a different route every year. It offers tons of amenities: beer garden with pizza, live entertainment on stage every night, massage, yoga, hot show- ers, and more. And it's for a good cause; the Cycle Oregon Fund has contributed millions to the communities it rides through, as well as a wide variety of cycling and other projects. Preregistration is in early February; this event typically sells out extremely quickly.

Cycle Oregon weekend, July; www.cycle oregon.com. A two-day version of the week-long tour, with a much more family-friendly setup in one spot. Multiple route lengths to appeal to all levels of riders, plus a Kids' Bike Camp.

Monster Cookie Ride, April; www.salem bicycleclub.org. An early-season ride, a metric-century loop from Salem north to Champoeg State Park and back. This is a good ride to get you ready for summer riding.

Race Across Oregon, July; www.race acrossoregon.com. Hands-down the toughest event in the state: more than 500 miles, nonstop (well, you can stop when you need to, but it's a race). Riders can do it solo, on a tandem, or as a relay team, all on the same challenging route, which typically features about 40,000 feet of climbing and takes roughly 25 to 30 hours. Riding in the middle of the night in the middle of nowhere is quite an experience.

Reach the Beach, May; www.reachthe beach.org. A variety of routes, from 26 to 100 miles, start in various towns but all end up in Pacific City with a rockin' party on the beach. Almost any rider can find an appropriate route, but the weather in May can be iffy.

Seattle to Portland (STP), July; www .cascade.org. A 220-mile ride that can be done all in one day or split into two back-to-back centuries, camping or staying in locals' homes halfway through. Upward of 10,000 people do this every year, so apparently it's not that hard. Other than a few rollers here and there, the toughest climb is over the bridge into Oregon.

Strawberry Century, June; www.santiam spokes.org. A Willamette Valley ride out of Lebanon that has some nicely forested roads early on, followed by wide-open valley flatlands. There's a shorter family route, and everyone gets strawberry shortcake at the end.

Vine Ride, August; www.vineride.com. A late-season roll through the orchards, farms, and vineyards of wine country, starting in Newberg. A beast of a climb in the middle, but it's not that long.

RECOMMENDED READING

Beyond other guidebooks, this list includes a few titles that will give you a better idea of what cycling means to Oregonians and how we got to be such a bike-centric place.

Birk, Mia. *Joyride: Pedaling Toward a Healthier Planet.* Portland: Cadence Press, 2010.

Kurmaskie, Joe. *Momentum Is Your Friend.* Halcottsville, NY: Breakaway Books, 2006.

Mapes, Jeff. *Pedaling Revolution: How Cyclists Are Changing American Cities.* Corvallis: Oregon State University Press, 2009.

INDEX

A

Albany 294
Alpine 125
Alsea 127
Applegate 150
Ashland 157, 160, 163, 167
Astoria 37, 41, 281
Athena 258

B

Baker City 265, 266, 305
Bandon 285
Banks 57
Bay City 285
Beaver 46
Bellfountain 125
Bend 234, 238
best of the best 34–36
Biggs 244
bike fit 17–18
Birkenfeld 39
Bridal Veil 180
Brightwood 197
Brookings 288
Brownsville 294
Buncom 156
Burns 273, 277, 280
Butte Falls 167

C

Camp Sherman 204
Cannon Beach 285
Cape Foulweather 49
Cape Kiwanda 46
Cape Meares 44
Carlton 68
Cascade Locks 184
Central Point 157
Charleston 287
check, bike 24–}25
check, safety 25
Chenoweth 189, 192

clothing 19–23
Cloverdale 46
Coburg 295, 303
Coos Bay 286
Corbett 175, 178
Corvallis 116, 121, 124, 294
Cottage Grove 53, 141, 214, 220
Cove 308
Crabtree 115
Crane 280
Crater Lake 167, 221, 224
Culp Creek 143, 214
Cycle Oregon 33–34
cycling advocacy groups 311–312
cycling events 312–313
cycling maps 312

D

Dayville 298
Depoe Bay 49, 285
Diamond Lake 217
Diamond 273, 277
Dorena 143

E

Elgin 258, 305
Enterprise 259, 308
Estacada 201
Eugene 131, 134, 137, 298

F

Florence 51, 286, 303
food 23
Forest Grove 61, 68
Fort Klamath 224
Fossil 246
Frenchglen 273, 277

G

Galice 148
Gardiner 286
Garibaldi 285

gearing 18
Glendale 144
Gold Beach 285
Government Camp 195
Granite 268
Gresham 100

H

Haines 265
Halfway 305
Harbor 288
Harrisburg 303
Hebo 46
Heppner 249
Hillsboro 64
Hood River 186, 187, 191, 193, 198
how to use this book 30–32

I

Imbler 308
Independence 294
Ironside 302

J

Jacksonville 153
Jefferson 113, 294
Jewell 39
John Day 302
Joseph 259, 305

K

Kamela 253
Keizer 294
Kernville 49, 286
Kings Valley 120

L

Lake Oswego 101
Lebanon 128
Lincoln Beach 49, 286
Lincoln City 286
Lorane 53, 139, 303
Lostine 308

M

Manzanita 285
Mapleton 51, 303
Maupin 228
McEwen 267
McKenzie Bridge 298
Meacham 254
Medford 158
Medical Springs 264, 305
Merlin 148
Mist 38
Mitchell 298
Monmouth 121
Moro 244
Mount Angel 111
Mount Vernon 302
Mountain Park 104
Murphy 152

N

Nehalem 285
Neskowin 286
Newport 47, 285
North Bend 286
North Powder 265
Nye Beach 49, 286
Nyssa 298

O

Oakridge 211, 216
Oceanside 43, 285
Oregon Scenic Bikeways Program 32–33
Otis 286

P

Pacific City 46, 285
Pedee 121
Pendleton 254, 256
Peoria 295
Philomath 116, 121, 127
Phoenix 158
Pondosa 264, 305
Port Orford 285
Portland 71, 75, 79, 82, 87, 90, 94, 98

Powers 144
Prairie City 269, 298
Prineville 238, 298
Prospect 167, 225
Provolt 151

R

recommended reading 313
Redmond 231, 238, 303
Reedsport 55, 285, 303
Rhododendron 195
Richland 306
Richmond 248
Ride Oregon 34
riding techniques 28–30
road biking clubs 311
Rockaway Beach 285
route selection 18–19
Rowena 189
Ruch 156
Rufus 242

S

safety 25–28
Salem 106, 294
Sandy 200
Sauvie Island 71
Scio 113
Seaside 285
Selma 152
Service Creek 246
Shaniko 229
Shedd 295
Siletz 47
Silver Falls State Park 112
Silverton 109
Sisters 208, 298
Sixes 287
Springdale 171, 175, 177
Springfield 303
St. Johns 73, 84
St. Louis 294
Sumpter 266
Sweet Home 128

T

Talent 158
ten essentials 25
Terrebonne 233
The Dalles 187, 191
Tillamook 43, 46, 285
Toledo 47
Troutdale 170, 177
Tumalo 237

U

Ukiah 249
Union Creek 227
Union 263, 305
Unity 298

V

Vale 302
Veneta 303
Vernonia 37, 57

W

Waldport 286
Wallowa 308
Wemme 195
Westfir 211
Weston 258
Wheeler 285
Wilderville 152
Williams 151
Winchester Bay 285
Wolf Creek 149
Wonder 152
Wren 121

Y

Yachats 285
Yamhill 70
Yaquina Bay 47
Youngs Bay 39, 40

Z

Zigzag 195

ABOUT THE AUTHOR

Jim Moore is a freelance writer who covers any topic he's assigned to. He owns Word Jones (www.wordjones.com), a virtual creative agency in Portland, Oregon. Jim moved to Oregon at age ten from his birthplace of Omaha, Nebraska, and he's deeply thankful to his parents for that decision. Travel and exploration have always called to him; as soon as he could drive, he started marking up an Oregon road map, highlighting all the roads he had driven and always looking for new ones to experience. When he began cycling seriously, he started a second map for that—which became a resource for this book. A University of Oregon journalism graduate, Jim sampled several careers before starting Word Jones. He currently does marketing and writing for Cycle Oregon, Travel Oregon, and other clients, and sells travel stories to subsidize his wanderings. He lives with his wife and son, who alternately enjoy and tolerate his need to hit the road.

THE MOUNTAINEERS, founded in 1906, is a nonprofit outdoor activity and conservation organization whose mission is "to explore, study, preserve, and enjoy the natural beauty of the outdoors . . . " Based in Seattle, Washington, it is now one of the largest such organizations in the United States, with seven branches throughout Washington State.

The Mountaineers sponsors both classes and year-round outdoor activities in the Pacific Northwest, which include hiking, mountain climbing, ski-touring, snowshoeing, bicycling, camping, canoeing and kayaking, nature study, sailing, and adventure travel. The Mountaineers' conservation division supports environmental causes through educational activities, sponsoring legislation, and presenting informational programs.

All activities are led by skilled, experienced volunteers, who are dedicated to promoting safe and responsible enjoyment and preservation of the outdoors.

If you would like to participate in these organized outdoor activities or programs, consider a membership in The Mountaineers. For information and an application, write or call The Mountaineers Program Center, 7700 Sand Point Way NE, Seattle, WA 98115-3996; phone 206-521-6001; visit www.mountaineers.org; or email info@mountaineers.org.

The Mountaineers Books, an active, nonprofit publishing program of The Mountaineers, produces guidebooks, instructional texts, historical works, natural history guides, and works on environmental conservation. All books produced by The Mountaineers Books fulfill the mission of The Mountaineers. Visit www.mountaineersbooks.org to find details about all our titles and the latest author events, as well as videos, web clips, links, and more!

The Mountaineers Books
1001 SW Klickitat Way, Suite 201
Seattle, WA 98134
800-553-4453
mbooks@mountaineersbooks.org

 The Mountaineers Books is proud to be a corporate sponsor of The Leave No Trace Center for Outdoor Ethics, whose mission is to promote and inspire responsible outdoor recreation through education, research, and partnerships. The Leave No Trace program is focused specifically on human-powered (nonmotorized) recreation.

Leave No Trace strives to educate visitors about the nature of their recreational impacts and offers techniques to prevent and minimize such impacts. Leave No Trace is best understood as an educational and ethical program, not as a set of rules and regulations.

For more information, visit www.lnt.org, or call 800-332-4100.

OTHER TITLES YOU MIGHT ENJOY FROM THE MOUNTAINEERS BOOKS

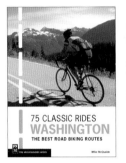

75 Classic Rides: Washington
The Best Road Biking Routes
Mike McQuaide
The "classic" routes for one of the nation's top cycling destinations—in full color

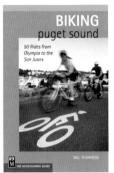

Biking Puget Sound
50 Rides from Olympia to the San Juans
Bill Thorness
The ultimate guide to exploring the Puget Sound region on two wheels

Bicycling the Pacific Coast
A Complete Route Guide,
Canada to Mexico, 4th Edition
Tom Kirkendall & Vicky Spring
If you're ready for the Big Ride, this is your guide.

The Bar Mitzvah and the Beast
One Family's Cross-Country Ride of Passage by Bike
Matt Biers-Ariel
The light-hearted and hilarious story of an ordinary family's extraordinary journey

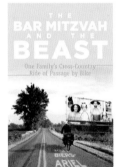

Cycling the Great Divide
From Canada to Mexico on America's Premier Long-Distance Mountain Bike Route
Michael McCoy
Get off the road and onto the rugged passes of the Continental Divide!

The Mountaineers Books has more than
500 outdoor recreation titles in print.
For more details, visit
www.mountaineersbooks.org